JOHN & BRYONY COLES

ENLARGING THE PAST

THE CONTRIBUTION OF WETLAND ARCHAEOLOGY

The Rhind Lectures for 1994–5

SOCIETY OF ANTIQUARIES OF SCOTLAND
MONOGRAPH SERIES NUMBER 11
and
WETLAND ARCHAEOLOGY RESEARCH PROJECT (WARP)
OCCASIONAL PAPER NUMBER 10

SOCIETY OF ANTIQUARIES OF SCOTLAND

MONOGRAPH SERIES

EDITOR ♦ ALEXANDRA SHEPHERD

This volume is published in conjunction with
WETLAND ARCHAEOLOGY RESEARCH PROJECT

EDINBURGH 1996

British Library Cataloguing-in-Publication Data.
A catalogue record for this book is available
from the British Library.

ISBN 0 903903 11 3 (SAS Monogr Ser)
ISBN 0 9519117 3 2 (WARP Occas Pap)

Produced by Short Run Press Ltd, Exeter.

ENLARGING THE PAST

JOHN & BRYONY COLES

Cover illustrations and design by Mike Rouillard

This book is dedicated to
Grahame Clark
(1907–1995)

CONTENTS

ILLUSTRATIONS

COLOUR SECTIONS

PREFACE

It was a great honour to be invited to deliver the Rhind Lectures for 1995 to the Society of Antiquaries of Scotland, and now to present them for publication as a Society Monograph. We are, we believe, the first pair of archaeologists to be appointed as joint Rhind Lecturers, but it is appropriate that we shared the lectures on wetland archaeology as we have shared the surveys, excavations and analyses for 25 years. For the lectures, and for this Monograph, we have selected a number of themes to examine, each of which will show how wetland archaeology has enlarged our knowledge about the past. Each of these themes was discussed by both of us, in turn, for the lectures and we have followed the same practice for the chapters of the book. We hope the joins are not too obvious but in any event what we present here has been thoroughly discussed, time and again, and we are generally in agreement about most aspects of our studies even if we may each have our own emphasis and expressions. As it happens, our wetland activities have diverged over the years and so it has been easy to divide up the preparation of this book.

Our individual interests in wetland archaeology began in the Somerset Levels, JMC in 1963 and BJC in 1970. We jointly directed the Somerset Levels Project from its establishment in 1973 to its self-administered demise in 1989, and other wetland projects have been in operation in the United Kingdom under our supervision since 1981. In bringing our wetland words to Scotland in 1995 we were aware that much was already going on and that even more was being planned, and we hope the views and comments expressed in this book will help in the furtherance of Scottish wetland archaeology. We received advice and information in advance of our lectures from the National Museum, the Royal Commission on the Ancient and Historical Monuments of Scotland, Historic Scotland and the Society of Antiquaries of Scotland, and we especially thank Alison Sheridan, Roger Mercer, Richard Hingley and Fionna Ashmore for their enthusiasm, inspiration and guidance. We are also indebted to our President, Gordon Maxwell, for his kind and skilful management of the occasion.

We have benefited greatly from our visits to wetland sites and contacts with wetland archaeologists in many places, and colleagues have been generous in supplying information and illustrations for the lectures and for this book, sometimes well in advance of their own final publications. A number of archaeologists have read parts of our text and have provided additional information as well as amendments and for this help we thank:

Katsuhiko Amitani, Béat Arnold, André Billamboz, Michel Colardelle, Richard

Daugherty, Tom Dillehay, Glen Doran, Michel Egloff, Bernhard Gramsch, Philip Macdonald, Mats P Malmer, Akira Matsui, Paul Mellars, Daniel Mordant, Bengt Nordqvist, Woitek Piotrowski, Flemming Rieck, Helmut Schlichtherle, Eric Verdel, Jürgen Weiner.

We also thank a number of people who have discussed aspects with us, or supplied information during site visits, or illustrations for the book:

1

Map to show location of the European sites described in the text.

Tomas Bartholin, Aimé Bocquet, Jane Brayne, Hans Browall, Wil Casparie, Ciara Clarke, Dale Croes, Anne Crone, Nicholas Dixon, Anders Fischer, Marion Gilliland, the late Hajo Hayen, Hans Göransson, David Hall, Mogens Schou Jørgensen, Leendert Louwe Kooijmans, Tom Lane, Bob Middleton, Aonghus Moloney, Claude Mordant, Robert Mowat, Francis Pryor, Barbara

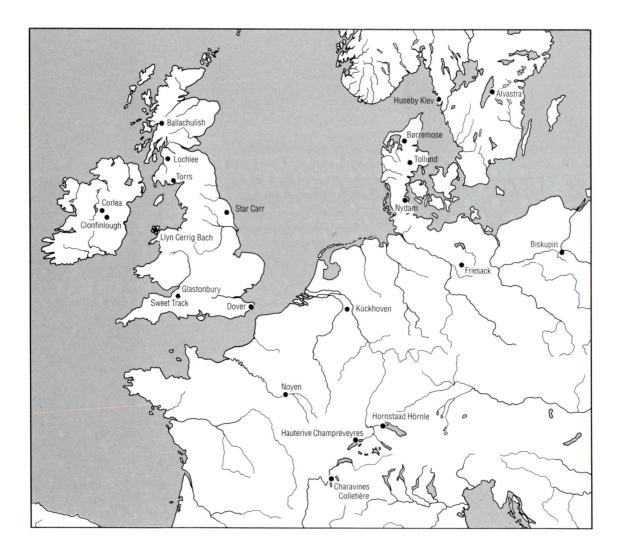

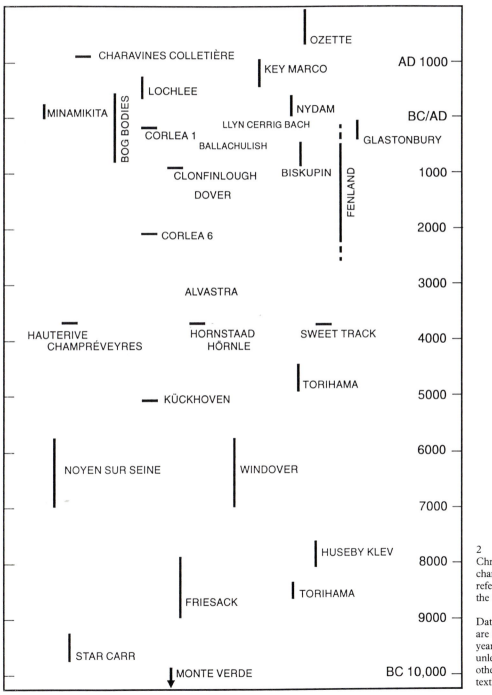

OZETTE

CHARAVINES COLLETIÈRE   KEY MARCO   AD 1000 —

LOCHLEE

MINAMIKITA   NYDAM   BC/AD —

BOG BODIES   CORLEA 1   LLYN CERRIG BACH

BALLACHULISH   GLASTONBURY

CLONFINLOUGH   BISKUPIN   1000 —

DOVER

FENLAND

CORLEA 6   2000 —

3000 —

ALVASTRA

HAUTERIVE   HORNSTAAD   SWEET TRACK   4000 —
CHAMPRÉVEYRES   HÖRNLE

TORIHAMA

KÜCKHOVEN   5000 —

6000 —

NOYEN SUR SEINE   WINDOVER

7000 —

HUSEBY KLEV   8000 —

TORIHAMA

FRIESACK

9000 —

STAR CARR

MONTE VERDE   BC 10,000 —

2
Chronological
chart of sites
referred to in
the text.

Dates. All dates
are in calendar
years BC or AD,
unless stated
otherwise in the
text.

Purdy, Barry Raftery, Denis Ramseyer, Ulrich Ruoff, Maisie Taylor, Rick Turner, Robert Van de Noort, Wieslaw Zajaczkowski.

Many of the illustrations in the book have been supplied by colleagues, as indicated in the captions, and copyright remains with them. A large number have not been published previously. We also thank Sue Rouillard for help with the illustrations and Jennifer Warren for typing the whole book. The book has benefited from the editorial work of Lekky Shepherd.

We thank the British Academy, English Heritage and the University of Exeter for supporting the research relevant to several aspects of this book. We hope that our selection of sites (illus 1 and 2) and themes, and our comments and opinions, will fairly reflect the work of our colleagues and provide some sort of wider or comparative context within the world of wetland archaeology.

Devon, summer 1995
(a very dry place)

John and Bryony Coles

1

IN AT THE DEEP END

Wetlands as an environment in which to live and work may not be understood by everyone, particularly those who dwell in cities; most of us are brought up to avoid the unpleasantness of rising damp, chilblains, chapped hands, colds and flu – and doubtless people in the past felt exactly the same. Yet many of them chose to live in, or beside, or near water, just as they do today in West Africa, Latin and South America, the Middle East, South East Asia and many other areas of the less industrialised world. Wetlands in the past were often very rich environments, with plentiful opportunities, not clogged by forest, easy of access, and offering a variety of resources all the year (illus Ia). In the western world, the tendency has been for many centuries to convert wetland to dryland, but here and there a tradition of wetland farming has developed as in the Marais Poitevin in western France. Other wetlands survive unfarmed, although few have escaped the effects of human exploitation in one form or another.

There is no single definition of 'wetland' that covers all the variations, except the most general one, that a wetland is any area of land covered by water for part of each year (daily or seasonally) or which has been drowned and waterlogged at any time in its existence. So climate and seasonal change are crucial elements, and no other landform is so susceptible to environmental change as a wetland.

Wetlands began to be explored, utilized and exploited as long ago as 10,000 years in many parts of the world – South America, North America, Europe, Africa and Asia all have prehistoric sites of this age in or beside wetlands, and some are far older. It was not until the 17th century AD that wetlands began to be described by European travellers, missionaries and explorers as they encountered a myriad of people who had developed close relationships with particular wetlands. These descriptions were mostly unscientific and they tended to reflect the individual traveller's first impressions of the wetlands they ventured to explore. One such commentary, based on a journey through south-west England, referred to the Rhind lecturers' own Somerset Levels as 'a gloomy waste of waters . . . a hideous expanse of reeds . . . impassable by human foot . . . an atmosphere pregnant with pestilence' (R Warner in 1826). And another, describing a different part of wetland Britain, 'the Air nebulous . . . the water putrid and muddy, yea full of loathsome vermine; the earth spuing, unfast and boggie' (Anon 1629). Quite clearly these travellers had had a bad time of it. But others, exploring southern Florida at the same time, wrote '. . . aquatic flowers of every hue and variety are to be seen on every side of this place of profound and wild solitude . . . pervaded by silence' (Buckingham Smith in 1847). The truth of these matters lies somewhere between, we think, and it all depends on your own traditions, instincts and emotions at the time of entry. Clearly, not all wetlands are the same and in this book we will be concerned with fens and rich tree swamps, ponds and lakes, barren boglands and floodplains once dry but overwhelmed by floodwaters.

FIRST SIGHTINGS

The first recorded discoveries of objects in peatbogs, swamps, river muds and lake silts were made from *c* AD 1400 onwards. Peat digging in particular was likely to reveal artefacts that had been put into the top layers of peatbogs, and human bodies were often discovered by peasant diggers; many were in fragments, partly rotted away, and some were clothed, but almost all were abandoned and lost through neglect and fear. By the early 19th century, wooden wagons, wheels, roadways, barrels and kegs were being found in the bogs of Ireland, Britain, the Netherlands, Denmark and north Germany. At Blair Drummond Moss in Perthshire, a disc wheel was discovered in 1830 and published as a shield until Stuart Piggott re-interpreted it as a wheel; it is now believed to be about 3,000 years old, one of the oldest such objects from Britain. It has suffered over the years and is now but a pale shadow of its original form.

Even earlier, quarrying and dredging of the River Clyde in Glasgow revealed a logboat of oak, and by 1850 so many other logboats were being hauled out of the ancient river channels that Daniel Wilson, one of the pioneers of archaeology in Scotland, was led to comment on one particularly fine boat:

3
Two 'savages' with an unlikely pig, embarking in a logboat. From the *Scots Pictorial* 1892, courtesy of the Trustees of the National Library of Scotland.

'The citizens of Glasgow having a reasonable conviction that boats lose their value in proportion to their age, the venerable relic lay for some months unheeded, until at length the Society of Antiquaries of Scotland made application for it . . . and . . . (it) is now safely deposited in their museum'.

Other logboats suffered even more, and some were photographed or sketched in undignified and terminal positions (illus Ib), while others were the subject of outrageous sketches; the *Scots Pictorial* of 1892 showed one logboat about to be boarded, and sunk, by two savages laden with a gigantic boar, with a crannog in the background (illus 3). Crannogs were being discovered in Scotland by agricultural drainage but most were abandoned, neglected or destroyed. John MacKinlay described one such structure on a low green island in a small loch on Bute which he had seen in 1812; it had a double wall of piles, a wooden floor and a bridge across to the mainland. By the end of the 19th century, some excavations were mounted on other crannogs (Morrison 1985) but the subject suffered from the notorious goings-on at Dumbuck where it seems certain folk were not content with the genuine artefacts found there, and created a more interesting lot. Crannogs in Ireland were equally trenched and quantities of (real) Iron Age and Early Christian relics were recovered (Wood-Martin 1886). One of the most intriguing of the Irish discoveries was the 'house' from Co Donegal, found in 1833 under eight metres of peat, with implements of stone and wood lying around; this may have been a Neolithic wooden tomb.

On the continent of Europe, the same kind of discoveries were made, and a few antiquaries were aware of the possibilities of discoveries in the lake muds, peatbogs and river valleys. But no one was ready for the flood of finds that was to come. Most readers will know of the beginnings of lake village research in Switzerland in the winter of 1853–54. The low water levels of that winter revealed wooden piles along the shore of several lakes, and dredging of the lake muds near Zürich brought up quantities of stone axes, bone points, pottery and wooden tools. Frederick Keller, President of the Antiquarian Society of Zürich, began to publish the discoveries in a series of fascicles, and the antiquaries of Switzerland, Germany, France, Italy and Austria began to attack many of the Alpine lake shores, dredging the lake muds with steam-driven mud engines, rakes and other ingenious tools, and recovering thousands of Neolithic and Bronze Age axes, pots, bones, wooden tools, metal ornaments and weapons (Keller 1878). The piles and timbers of the structures that once had supported the owners of these items were mostly ignored and swept away by the enthusiasm for 'real' objects. It was fondly and universally believed that the lake dwellers had built their houses on piles, set in the open water offshore for protection from land-based marauding animals, including humans. Many romantic reconstructions of the lake dwellers were created by a host of painters, some more sober than others.

Of excavations there were few as most of the sites lay beneath the lake waters or were buried beneath silt or peat. One site, Robenhausen, had existed in or beside a small lake which had mostly infilled with peat and a vigorous campaign of excavation was mounted by an amateur archaeologist whose recording techniques and thought-provoking analyses were well ahead of his time. This man, Jacob Messikomer, was surely one of the true pioneers of archaeological studies, as he argued the primary importance of stratigraphy, context, economy and environment (B & J Coles 1989, 26-31). A second settlement in the same lake was less instructive for structures but had somehow preserved some quantity of Neolithic textiles, including highly decorative pieces. These two sites, Robenhausen and Irgenhausen, were probably the best-preserved ancient settlements in the whole of Europe; had they been saved for today, we would know much more about the Neolithic, but the likelihood would also be that the sites had deteriorated through drainage and we should be thankful that Messikomer was there instead of a 'professional' antiquary.

Another pioneer in this story of the lake dwellings was Adolphe von Morlot, the first underwater archaeologist, who explored a site in Lake Geneva in 1854, wearing lead boots, a bucket over his head, and carrying a pick and butterfly net. He drew a picture of himself at work, and described the scene: 'It was strikingly poetical to stand amidst those ancient posts in the bluish twilight'. Not long after, the Rev RJ Mapleton employed two divers from the Crinan Canal to explore a crannog near Lochgilphead in Argyll. Each diver needed two men to pump air, and two more to manage his life and air lines (Mapleton 1867); this was probably the first underwater excavation in Britain.

A PIONEER IN SCOTLAND

In Scotland, one pioneer of wetland archaeology began work in the late 19th century. Robert Munro is a well-known figure in the history of British archaeology, always an amateur but extremely vigorous in his pursuit of sites and discoveries. He abandoned his medical career at a relatively early age to devote himself to archaeology, and visited the Swiss lake dwelling sites soon after Keller's work had appeared in an English translation (1878). Munro excavated several Scottish crannogs, by cutting trenches into them, and Lochlee in Ayrshire saw one of his more extensive forays into these structures (illus 4). His technique, and that of his contemporaries, was probably not up to much of a standard, and reports indicate that the spoil heaps were often trawled by the public, seeking relics. In the market place of Kilmarnock, the sale of artefacts was brisk (Dixon 1991, 2). In 1882 Munro published his book on *Ancient Scottish Lake Dwellings or Crannogs*, and his contribution has recently been assessed by Historic Scotland through the work of Barber and Crone (1993). Munro died in 1921 and his obituary in the *Journal of the Society of Antiquaries of London* notes his 'absorbing enthusiasm and . . . sense of good fellowship', and also that he was 'a sturdy antagonist in argument and was loath to leave a controversy even although the issue had ceased to arouse interest'; nothing changes in archaeological discussion.

The importance of Munro in the context of this book is that he was asked to give the Rhind Lectures for 1888 and his subject was *The Lake-Dwellings of Europe* (and published under the same title in 1890). His reaction to the invitation was: 'My first and almost immediate step was a hasty run to the principal centres of lake-dwelling researches in Europe . . . it was only then that the magnitude of the labours I had undertaken dawned upon me'. Our own reaction to the invitation to give the 1995 Lectures was just about the same except that, thanks to air travel, we could aim for a wider coverage. So while Munro journeyed to about 10 European countries and visited 51 museums, we were able to visit 23 countries from western Canada eastwards to Japan, looking at wet site archaeology and wetlands; we lost count of the museums in which we could examine material but there were over 20 in Japan alone. Along the ways, we sampled a sometimes disconcertingly wide variety of foods, both cooked and raw, obtained from wetland contexts, and on one site were invited (and agreed) to walk out upon the 3,000-year-old timbers of a freshly-exposed wooden roadway – in the light of our own experiences with such things in the Somerset Levels, we were wholly unnerved at the prospect.

Before leaving Munro and his formidable contribution to wetland archaeology, it will be worth noting that he was one of the main supporters and advisors called in to help a young wholly inexperienced amateur who had discovered a 'lake village' in Somerset. The young medical student, Arthur Bulleid (illus 5a), had been encouraged by Keller's book on the Swiss Lake Dwellings and perhaps had seen Munro's book of 1890 as well, but by then Bulleid was searching the peat moors of the Somerset Levels for the tell-tale bumps that might identify a buried village. In 1892 he discovered a field with suitable mounds and soon was able to announce the existence of the Glastonbury Lake Village, probably England's best-known prehistoric site other than Stonehenge. Munro was Bulleid's most

4
View of Robert Munro's trench through the crannog at Lochlee, Ayrshire in 1878–79. From Munro 1882.

assiduous advisor and contributed a very long introductory chapter to the final monographs on the site; the Lake Village is further described in Chapter 4.

A FLORIDA MAVERICK

Bulleid was a scientist, quiet, calm and methodical in all his work, approaching his site with clear aims and dedication. In contrast, one of his exact contemporaries in America was as different as it is possible to imagine. While Bulleid was digging at Glastonbury, there were new settlers and exploiters arriving on the south-west coast of Florida. The region was almost wholly undeveloped, no road or rail links to the north, and the coastline was choked with mangrove swamps and other dense vegetation. A few entries had been made by 1895, mostly to exploit, and eventually exterminate, the animal life, but various small orchards were being created on the rich soils on and around some of the ancient shell mounds. In early 1895 the digging of peaty soils at Key Marco revealed some artefacts of bone, shell and wood. By pure chance, a Colonel of the British Army got hold of them, and they, and news of the find, filtered to the University Museum in Philadelphia. Here was a visitor, a specialist in the Zuni Indians of Arizona, who had also read about the Swiss Lake Dwellings. Frank Cushing was by all accounts the opposite of Arthur

5
Two pioneers of wetland archaeology. Left a) Arthur Bulleid standing in the doorway of his excavation hut at the Glastonbury Lake Village, 1906; right b) Frank Cushing dressed as a Dakota warrior; late 19th century. Photo of Bulleid courtesy of Glastonbury Antiquarian Society; photo of Cushing courtesy of Smithsonian Institution, Washington.

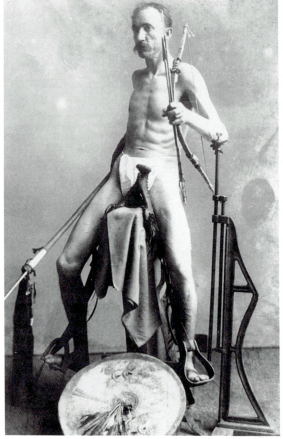

a   b

Bulleid. Cushing (illus 5b) was a maverick, a showman, and a controversial figure but above all a dedicated and determined archaeologist. He decided to check the site and assess its potential for further work. In the two weeks it took him to get from New York to Key Marco, he travelled by steamboat, river boat, train, horseback and sloop (Gilliland 1989). He dug a test pit, negotiated with the owner of the orchard (who only wanted the peaty soil for his orange grove), secured funding, and by the autumn of 1895 he was back with a team of sailor-diggers, a draughtsman, a field secretary, and his wife as conservator; they had a schooner as a base camp anchored just off the island of Key Marco. The draughtsman Wells Sawyer, who turned out to be the saviour of the whole enterprise, described the site as a 'muck hole'; there were 'many curious weeds . . . underlain by foul-smelling black muck . . . the whole place was like a thick sponge saturated with water holding a great deal of salt and a large variety of smells. Almost to a man they looked with absolute revolt upon the unpromising hole. Cushing waded into the mud . . .' (illus 1c). Soon, the yield of finds enthused the whole team and the slime, heat, mosquitoes and sand-flies were forgotten, or at least ignored.

The site was, or had been, an ancient marina of the Calusa Indians, where canoes had been lodged out of the Gulf of Mexico storms, and where, upon the mounds and banks of shell piled up to provide safe ground, various activities had taken place. The structures of wood, embellished by carvings and paintings, had collapsed into the water, and the debris of activities on the shell mounds had similarly come to rest in the pond. At abandonment, perhaps because of a destructive hurricane, the pond had silted up and, over time, sealed the levels of debris, preserving them immaculately. Alas, the recovery of the relics by Cushing and his team was a battle against their fragility and the exposure to the air, and the lack of facilities for sealing and protecting the objects. The team had to dig into the soft peaty soils with bare hands, mostly feeling their way due to the muck and murky water, and often while standing in the deposits. The bone and shell were still hard and could be retrieved, but much of the wood, carved and painted, was

6
Three wooden masks with inset shell eyes from the excavations at Key Marco. This is a field photo taken just after recovery; Wells Sawyer made watercolour paintings of some masks, and few survived the attempts at conservation. Photo courtesy of Smithsonian Institution, Washington.

like soft butter and was often squashed before or during recovery. Cordage and nets were barely distinguishable from the masses of rootlets, and the removal from the site of wood and nets was achieved only with the greatest of difficulty. Cushing and his wife tried everything they could to conserve the objects, or at least to hold them in an identifiable condition – glue, shellac, soda, sand-drying were tried, all of them unsuccessfully. Sawyer made drawings, and photographs were taken and casts were made of as many artefacts as possible, and these are basically all that remain other than dried-out, shrunken and warped pieces in various collections today.

Key Marco was probably the richest site in all of North America for artistic decoration of organic materials (Purdy 1991). The marina had been constructed over 1,000 years ago (AD 650–900), was clearly a very elaborate structure and had housed and supported a wide variety of events commemorated by the carving and decorating of masks (illus 6), figures, engraved and painted boards, models of larger objects like canoes, and doubtless major ceremonial structures; tools and weapons and other domestic debris were also well-represented in the array of materials coming to rest in the pond. Today the site is obliterated by a condominium city and the location itself is lost. What should Cushing have done? Had he ignored the first few artefacts that arrived in Philadelphia, had he not been there at the precise moment, it is possible that the site would be almost wholly unknown, as the digging of the muck was already under way. Cushing's team was inadequate for the task and it is easy to criticize his result. We prefer to see him as a major figure in the development of an appreciation of wetland archaeology for the contribution it can make to the wider field of archaeological endeavours. Without Key Marco as a marker in Florida's prehistory, we would be much the poorer.

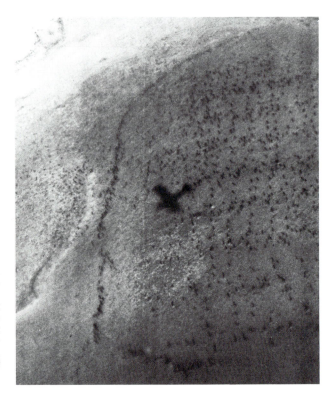

7
The first aerial photograph of a submerged lake-dwelling, at Cortaillod in Lake Neuchâtel, about 1925. Photo by Paul Vouga courtesy of Michel Egloff.

By 1900, Cushing was dead, his site published only as a preliminary note, although it is a rewarding 118 pages (Cushing 1896). Bulleid had halted his excavations at Glastonbury, due in part to the quantity of finds, and Munro was less actively promoting the sites he had adopted. It was the beginning of a long period of only sporadic research, Bulleid finally completing his Glastonbury excavations in 1907, the Rev Odo Blundell donning a cumbersome diving suit and 56lb boots to view a crannog in the Crinan Canal, and R Schmidt and H Reinerth working on and questioning the Alpine lake dwellings. Paul Vouga deserves a mention here, for taking the first aerial photographs of drowned settlements beneath the cold still waters of Lake Neuchâtel (illus 7), and he is the person who conceived the idea of a coffer-dam for excavations in shallow waters; at Cortaillod, he sank long metal pipes onto the settlement, pumped the water out and descended a ladder to stand on the ancient debris. He was confident of the success of the venture as he did not bother to change out of his dark suit and fedora.

By 1930, the lake dwelling theory was under serious attack, new wetlands were being explored, and major sites were either discovered or were soon to be found. Alvastra in Sweden (Chapter 2), Biskupin in Poland (Chapters 2 and 5), the terps of the Netherlands and north Germany, the perplexing fish weirs in Boston USA, and the establishment of multi-disciplinary work in the Fenlands of eastern England (Chapter 5), all came into active periods of research leading up to and/or after 1930. But it was all isolated and individualistic, and no real theory or even an agreed set of principles existed. The period of trial and error, mostly error, came to an end with the innovative work of Grahame Clark and his team at Star Carr in Yorkshire.

MULTI-DISCIPLINARY WORK

Clark excavated at the site of Star Carr in the Vale of Pickering in northern England from 1949 to 1951, not continuously but for three summer seasons. The site had been found by a local archaeologist, John Moore, who collected Mesolithic flints from the surface of a pasture field. Excavation showed the flints to be scattered across a sandy slope leading down to waterlogged peats where wood and bone were well preserved. Publication followed promptly (Clark 1954). The excavation team consisted mainly of undergraduates and research students from Cambridge, many of whom went on to distinguished careers in archaeology, particularly those who attended all three seasons. Clark's budget was small, each season of excavation was relatively short, equipment was limited, and only small areas of the site were opened at any one time (illus 8). The size of the excavations was governed by the capacity of the pumps as much as anything, and the heavy waterlogging of the site threatened logistical problems that we could only wish still existed today. Despite these limitations, several new pieces of equipment were tested on site, including 'Apparatus for impregnating animal remains under vacuum conditions'. Probably the treatment worked, for the Star Carr bone and antler has survived fit for subsequent re-interpretation.

Clark's focus on archaeology was complemented by the palaeoenvironmental researches of Harry Godwin and Donald Walker; they worked out the environmental setting of the site at the time of its occupation early in the post-glacial period by a small group of hunter-fisher-gatherers. Godwin had already collaborated with Clark in the Fens, and with Arthur Bulleid in the Somerset Levels; his work at Star Carr is usually overshadowed by the archaeology, but Clark rightly emphasised that 'the value of interdisciplinary team-work is not to be measured by separate contributions so much as by the total result' (1954, xxii). The Mesolithic settlement, it was found, had been made on the northern shore of a lake, one of a series of irregular bodies of water drained by the river Derwent and fringed with reeds and occasional trees. The dry land was covered with light birch woodland, probably with some pine, and willow in the wetter places. The people who lived at Star Carr probably made use of all three zones: the birch woodland, the reedswamp and the open water (illus 9). It is the evidence from the wetland zone, the reedswamp, which was preserved and in due course excavated.

Perhaps because of all those students who went on to become University lecturers and professors, and no doubt included Star Carr in their courses, and perhaps because the bone and antler was professionally treated on site and published in detail, Star Carr has undergone many subsequent re-interpretations, many of which have focused on the animal remains and on the flint. There has been much discussion of the likely season of occupation of the site and the significance of the antler industry, but little agreement. Some of the arguments are presented in Legge and Rowley-Conwy's *Star Carr Revisited* (1988), Clark's own reappraisal of the site being published in 1972.

One common factor of the re-interpretations is that they have paid little attention to the wetland context of the site. This must have influenced the activities of the

8
Grahame Clark's 1950 excavations at Star Carr, looking south across the former lakes of the Vale of Pickering to the Yorkshire Wolds in the distance. The photograph was taken from approximately where the Mesolithic settlement had been, on the dry slope leading down to the lake. From Clark 1954.

original inhabitants, who as hunter-fisher-gatherers were attracted to the spot as a base for easy access to the resources of open water, reed-swamp and birch forest hinterland. The waterlogged conditions preserved a range of artefacts indicative of a more varied and interesting material culture than is known from the dryland sites of the period. There were, for example, a birchwood paddle, an elk-antler mattock with the remains of its wooden handle and several largish rolls of birch bark which Clark thought might have been used to produce resin or pitch for hafting flints.

Felled birch trees made up the lake-side platform for which Star Carr is renowned. The excavated wood was planned and photographed, but surviving records show insufficient detail to discuss woodworking techniques, and it is little wonder that the wood has been largely ignored in the various re-interpretations of the site. However, one of us (JMC) re-discovered the worked end of one of the Star Carr branches in a jar of preserving fluid on a shelf in Cambridge. This was the only platform timber to be illustrated in the publication, other than the wood shown in general site views. At the time of rediscovery, we were studying wood from the Somerset Levels which carried somewhat unusual traces of working, similar to those preserved on the Star Carr piece. Thanks to the Somerset work, and to our own fieldwork in Canada, we immediately recognised that the particular bit of Mesolithic platform wood in front of us had been felled by beaver not humans, the facets being tooth not axe-marks (illus Id, e). It seems probable, looking at the site photographs and reading Clark's description of angles of felling, that much of the Star Carr platform was made up of beaver-felled wood. We can visualise the canny Mesolithic gatherers making good use of the largesse of felled wood strewn along the lake shore by the beaver, who were their neighbours and occasionally their victims (Coles & Orme 1983; B Coles 1992b).

We are not proposing yet another re-interpretation of Star Carr on the basis of the beaver wood. Its identification merely adds another dimension to the resource base of the site. The re-interpretations of the future will come from two current programmes. One, directed by Tim Schadla-Hall, aims to broaden knowledge of Mesolithic settlement and exploitation of the Vale of Pickering. The second, and more recent development, is a programme of renewed excavation at

9
The Star Carr site and its immediate surroundings, based on the evidence retrieved by Clark's excavations and Godwin and Walker's palaeoenvironmental analyses. From Clark 1954.

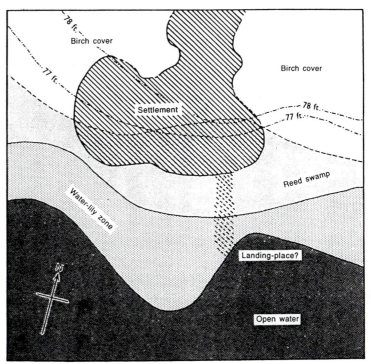

Star Carr itself, directed by Paul Mellars, with investigation of the palaeo-environment by Petra Day. Occupation evidence has been found beyond the limits of the area opened by Clark and wood still survives, more substantial than that recorded by Clark and some of it possibly split timber. Day's detailed palaeo-environmental work has identified two separate phases of human activity in the region, the first contemporary with the timber platform and lasting for about 80 years from about 10,700 years ago. The second phase began about 10,550 years ago and lasted for approximately 120 years (Day & Mellars 1994). Charcoal associated with the occupation derives almost entirely from *Phragmites* reeds, as if people were burning off the dead reeds to clear their access to the lake (Mellars pers comm) The new fieldwork, both archaeological and palaeoenvironmental, indicates that people were using other wetlands of the Vale of Pickering during and following their activities at Star Carr itself. Future re-assessment of Clark's excavations will need to recognise that Star Carr was but one of several, possibly many, lowland encampments in the immediate area.

ACROSS THE EUROPEAN PLAIN

Another avenue to the greater understanding of this classic and influential site is the investigation of contemporary peoples in other regions. Ten to eleven thousand years ago, had they so wished, the people who lived at Star Carr could have undertaken a long and probably arduous walk overland to another region of freshwater lakes and low rolling hills, just to the northwest of present day Berlin and Potsdam. The walk would have been possible thanks to the low sea-levels of the period when much water was still locked in the ice-sheets; the southern part of what is now the North Sea was low-lying land, traversed by slow-flowing rivers, often marshy, and broken by the occasional hill such as Dogger Bank.

10 Friesack, Germany: a view of the recent excavations. Note the flat character of the landscape and the wide drainage ditch to the left where the Mesolithic site was first recognised. Photograph courtesy of Bernhard Gramsch and Brandenburgisches Landesmuseum für Ur-und Frühgeschichte.

I

a Brackagh Moss, N Ireland: a former raised bog previously exploited for peat and now managed as a nature reserve. The abandoned peat-cuts have filled with water, allowing fish and aquatic and emergent plants to colonise, whilst trees such as birch and willow are spreading on the drier ground. The range of plants and animals reflects the variety found in many temperate wetlands of the post-glacial period. Photograph Bryony Coles.

b

c

I

b Two logboats from Springfield, Glasgow, recorded in a watercolour of 1847 by A McGeorge. Reproduced by kind permission of Dr C Batey from the collection of Glasgow Museums and Art Galleries.

c Key Marco, Florida, in 1895. This was the area of Cushing's excavations. Watercolour by Wells Sawyer, courtesy of Marion Gilliland.

d Beaver-felled wood: the Mesolithic birch stem from Star Carr.
e Modern beaver-felled wood from Ontario.
The facets on the Star Carr wood show the same pattern of parallel grooves in groups as seen on the modern wood, each group consisting of the grooves left by a set of beaver-teeth as the animal took a bite. Photographs John Coles.

Noyen-sur-Seine, France.
f A view of the Mordants' excavations of the Mesolithic peats preserved in an ancient channel of the river Seine.
g Preparing to lift one of the Mesolithic fish-traps. The long, supple stems used to make this trap were subsequently identified as privet.
h Mesolithic basket, one of the earliest known from Europe, woven from willow stems of varying colour, with a privet rim. Photographs courtesy of Daniel Mordant.

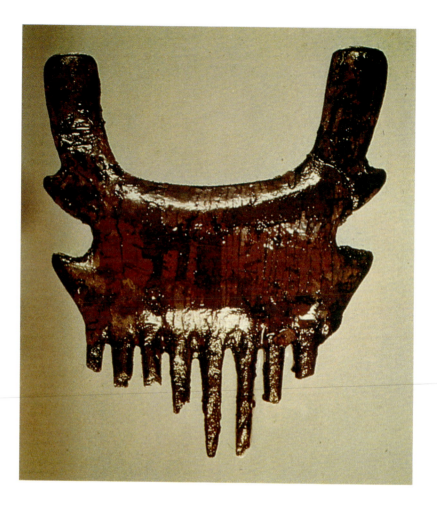

I

i Wooden comb, of *Camellia japonica*, painted with lacquer from Torihama, Japan. About 6,500 years old. Photograph Torihama Shell-Mound Research Group.

The land between Potsdam and Schwerin was once sprinkled with small shallow lakes and peatbogs. As in many other parts of Europe, technical developments in recent decades have made it possible to drain the organic soils for agriculture. Following drainage, the peaty soils have shrunk and wasted away, exposing previously buried islands and archaeological features, both of which may also be cut through by drainage ditches. Early in the 20th century, an island and associated Mesolithic material was discovered at Friesack and when a new drainage scheme was proposed for the area in the early 1970s, excavations began, directed by Bernhard Gramsch of Potsdam Museum (Gramsch 1992).

The investigations at Friesack continued until 1989 (illus 10), revealing a long stratigraphy of archaeological layers and natural sediments, representing periods of human settlement on the shore of a former lake, interspersed by periods of abandonment. As at Star Carr, a small group of people had probably visited Friesack on a regular basis, settling by the lakeshore for a few weeks, moving on to another ecological zone as the seasons changed, returning to Friesack another year at much the same season as before. Analysis of seasonal indicators such as food remains indicates that people were usually present between March and May. Radiocarbon dating indicates that the site was in use for longer than Star Carr, probably for over a thousand years from about 11,000 years ago, during the Early Mesolithic. There were 10 to 20 occupation episodes in every two to three centuries, interspersed by a century or so with no evidence for people's presence. A later series of occupations need not concern us here.

The combination of wetland location and continuous waterlogging (until the recent drainage) has resulted in very good preservation of the artefacts and debris that people left behind them, including bone, antler, wood, bark and other plant materials. The undisturbed stratigraphy combined with radiocarbon dating of many of the layers has allowed the relatively precise dating of much of the archaeological and environmental evidence, and some interesting interpretations of the sequence of events at the site. But to appreciate these it is necessary first to look at the artefacts.

11
Friesack, Germany: an antler axe-head and its wooden haft. Photograph courtesy of Bernhard Gramsch and Brandenburgisches Landesmuseum für Ur- und Frühgeschichte.

Friesack has produced a range of organic objects, and things made from a combination of different materials which might sometimes include an inorganic element such as a piece of flint. The finds include an antler axe complete with wooden haft (illus 11), a more complex axe with a flint blade set in an antler sleeve, again with its wooden haft, and another axe, this time without its blade, but with an alder-wood sleeve, probably rootwood, a good choice to withstand the shocks of use. Other wooden artefacts include a rowanwood paddle, pinewood

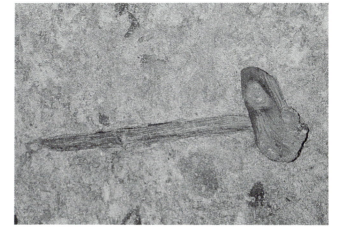

arrows, and parts of pinewood spears. At the base of a waterlogged pit, possibly a well, a container was found made from folded birch bark. Nothing of these varied artefacts would have survived on a dryland site in the same region, apart from the flint axeblade.

Bone and antler artefacts are known from dryland sites, with finds similar to Friesack's pierced teeth and decorated pieces. Projectile points, usually made of bone and sometimes barbed, have an added dimension at Friesack due to the combination of waterlogged and undisturbed conditions. Some of these points retain the birch-bark pitch that was used to attach them to a wooden shaft, with maybe a fragment of shaft as well. Others, hafted in a different way, still have strips of willow-bast binding wound around their lower half.

More remarkable, perhaps, is the survival of rope, string and netting, also made from willow-bast (illus 12). The willow-bark fibres were rolled and twisted to make a yarn, which for strength was then either plaited using three yarns, or plied using two yarns. When making nets, the two-ply cordage was used, and the nets were made either by knotting, or by using a knotless technique not unlike a form of knitting.

Gramsch has noted that technological differences in the material culture from Friesack show an interesting chronological patterning (illus 13). In the first sequence of visits, covering maybe as much as three centuries, people used birch-bark resin to haft their bone points, they made nets in the knotless manner, and their rope, apart from that used for nets, was plaited. During the next sequence of visits, spread over perhaps two centuries, the people on the Friesack lake shore

12
Friesack, Germany: left a) a large piece of knotless netting, made from twisted willow-bast cordage. Nets such as these may have been used for carrying things, or for catching birds and small mammals or fish; right b) a short length (c 25cm) of rope made by plaiting together several willow-bast strings. Photos courtesy of Bernhard Gramsch and Brandenburgisches Landesmuseum für Ur-und Frühgeschichte.

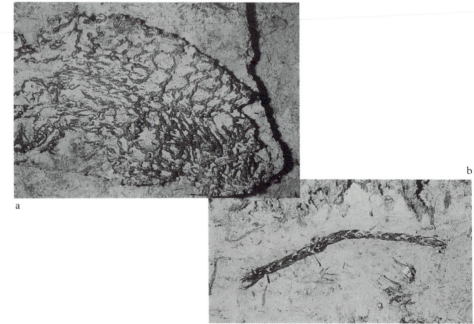

used willow-bast strips to haft their bone points, they made nets in the knotted style, and all their string and rope was plied. The third sequence of visits, spread over about three centuries, saw a return to the use of resin for hafting, knotless nets and plaited string and rope.

It has been suggested by Gramsch that these changes in material culture are a

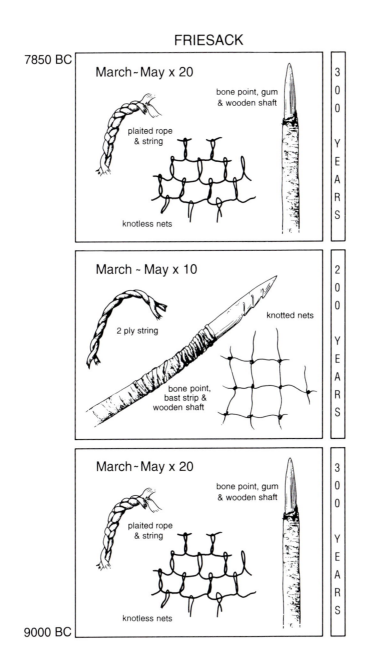

13
Chronological chart illustrating the changes in organic material culture seen at Friesack from the early phases of occupation (base) to the more recent (top). Drawn by Sue Rouillard based on information supplied by Bernhard Gramsch.

reflection of shifting tribal boundaries. Two groups of people with slightly different cultural traditions may have been using the general area, with the boundary between them moving first this way then that as the centuries passed and first one group then the other having the Friesack lake within their territorial range. Other explanations could be put forward, such as the use of knotless nets to catch a particular species of waterfowl, and knotted nets for another species, and the changes in material culture therefore stemming from changes in prey. Or maybe the knotless nets served as carrier bags, and were not hunting or fishing gear at all. The explanations are not necessarily mutually exclusive, and no firm conclusions can be reached until Friesack has been fully studied and published. Already, however, we can see that it is the organic material culture which has provided the evidence for discussion, rather than the many thousands of flints and other stone artefacts recovered from the site. In fact the differences in hafting, cordage and nets all relate to the ways in which willow-bast was used. Without a waterlogged, undisturbed site we would not even know that people used willow-bast, let alone the technical and cultural quirks of how they used it; it is the wetland context that has provided an opportunity for a more complex interpretation of the past, hanging from little bits of string.

FRENCH FISHERMEN

A third Mesolithic site from Europe, later in date than Star Carr and Friesack, shows further aspects of the advantages of wetland preservation. The site is Noyen-sur-Seine, about 100km upstream from Paris, excavated by Daniel and Claude Mordant in advance of gravel quarrying during the 1980s. Their work at Noyen (illus If) was in fact prompted by the discovery of a Neolithic causewayed enclosure set on a meander of the Seine, a dry site but with an ancient channel of the river along its eastern edge. Hoping to find Neolithic organic material in the peaty waterlogged fill of the channel, the excavators soon exposed a wooden fish-trap. It was sampled for radiocarbon dating, and the result showed that the trap and associated peats were Mesolithic not Neolithic. Subsequently, the Mesolithic occupation at Noyen has been shown to extend from about 9,000 to about 8,000 years ago (Mordant & Mordant 1992).

The Noyen archaeological material, like that from the previous two sites, consists largely of the abandoned artefacts and debris of hunter-fisher-gatherers who came seasonally to the water's edge, with repeated short visits over a long period of time. One important difference in terms of the archaeological evidence is that the Noyen settlement was on the bank of a river channel, not a lake. It was for the most part a backwater, allowing the peaty fill of the channel to accumulate. But from time to time floodwaters caused erosion, and the Noyen record may have been truncated in places. The character of the riverine wetlands must have been different from that of the Star Carr and Friesack lakes in various respects, although backwaters and recently cut-off channels may have offered many of the same resources as a freshwater lake. Being later in time, further south and located by a major river, Noyen had the wider range of plant and animal species, except perhaps for waterfowl; the hinterland carried relatively dense forest which at the time of first occupation was shifting from pine to a preponderance of deciduous trees, mostly hazel, oak and elm.

A bare 1,000 flints were found in the course of excavation, most of them undiagnostic in terms of relating Noyen to the Mesolithic of the wider region, and varying little from beginning to end of the life of the site. However, the peaty fills of the channel can be separated into a lower, early, layer and an upper, later, layer; several interesting changes in the lives of the bankside settlers can be suggested on the basis of differences in the evidence from the two layers.

The earlier occupants used a variety of wooden and basketry artefacts, and left behind them a canoe which is one of the earliest known from Europe. The pinewood tree trunk had been hollowed out using fire and an axe or adze blade to make a boat at least 5.0m long and about 0.5m wide. Six fish-traps were recovered, including one made from long thin stems of privet, a shrubby species that grows very long thin whippy branches when not trimmed into suburban submissiveness (illus Ig). Privet was also used for the rim of a basket, the body of which was woven from willow stems of several different colours (illus Ih). A fragment of hurdle-work about 1m square may have belonged to a fish-weir, or fallen from an abandoned dryland shelter. Together with the canoe, the basket and hurdle-work are amongst the earliest examples of their kind known from Europe.

The fish traps of the lower peats may well have been used to catch eel, for eel bones predominate amongst the identified fish bones from these levels. Many were caught in the summer months, and the presence of burnt vertebrae suggests that the eels may have been split and smoked, perhaps for later consumption, although eel is very tasty when smoked and eaten directly it has been caught. Amongst the other animals trapped or hunted from the river were beaver and otter. Wolf, fox, aurochs and roe-deer were hunted along the woodland edge and red-deer, pig and lynx or wildcat from the thicker forest. Some of these animals were hunted for their pelts as much as their meat, and although there is no doubt that pig and deer, for example, were butchered and cooked, deer-hide and pigskin, antler and tusk, bristle and bone may also have been valued. As for the cooking, it seems that the larger animals were butchered where they were killed and brought back to the riverside settlement in quarters. There, the carcasses were chopped up and cooked over a fire, the meat still on the bone. Long bones were split to extract the marrow.

The upper peats held no fish-traps or other wooden artefacts. Possibly they were carried away by flood-waters, but it seems likely that fish-traps at least had gone out of fashion, to be replaced by fish-hooks made out of bone; the catch was mainly pike. A variety of animal species was hunted, as before, but pig was now the preferred quarry. The carcasses were predominantly those of young pigs, brought back whole to the site where the meat was cut off the bone.

Whoever lived at Noyen in this second phase of Mesolithic occupation had ideas different from their predecessors about what to eat and how to cook it: pike rather than eel for fish, pork for meat, kebabs or stew as a method of cooking rather than meat roasted on the bone. Some of the differences will have been due to changes in the resource base as climate and vegetation changed with time. Others may reflect developments in domestic technology, the introduction of cooking vessels for example (although it must be said that none has been found at Noyen). The Noyen record is more patchy and disturbed than that from Friesack, and it does not have the same degree of chronological precision. Nevertheless, the wetland context has preserved evidence for choice and change in an area of human activity – food and its preparation – which is close to the heart of many a present-day French person.

One of the features of hunter-fisher-gatherer sites is their unpredictability, turning up in unexpected and unanticipated places. We now move out of Europe to look at two sites, entirely different in character, but each of which has already contributed to our knowledge of early societies in Japan and in America. The two sites, Torihama and Windover, like those we have already discussed, show the expansion of information that comes from sites where we might have expected only slender traces of the past to have survived. They also show how archaeologists have deliberately or inadvertently gone In at the Deep End.

A GLUT OF ORGANICS

The islands of Japan are geologically unstable and many earth movements and volcanic activity have created an archipelago of high, steep hills and mountains, often forested, with relatively few caldera and alluvial plains, river and coastal terraces. The plains and terraces are used today for agriculture and settlement. Most of the archaeological sites lie on these plateaux but an increasing number are now known from low-lying wetlands in river basins and other waterlogged areas. Here the preservation by flooding silts or peat is often very good (Matsui 1992). Some of these sites are of the Jomon period of Japanese prehistory, an episode dated from *c* 10,500 BC to *c* 400 BC, and one site in particular has been selected to represent all that is best in wetland archaeology, and equally to demonstrate some of the problems we face today.

Torihama was an ancient hunter-fisher-gatherer site on the shore of an inland lake , near the northern coast of Honshu. On the shore of the lake, various ancient settlements once existed, and parts of them became covered and sealed by lake silts. Today, the flat low wetlands at Torihama are cultivated for rice (illus 14). Many years ago, the river Hasu exposed the midden of an ancient settlement and, in more recent years, river improvements to prevent flood damage threatened the site. As is usual with most development projects, archaeological sites, once discovered, are difficult to preserve, and at Torihama very extensive rescue excavation was done, by building coffer dams around the midden and pumping groundwater out.

The excavations, directed by Katsuhiko Amitani, revealed various separate and distinct midden levels, the earliest being c 12,000 years old, but the main occupation appears to have been c 4,500 BC. Early Jomon settlements usually consisted of semi-subterranean houses, thatched to ground level, with various pits perhaps used for storage. At Torihama, the dwellings were on the dry ground but the shoreline had various structures such as boathouses, piers and stakes for boats, perhaps food-processing huts, and places for disposal of the rubbish. The middens thus created in the lake waters were enormous (120m long), the lowest levels separated from the upper levels by volcanic-derived sediments, mud and a natural shell bed. That the actual buildings of the settlement were near the lake edge is shown by the 1,000 boards and planks, from dismantled or collapsed structures, that came to rest in the midden levels.

The excavators of the midden, working under rather constricted conditions and under pressure to complete, admit that they undertook the work full of anticipation for good results without realising the enormity of their task. The midden yielded two tonnes of bone, thousands of pieces of wood, huge quantities of shells, seeds, bark, fish scales, insects, and many fragments of stone, pottery, rope and baskets. In the county museum we saw about 10,000 large plastic bins of midden awaiting separation and analysis. Already a series of preliminary reports has appeared but it will be a long process before the definitive report emerges. (Preliminary reports, Torihama Shell-Mound Research Group 1979-1987; also, Kasahara 1981, 1983; Hongo 1989).

The ancient Jomon people of Torihama were utilising over 100 different elements in their diet by c 4,500 BC. Over 20 species of nut (walnut and water chestnut

14
Aerial view of the Torihama area of Japan, looking over the site to the lake waters, and the islands beyond. The river channel cuts through the ancient midden at the bridge, with the wooded ridge immediately adjacent. Photograph from Torihama Shell-Mound Research Group.

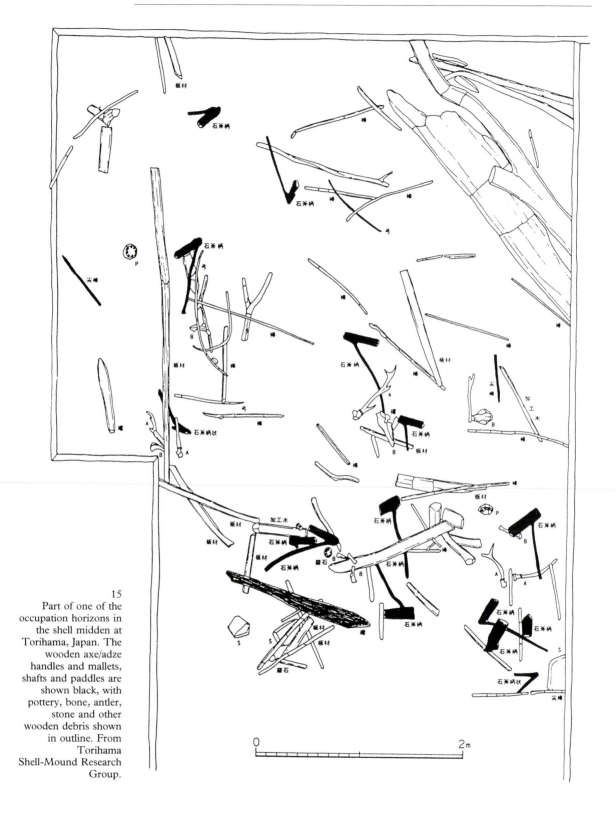

15
Part of one of the
occupation horizons in
the shell midden at
Torihama, Japan. The
wooden axe/adze
handles and mallets,
shafts and paddles are
shown black, with
pottery, bone, antler,
stone and other
wooden debris shown
in outline. From
Torihama
Shell-Mound Research
Group.

0   2m

among them), 18 species of fish and sea mammals (particularly carp, but also sea lion, dolphin, shark, whale, porpoise, puffer, bream, mackerel and sardine), 12 species of land mammals (deer, boar, raccoon and monkey included) and 33 species of shellfish have been identified to date, and some spade-cultivated beans, gourds and burdock seeds as well. All of this led to the deposition of dog and human excrement, and the coprolites will yield interesting analyses. The seasonality patterns suggest that this was a permanent settlement, by a small group of people numbering perhaps only 15 at any one time, but the community persisting in a richly varied environment for many decades. Environmental analyses suggest that a beech forest existed at the onset of settlement, but the effect over time of the Torihama settlement has yet to be elucidated. The people were ranging widely, as some open sea animals were taken, and a logboat in the later level shows that the waters of the lake were doubtless a part of the normal routine of food procurement.

Because of the very good conditions for preservation of organic material, Torihama is the most prolific Japanese site for early prehistoric wooden artefacts (illus 15). Here in Britain we are rightly excited to find one prehistoric bow or axe handle, and the recent discovery of the bow from Rotten Bottom in Dumfriesshire, dated by radiocarbon to *c* 4,000 BC is a very important find, and the oldest dated bow from Britain (Sheridan 1992). At Torihama, about 500 years earlier, the people left a quite extraordinary amount of material that became incorporated in the midden, and already there are 196 bows identified, as well as 31 smaller bows for drilling. The preliminary reports note 66 paddles, 186 wooden handles for axes or adzes and many other less-identifiable pieces of tools that, when broken, did not reach the consuming fires. Quantities of stone and bone tools, and pottery, were also recovered from the midden. More interesting are 148 pieces of rope, 28 pieces of baskets or mats, and textile woven from hemp in a 2-ply twist; such materials are hardly known from most hunter-gatherer sites in Europe although there are notable exceptions as we have already seen in this chapter. Unique for this period is lacquer work, the paint made from the sap of *Rhus verniciflua* mixed with either red haematite or black carbon. So far, 77 wooden objects and 111 pots have been identified with lacquer, including bows and a fine wooden comb made of *Camellia japonica* (illus Ii).

Torihama has already rewritten Japanese prehistory; the standard texts on Jomon culture are now peppered with exceptions and additions, all from Torihama. The materials recovered are now being assessed for a dedicated Torihama museum, as a major cultural centre for the public. This is another example of the way heritage centres are being developed, specific to a site, rather than to a regional overview with little focus. Torihama is, at the moment, an artefact-based site, and future analyses of the evidence about the environment, seasonality, cultural relations, and structures are expected. When these are delivered and assessed, the Torihama midden will become one of the world's most significant hunter-fisher-gatherer sites in enlarging our knowledge about the past.

BRAINS

It would be inappropriate to neglect one final hunter-gatherer site in this theme, because by any reckoning the site of Windover in Florida has enlarged the past of the south-eastern United States and has exposed the anthropologists called to the site to all manner of problems. Following the exploits of Frank Cushing in the late 1890s at Key Marco, wetland archaeology in Florida was more or less moribund for decades, until a few people in the 1970s and 1980s began to realize the huge losses of unique well-preserved sites that were being drained and dredged out of the peat soil, as 'development' took place for orchards, houses, industries and tourism. The demand for water from the freshwater interior lakes and rivers to be pumped to the coastal resorts and cities was one of the major reasons why lakes and marshes began to dry out, and with them many ancient settlements and burial grounds were damaged. Funding for rescue archaeology was slender, and only a few archaeologists, Barbara Purdy among them, persisted in efforts to retrieve some of the evidence.

In 1982 all this changed for one site. At Windover near Cape Canaveral on the Atlantic coast of Florida, dredging for a housing development began to bring up pieces of wood and human bones. Glen Doran, an anthropologist, was called in with a small team and soon could demonstrate that the human bodies were well-preserved, as skeletons, some had pieces of cloaks or blankets associated, and various other artefacts were also present. Some radiocarbon dates were obtained and suggested that the site was in use about 8,000 years ago, and thus one of the earliest hunter-fisher-gatherer sites in eastern North America (Doran 1992; Doran & Dickel 1988).

16
The Windover, Florida, burial swamp after excavation. Part of the swamp deposits remain sealed behind the sheets, now protected by back-filling and water. The area in the foreground yielded over 160 bodies. In the background is the development that resulted in the discovery of the site. Photograph John Coles.

Armed with this information, the developer re-aligned his plan for the site to avoid further disturbance, and helped to get major funding of about £600,000 (equivalent) to allow part of the site to be properly investigated (illus 16). In the event, about half of the site has been excavated, the rest sealed and waterlogged for the future. The site was a burial pond in which wrapped or clothed bodies had been laid, sometimes staked down to keep them in place. Almost 170 bodies have now been recovered, with perhaps 100-150 remaining undisturbed. This is one of the largest assemblages of human remains of this antiquity in the New World. The condition of the bodies shows that they were buried in the pond within 48 hours of death, in conditions of nearly neutral water (pH 6-7) so bone survived well although the skin and flesh was dissolved out. The fabrics on or over the bodies were astonishing, with five variants of twining or weaving so far identified. Fine tunics at up to 10 strands per cm were found along with blankets, mats, bags and rope with heavier 3-strand twining. The Sabal palm or Saw palmetto was probably the source of the fabrics, and perhaps it was masticated in the preparation. The fabrics are unique for North America at this early time.

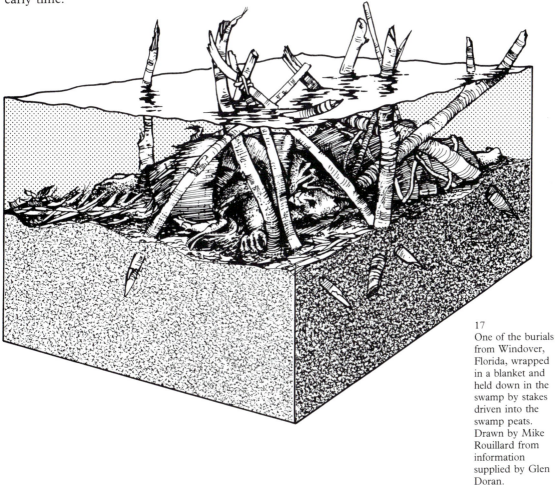

17
One of the burials from Windover, Florida, wrapped in a blanket and held down in the swamp by stakes driven into the swamp peats. Drawn by Mike Rouillard from information supplied by Glen Doran.

The dead were laid in the burial pond (illus 17) with various grave goods such as bone and antler points and pins, antler hammers and antler hooks, and shark teeth or dog canines glued to wooden hafts. The animals that provided this material included deer, manatee (sea cow), cat and dog. In addition, bottle gourds were among the offerings, again by far the earliest gourds in North America. Some wooden bowls, pestles and a spring trap were also in the pond sediments along with numerous wooden stakes that held the bodies down. All of these objects and materials are organic, and most would have vanished had the site been drained. There were fewer than 10 stone tools in the part of the site excavated, for 168 burials. This places lithics where they belong, in our opinion.

The humans were of mixed ages, very young and up to 65-70 years old; 74 were adult, and 11 of these had suffered broken arms during their working life, and three had had skull fractures, all of these wounds healing. One 47-year-old had had an orbital blowout, probably because he got a point stuck in his right eye; his left arm had been broken, perhaps as he flung it up to ward off the blow; he survived the damage but had had to adapt his posture in order to see and move forward. One child had spina bifida and osteomyelitis; it had a severe leg infection and had lost the right foot, yet the child survived until the age of 15 when renal failure finally overcame the life. This is the sort of information that brings archaeology closest to the humanity of people. We generally deal with the anonymous past, with bland populations building houses, eating animals, burying the dead – all unnamed and mostly undifferentiated. Rarely do we get closer to individuals, to one person's own circumstances, in this case illness, injury, being cared for and looked after with affection during his or her lifetime of 15 years, and then buried with care. From what we know of this person, there was severe disability and great pain at times; yet the life went on, not contributing at all to the quest for food, or the gathering of firewood; perhaps he or she helped with the preparation of fibres for rope or cloth. Whatever the case, we can identify with this life and its supporters.

Conditions of preservation in the burial pond were such that the stomach contents of some of the bodies could be identified, and apart from the foods consumed just before death some indication of seasonality could be determined; late spring/summer/early autumn are the periods for a number of the burials. In general, the people had a freshwater aquatic diet but there are some exceptions. One adult male had consumed 550 elderberries, 40 grapes and a prickly pear cactus fruit just before he died, perhaps not unconnected events. But what got the Florida State legislators and the public really excited about the Windover pond was the realisation that brain tissue was still present in the skulls – in 91 of the skulls by the end of the excavation. Although brain tissue had been previously found at another Florida site a few years before Windover was discovered, the quantity of burials and the excellent condition of the bodies at Windover created much interest and great misguided enthusiasm. There were hopes expressed that DNA could be compared and potentially matched with the Amerindian peoples, but this has so far been unrealised. There were claims advanced that somehow we could read the thoughts of these people, and the anthropologists were quick to close down that wild idea. And some of the more outrageous suggestions are, in a way, summed up by a reported headline in a local newspaper when the Windover find was announced: 'Brains discovered in Florida'. This is surely too good to be true.

JOINING THE DOTS

On dryland sites, the excavation, identification and interpretation of post-holes has taken up much archaeological time, and space in the literature. From the possible wind-breaks of Mesolithic camp sites such as Morton in Fife (J Coles 1971) to timber structures of the scale of the Neolithic building at Balbridie (Fairweather & Ralston 1993) and the complexity of the Dalladies long barrow in its wooden phases (Piggott 1971), part of the fascination and frustration of posthole sites has been the scarcity of sound evidence for sorting out the postholes into structures of known shape, size, date and sequence. Sometimes it is possible to determine the length and width of a structure with some certainty, as at Balbridie where a rectangular structure 22m x 11m is outlined by the postholes.

Very often there is charcoal or other organic matter associated with the postholes which can be used to obtain a radiocarbon date. But we have long recognised the imprecision of such dating, arguing for example that the Dalladies dates could be significantly older than the building of the timber mortuary structures, if the charcoal taken for radiocarbon assay came from the inner rings of mature trees (J Coles & Jones 1975). Such deviance is quite apart from the normal standard deviation which, as we all well know but do not always take on board in practice, means that dating by radiocarbon yields time-spans not single years. The need to calibrate radiocarbon dates is also well-recognised; today calibration is on a much surer footing than even a decade ago but liable, in its refinement, to convert the timespan of an uncalibrated date into two or three separate series of years. To take an example from our own work in Somerset, one of the peat samples from the Glastonbury Lake Village has a calibrated result at one standard deviation of 8 BC–AD 143 and AD 165–AD 188; at two standard deviations the span is 94 BC–AD 236 (Q-2629: J Coles & Minnitt 1995, 179). As we shall argue in this chapter, how much better to have a post with its tree-rings ready to be counted.

DATING A TRACKWAY

Our conversion to a belief in the superiority of posts can be traced easily to the discovery in 1970 of one particular structure in the Somerset Levels, the Sweet Track. This was a plank walkway providing a narrow raised footpath across a reed-swamp, which we knew from an early stage in our investigations to be Neolithic in date. Three separate categories of evidence were relevant: the trackway occurred low in the peat stratigraphy of the Levels, in the first season of excavation a flint axe-blade and flint leaf-shaped arrowhead were found lying beside it, and a short series of radiocarbon dates indicated a date of about 3200 bc (uncalibrated). Soon the discovery of round-based pottery confirmed that the trackway belonged to the earlier Neolithic (J Coles *et al* 1973).

Even at this level of dating, the wooden structure had various implications for Neolithic studies. For example, the use of long straight oak and ash planks and even longer roundwood poles, either of which might have well-cut mortice holes, indicated more developed wood-working skills than most archaeologists at work in the early 1970s normally associated with stone-axe-wielding early farmers. Indeed, the Sweet Track (illus IIa, b) provided a visible, three-dimensional demonstration of the use of wood to confirm a Neolithic date for the technological skills required to put up the Balbridie building, when the age of the latter was still under discussion. Furthermore, we had the undisturbed context and undoubted direct association of trackway, flint axe-blade, leaf-shaped arrowheads, round-based pottery and, by 1973, a beautiful polished axe-blade of jadeite (illus 18). The artefacts were contemporary with each other and with the trackway, and the dating of any one item therefore helped to date the others. The jadeite axe, by virtue of its association with the track, became associated with the round-based pottery, and with the suite of radiocarbon dates placing trackway wood in the later 4th millennium bc (uncalibrated). Previously, little was known of the period when jade axe-blades were in circulation in Britain, since most were stray finds; here was one of undoubted earlier Neolithic age.

As a linear structure, the Sweet Track could be comprehended without the precise dating of individual elements. Without knowing how long it took to build, how long it remained in use, and whether or not it was repaired at intervals, we could assume that all parts of the track were in simultaneous use: it could not otherwise have functioned as a pathway enabling people to walk from the Polden Hills to a

18
Sweet Track, Somerset Levels. Uncovering the jadeite axe-blade discovered beside the trackway during the 1973 excavations. Much of the peat covering the track has still to be removed but the piece of wood visible beside the axe-blade is a part of the track and not a haft for the axe. Photograph Somerset Levels Project.

19
The Sweet Track
and associated
range of artefacts.
The track was
built in 3806 BC,
used and repaired
for ten years, and
abandoned by
3791 BC. All of
the artefacts were
dropped or
deposited along
the track during
these years.
Drawn by Sue
Rouillard.

large island in the middle of a reed-swamp. The arrival of Ruth Morgan (then Jones) in the Somerset Levels in 1973 was soon to refine the dating of the Sweet Track further, through her researches on many aspects of tree-ring analysis. The results were to open new possibilities of interpretation previously unthought of in the context of prehistoric archaeology.

Studying mainly oak, ash and hazel, Morgan established that the bulk of the wood used to build the trackway had been felled in one and the same year, probably in the winter. This was evident from the floating chronologies established for each species, based on the planking split from oak and ash tree-trunks and the roundwood pegs and poles cut from younger growth of all three species (Morgan 1988). During excavation many wood-chips and trimmings were found, indicating that the various elements of the structure were cut to size or axed to a point on location, down in the reedswamp.

3806 BC

Experimental wood-working using stone axes and the same species of trees as those used in the Sweet Track indicated that the cutting of wood into lengths, splitting trunks into planks and axing poles to a point should be done before the wood becomes seasoned. Oak may take up to two years to season, hazel perhaps six months. Willow, a species used particularly in the middle stretch of the trackway, can turn to unworkable hardness within a month or so of felling and later becomes brittle.

From the two sets of observations we concluded that the wood was worked during building of the structure, which happened shortly after felling. Coupled with the tree-ring evidence for felling of the bulk of the wood in a single episode, this indicated that the full length of the trackway was built within a few months of the felling.

Early in the 1980s, we built a replica of the Sweet Track in the reedy vegetation of an abandoned peat cut, using wood of approximately the correct size and species. We were amazed at how quick and easy it was to put the components together to make a firm walkway, and we subsequently suggested that two small teams could have built the original track in a single day, provided that the components were already assembled. Later reconstructions by other people have confirmed the ease and speed of building.

Morgan continued to study the Sweet Track wood, and identified a few pieces of ash and hazel wood that had grown for up to ten years after the track was built, and she suggested that they had been cut to repair areas of minor damage. From this evidence we could argue that the trackway was in use for a decade. The lack of evidence for any later repairs, together with the relatively low level of fungal attack on the wood of the structure, indicate that it fell out of use within at most 15 years of building.

The oak tree-ring chronology of the Sweet Track was by this stage over 400 years long, but it could not be matched to any of the dated master chronologies from north-western Europe. Thus, although we knew that the wood had been felled and the whole track built within a single year and that within 15 years it had gone out of use, we could not say exactly when this happened. The best we could do was to quote the mid-point of the radiocarbon dates: when calibrated, soon after 4000 BC.

In the meantime, Jennifer Hillam in Sheffield and Mike Baillie in Belfast, with their respective colleagues, were researching various different aspects of dendrochronology. Their work led, amongst other things, to the cross-matching of several previously isolated floating chronologies of Neolithic age from England. One of these was the Sweet Track chronology. The establishment of an English Neolithic master chronology for oak, with the Sweet Track chronology as an integral part of the dated sequence, led rapidly to the publication of the first dendrochronological date for a Neolithic structure from Britain: the wood for the Sweet Track was felled over the winter of 3807/6 BC, the trackway was built in 3806 BC, it was kept in repair until 3796 BC, and by 3791 BC it had gone out of use. The pottery and axe-blades and other directly associated artefacts belonged to these years, 3806–3791 BC (illus 19) (Hillam *et al* 1990).

20
A view of Hauterive-Champréveyres, Switzerland. Lake Neuchâtel is held back by an encircling coffer-dam; the trees to the left mark the present shore-line; the shelter covers one small part of the multi-period site, all of which was excavated prior to road-building. Many of the ancient wooden posts are visible amongst the modern scaffolding and plank walkways which allow access to the excavations without trampling the organic, waterlogged archaeological layers. Photograph John Coles.

DATING A SETTLEMENT

The accuracy and precision of dendrochronological dating is such that we can identify a site where people lived at exactly the same time as the Sweet Track was built and used, but hundreds of kilometres away in the Alpine foothills: the site is the Neolithic village of Hauterive-Champréveyres on the shore of Lake Neuchâtel. We are not proposing a historical link between the two sites, but in selecting a settlement to illustrate the full advantages of posts over postholes we thought to underline the power of dendrochronological dating by choosing a site exactly contemporary with the Sweet Track.

Hauterive-Champréveyres is one of a number of large sites excavated in advance of road construction along the northern shore of Lake Neuchâtel. The work has been carried out by Béat Arnold and colleagues under the overall direction of Michel Egloff. We visited the site in winter 1983–84 (illus 20), shortly after a Late Palaeolithic series of hearths and associated artefacts had been found, but our visit was focused on the excavation of Neolithic and Bronze Age cultural layers and associated parts. We saw an impressive array of sieving equipment, many hundreds of artefacts in the early stages of post-excavation work, and site plans that presented a bewildering mass of wooden posts. A number of posts could be seen on the site itself, romantically blanketed in snow. At times, it must be confessed, the snow made it hard to distinguish the prehistoric posts from the modern low scaffolding and walkways designed to give people access to all parts

21a
Prehistoric posts exposed on the shore of Lake Neuchâtel at Auvernier during the winter of 1880, when the lake level was artificially lowered. From Egloff in Coles & Lawson 1987.

of the site without trampling the deposits. Even without the scaffolding, the posts did not resolve themselves into a pattern of structures, for those who contemplated them *in situ*.

The site plan for a major episode shows the many posts, their distribution clearly not random but still difficult to understand in terms of structures. The plan presents the same overload of information that the 19th-century archaeologists faced when the lake villages were first recognised, an overload that contributed to the genesis of the pile-dwelling myth (illus 21). Sampling of the posts, identification of species, and dendrochronological analysis combined with evidence such as the location of hearths and the distribution of artefacts have provided the key to understanding the settlement. Full publication of the results has yet to come, but Egloff has provided a preliminary outline of the sequence of events for just one of the several episodes of occupation at Hauterive-Champréveyres, the one that happens to be contemporary with the Sweet Track (Burri *et al* 1987; Egloff 1989).

Over the years that they lived at Hauterive, the Neolithic people set some 1900 posts into the lake marls (illus 22), most of them oak (1169 posts) but also poplar (483 posts) and the remainder alder, birch, hornbeam, beech, ash, willow, maple and hazel. It was fortunate for the present studies that oak was the preferred species, as this is the best species for dendrochronological dating. The preliminary results indicate that the oak posts were set up in the 17 years from 3810 BC, with several separate episodes of building being identified.

The sequence begins in the spring of 3810 BC when young oak trees, 20–23 years old, were felled and used to build a rectangular structure 7.0 x 3.5m. The long axis of the structure was perpendicular to the lake shore, and subsequent buildings followed the same orientation (illus 23). Later in the same year, two houses went

21b
A 19th-century interpretation of posts as the supports for an extensive platform, in this case based on the posts exposed at Ober Meilen on the north shore of Lake Zürich in the winter of 1853–54. From Speck 1981.

up to the east of the first one and three to the west. Minor repairs and alterations followed almost immediately, and were to continue throughout the life of the settlement.

22
Plot of the posts
belonging to the
Neolithic
settlement at
Hauterive-
Champréveyres.
Some patterning
can be discerned,
but few if any
individual
buildings can be
identified with
confidence.
Drawn by Sue
Rouillard from
Egloff 1989.

In 3807 BC, three years after the row of six houses went up, a smaller squarish building was put up between them and the lake shore. In 3804 BC, another small square building appeared. In 3801 BC, a further big rectangular building was added to the west end of the row of houses, several little buildings were added to the foreshore grouping, and a solid oak fence was put up along the edges and shore-side of the village. The posts for the fence had been felled in winter. In 3800 BC, the villagers built two more of the smaller structures and a small square setting of split oak posts. For another seven years, until 3793 BC, the minor repairs and alterations continued, but no later felling has been identified. Given that repairs were needed somewhere in the village every year until then, it has been concluded that the repairs stopped because people had abandoned the site, probably by about 3790 BC.

Several structures have been identified but not dated. These are the buildings and

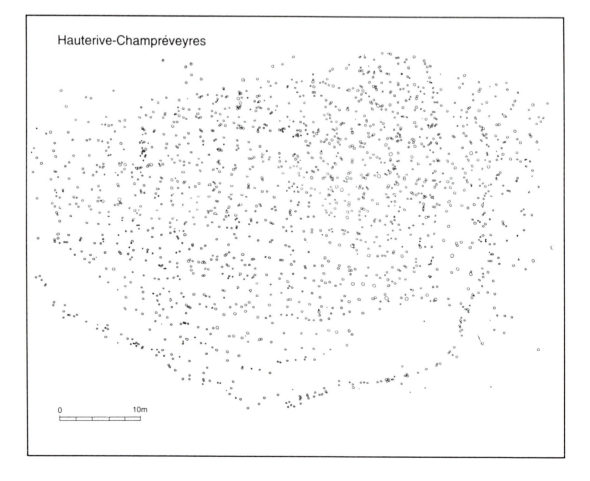

Hauterive-Champréveyres

0   10m

fences where species other than oak were used, for example the poplar fence which can be traced inside the oak fence, and several of the smaller buildings. In due time, it may be possible to match the site chronologies for different species, as Morgan has done for the Sweet Track, Billamboz for sites in southern Germany and Bartholin at Alvastra (see below). Then some of the non-oak structures within the Hauterive-Champréveyres village will be precisely dated. But it is clear from the layout of the site and from the associated material culture that the undated structures are contemporary with the rest of the village. The size of the first settlement must imply a large group of people moving to the lakeside, enough to fell, split, haul, shape, erect, roof and furnish six large houses in the first summer.

The settlement and the material culture of Hauterive-Champréveyres can be assigned to the years 3810–3790 BC, and the Sweet Track and its associated material culture can be assigned to the years 3806–3791 BC. The evidence from posthole excavations would be most unlikely to reveal either the exact contemporaneity of the two sites or their surprisingly short duration. Dendrochronology has shown that a number of prehistoric settlements and structures were equally short-lived, and we shall return to this point. But, before leaving

23
The posts of Hauterive-Champréveyres resolved into a village on the basis of dendrochronological analyses. Building began in 3810 BC and was completed by 3800 BC. Repairs and alterations continued to 3793 BC, soon after which the inhabitants moved away. Drawn by Sue Rouillard from Egloff 1989.

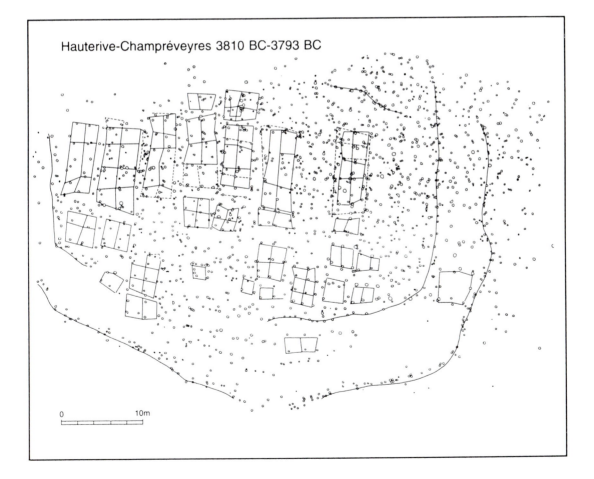

Hauterive-Champréveyres 3810 BC-3793 BC

0   10m

Hauterive-Champréveyres and the Sweet Track, we would like to point out that in the same years that people built and lived in the circum-Alpine village, somebody who walked along the Sweet Track dropped or deliberately placed just beside it the axe-blade – made of jadeite from the circum-Alpine region.

DATING A NEIGHBOURHOOD

At present, the earliest wetland settlements to be dated by dendrochronology come from the peaty surrounds of the Federsee, a relatively shallow lake in southern Germany much reduced from its former size. A number of sites were excavated in this region in the earlier half of the 20th century; renewed work in recent years has re-located known sites, identified new ones and dated several of the settlements thought on typological grounds to be amongst the earliest. Oak samples from the settlement of Henau Hof I and from Hartöschle suggest construction before 4000 BC. Shortly after, the first settlements on the shores of the Bodensee appear; a small group of sites on the western arm of the lake has been particularly well-studied by Helmut Schlichtherle and his colleagues, with dendrochronological analysis by André Billamboz (Billamboz 1990; Dieckmann 1990; Billamboz *et al* 1992).

One of the sites excavated and analysed in detail is known as Hornstaad-Hörnle I (illus 24). There were several phases of occupation, and the following paragraphs are concerned with the earliest of these, Hornstaad-Hörnle IA (the overlying Hornstaad-Hörnle IB which we discussed in *People of the Wetlands* is later by three centuries). As with Hauterive-Champréveyres, the interpretation of the development of the village depends upon a combination of archaeological evidence and dendrochronological results. At Hornstaad-Hörnle IA (referred to simply as Hörnle I below) spreads of daub from collapsed walling have been particularly important in the identification of buildings.

24
Hornstaad-Hörnle IA, Germany: excavation of a part of the Neolithic settlement showing the density of constructional posts; some of the horizontal timbers probably belonged to the superstructure of houses, and have been preserved following collapse of the house. Photograph Bryony Coles.

Young oak trees were felled from 3913 BC to build the village, and it looks as though most of the building took place in 3912 BC. Some 20 houses have been identified (illus 25), and Billamboz suggests that there was room for up to 40 within the area of occupation, but only a part of the site has been excavated and one cannot be sure of the number of buildings

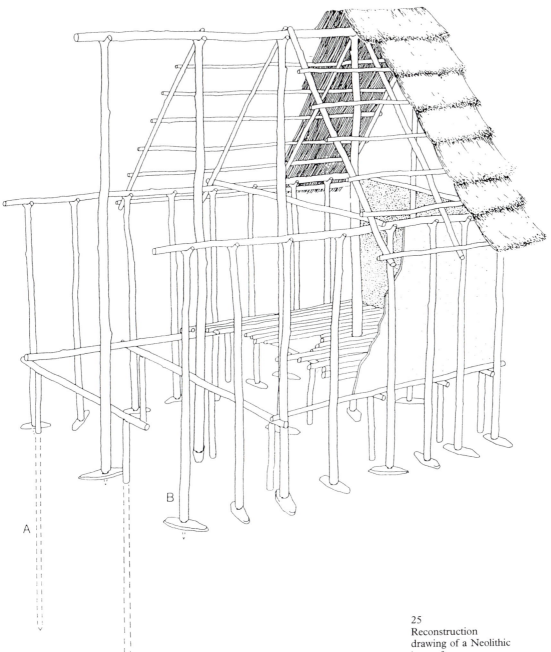

A

B

25
Reconstruction
drawing of a Neolithic
house from
Hornstaad-Hörnle,
based on excavated
timbers. Courtesy of
Landesdenkmalamt
Baden-Württemberg.

occupied at any one time. What is sure, both from the well-stratified archaeological deposits and from the record of the posts, is that a disastrous fire spread through the village, probably in 3910 BC; there was no break in occupation, houses were immediately rebuilt and some new ones set up. Building and repair work continued to 3904 BC; occupation may have lasted beyond this date, but in view of the accumulating evidence for constant repair to prehistoric wooden structures and settlements, we would suggest abandonment within 5 years at most of the last identified felling.

Within 5 kilometres of Hörnle I, and at much the same time as it was abandoned, two new villages were built on the lake shore (illus 26). One, at Hemmenhofen – Im Bohl, is estimated to have begun in 3900 BC and the second, at Gaienhofen-Untergarten, no earlier than 3890±10 BC. These dates are estimates because the wood sampled has sapwood but no bark edge in the first instance, and no sapwood in the second instance; without the final outer ring, an exact felling date cannot be given. In 3869 and 3868 BC, ash trees were felled to build Hornstaad-Hörnle II, adjacent to and some 40 years younger than Hörnle I. The ash is dated by the overlap of its ring sequence with that of the ash from Hörnle I, which in turn is dated by its match with the oak chronology from the site. Ten kilometres westwards along the shore and some 45 years after Hörnle II, in 3825 BC, wood was felled for a village at Wangen-Hinterhorn.

The lakeshore villages do not represent the complete settlement pattern of the region, for several reasons. Fluctuations in lake level mean that some shoreline settlements will not have been preserved. Others may remain to be discovered. Some have yet to be dated by dendrochronology, although typology and radio-

26
Map of the western end of the Bodensee, showing the known lakeshore settlements of one Neolithic phase covering about a century. It is likely that each village was occupied for between one and three decades, and perhaps only one or two villages existed at any one time. The map does not show the complete settlement pattern of the period, for there was also dryland occupation, and there may have been lakeshore villages that left no trace due to fluctuations in lake level, or villages that have yet to be identified. Drawn by Sue Rouillard based on dendro-chronological information provided by André Billamboz.

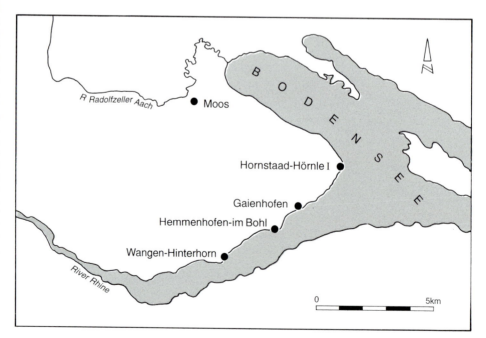

carbon dating allow for reasonably accurate placement in time in relation to the villages dated to calendar years. Settlement also took place away from the lake shore, and these villages are at best posthole sites or maybe only known from artefact spreads in the ploughsoil. Occasionally, the shadow of the missing settlements is to be detected in the tree-ring evidence, and the overall settlement pattern becomes that little bit more complete.

The oakwood from Hörnle I preserves evidence for probable human activity before the village was built. The oak was young, and it had grown rapidly. By sectioning one post which had fallen, and which was therefore well-preserved for a length of 2.8m, Billamboz found that the top had only three fewer rings than the base, indicating 2.8m of growth in three years. He suggested, on the basis of this and other growth characteristics, that the posts came from the re-growth of trees felled some 30 years earlier around 3940 BC. Calculating that approximately 150 trees were required to yield the oak posts used at Hörnle I, and noting that the similarity in growth pattern of the wood indicated a common origin in a restricted area of forest, Billamboz suggested that people had harvested the oak trees from the same area a generation or so earlier, to build a village that has yet to be located.

One settlement that could be of about the right date has been identified, the site of Moos, about 7km northwest of Hörnle I. Moos is not far from the lake shore, on the bank of a watercourse that meanders through a previously marshy zone to reach the lake within about 1km of the site. It is, however, a dryland settlement. The typology of the pottery and other artefacts found at Moos suggest that it belongs slightly earlier in time than Hörnle I and it could be that the people who built the later village came from here. The two settlements being about 7km apart, we could speculate that they made use of the same few hectares of forest for their building materials, the Moos people transporting their posts 4km to the west and, 30 years later, the Hörnle I people taking their posts 4km to the east. Although felled trunks can be moved quite easily by water, is this a likely scenario for the period?

The tree-ring record provides some further details about forest exploitation in the immediate region at this time, which may help to answer the question. Relatively young roundwood poles were used to build Hörnle I, mostly oak and ash with a little alder, beech and hazel. The tree-ring sequences for all five species have been matched, making it possible to date structures whether or not oak was used in their building. Following the fire, the inhabitants rebuilt their village mostly in ash, using trees which were large enough to have been used at the time of first building. It is thought that by 3909 BC the Hörnle I people had either run out of suitable oak within their part of the forest, or at least no longer had any close enough to use for re-building their houses.

When the settlements at Hemmenhofen and Gaienhofen were built, only 10 to 20 years had passed, not time enough for the Hörnle I forest to have grown to building size again. A different forest zone was used, which yielded oakwood old enough for the trunks to be split into several posts each. Forty years after the building of

Hörnle I, enough time had passed for re-growth from the oak stumps (stools) to have reached building size, but the adjacent village of Hörnle II was built almost entirely using ash posts, not oak. Willow and alder were also used for Hörnle II posts, with some maple, hazel, poplar, elm and birch and just a few oak and beech posts. Had the ash colonised the area previously cleared of oak, or was it re-growth from the stools of the ash used following the fire of 3910 BC?

The question does not have to be answered for us to begin to see that the forest of the region was a patchwork of growth at different stages. A range of species was present, in places fairly mixed and elsewhere dominated by one particular species like the stand of oak that supplied Hörnle I. Already the evidence suggests that people felled trees within a kilometre or so of where they were to build, since Hörnle was using a different source to Gaienhofen and Hemmenhofen. When Wangen-Hinterhorn was built, 5km further westwards along the shore, the ash and oak used were large, mature trunks, characteristic of primary forest. It would seem that people did not range far and wide for construction wood, if primary forest could survive for a century whilst people within 10km were apparently exhausting local supplies of their preferred building materials. The early settlement of Moos, we might conclude, was too far away to be the village whose shadow falls on the Hörnle I tree-ring record.

We have assumed, in all this, that oak was the preferred species for building, and the use of oak for Hörnle I, followed within two to three years by ash for the rebuilding after the fire, would seem to confirm this. We are not quite so sure what sort of oak was preferred, whether people sought out large trunks that could be split into many posts, or whether they went first for the long straight poles grown from the stump of a felled tree, poles which needed little further preparation for use. Likewise, we cannot yet say whether people exploited the forests close to home from choice, for example to minimise the task of transport, or whether they knew of good sources of construction wood at a distance but had no rights of exploitation in those places. However, the dendrochronological analyses of Hörnle I and neighbouring settlements continue, and these arguments may need modification as further details of the patterns of forest exploitation are revealed. At the time of writing, for example, Billamboz reports the possibility of regular alternation between ash and oak as the main species for house construction at Hörnle I (pers comm).

The present evidence from the neighbourhood of Hornstaad-Hörnle I seems to indicate successive villages, each one occupied for one or two decades only. If, and it is a big 'if', there was but one village in the neighbourhood at any one time, exploitation of the forest for construction wood was probably governed more by concerns over transport than by restrictions on territorial rights. Beyond one or two kilometres, it was not worth the effort to go for best building wood, and next best closer to home was used instead. In this, is there a clue to the short life of the villages, and to their spacing along the lake shore?

POSTS AND PEOPLE

The three sites discussed so far, the Sweet Track, Hauterive-Champréveyres and Hornstaad-Hörnle IA all have well-preserved wood, and the analysis of the wood in conjunction with other sources of evidence from each site has been remarkably informative. Date, duration of use or occupation, exploitation of territories and relations between groups of people are all better understood thanks to the unlocking of some of the information held in the posts, and there will be more to come as the science of dendrochronology develops. A few general comments on how the results from these sites have affected our own understanding of Neolithic peoples may be appropriate here.

First, there is the speed of building: in the Somerset Levels, two kilometres of trackway in a season, or a month; six substantial houses between spring and autumn for a Neuchâtel village; a Bodensee village rebuilt immediately following a fire and only two to three years after the settlement was founded. How did people find the time for felling and trimming and transporting and processing, not to mention the actual building, or was it all much easier than we suppose?

Secondly, there is the heavy consumption of wood. Although Morgan has calculated that seven large oak trees and about four smaller ones were all that were needed to supply the Sweet Track planks, which does not seem excessive, Billamboz reckoned that 150 oak stools were needed to supply the posts for the first set of houses at Hörnle IA. An equal quantity of wood, if not from the same species, was needed for the rebuilding and more still for later additions and repairs, all within a mere 10 years of the first building – and then people were off to start all over again somewhere else. As hinted above, perhaps it was exhaustion of local building materials that prompted people to move, rather than exhaustion of the soil. Indeed, one begins to think that fields may have been a by-product of the profligate use of timber rather than *vice versa*. These people, like the Iban of Sarawak in later times, could be dubbed *mangeurs de bois*.

Thirdly, and already discussed to some extent, there is the short life of settlements. Hauterive-Champréveyres, the one site of those under discussion that has been fully excavated, epitomises this: begun in 3810 BC and gone by 3790 BC, if not a little beforehand. Did people shift their farmed land as readily as their houses? Perhaps not, if it was timber rather than soil exhaustion that prompted the move, although the continual onslaught on the forest must have provided many new openings for cultivation and plenty of browse for cattle. Short-lived settlements succeeding each other rapidly within a region: would their separation in time be evident from the dryland record, or indeed through pollen analysis? Probably not. Studies which have used a combination of typology and radiocarbon dating to identify contemporary and adjacent groups of people with small differences in material culture, should perhaps be reconsidered in the light of the dendrochronological evidence for settlement shifts every decade or so. The people may not be contemporary but successive, the differences in material culture may be a reflection of time passing and not of the desire to be just a little bit different from one's neighbours, but a little bit different from one's parents. The region as a whole may be less densely populated than previously assumed.

If we are to use the evidence of the posts to provide a better understanding of postholes, we have also to ask if wetland settlements were typical or not. It could be that their location made them particularly short-lived. If so, why were they put there in the first place? In due course, typological studies of the evolution of artefacts such as pottery and flint on wetland sites of known duration may begin to give us an idea of the duration of dryland sites with the same artefacts. And, as we shall see later, there are exceptional dryland sites with waterlogged features that may also contribute to the discussion.

SOLVING AN OLD PUZZLE

Through the work at Hornstaad-Hörnle and Hauterive-Champréveyres we see the finest and most precise results of dendrochronology – the absolute dating of the individual components of a settlement and a settlement pattern. These sites, and there are increasing numbers of such sites, have the advantage of some construction in oak, a fine building material and one that is the basis of European dendrochronology. At some sites, large oak trees were being used, with long tree-ring sequences, so dendrochronological work is relatively easy although it has taken many years to bring agreement to the subject on a pan-European basis. Not all prehistoric sites have the advantages of oaks in their constructional phases, and it has taken some persistent and imaginative work to extend the concept of dendrochronology into new and surprising areas. We take as an example of this an old site that was in effect stuck – excavated long ago but incapable of a sensible and balanced interpretation. Because it was, or had been, a very wet site, the potential existed for new experimental techniques to be tried, and their success can be gauged by what follows below.

The site is Alvastra in central southern Sweden, near the eastern shore of Lake Vättern. It was substantially excavated in that rather depressed period of wetland archaeology, from 1909 to 1930, by O Frödin, who was not able to publish a full report (Frödin 1910). The site consisted of a platform of posts and logs covering an area in excess of 1000 sq m (illus 27). The wood had been laid in a small peatbog near a spring with a much larger bog stretching away to the north. The platform was positioned well away from the edge of the bog, about 75m from the nearest dryland, and it was clearly a deliberate decision to place the structure in the very wet spring-fed mire. There were over 100 limestone hearths placed on the platform, in a relatively structured manner, and the excavators attempted to work out the sequence of hearth-building on the basis of the formation of peat, and the wooden layers and artefacts of the platform, but this was very difficult to maintain in the absence of decisive chronological indicators.

A great deal of debris lay about on the platform, fire-cracked stones, animal bone, human bone, stone battle axes, pottery (much of it of high quality), and heaps of cereals. The animals brought to the platform included domestic cattle, sheep and pig, and wild animals such as deer, elk and pig, and fur-bearing bear, beaver, badger, marten and lynx. Some wild plants were also recovered, including apples and hazelnuts. A wooden trackway led into and through the platform from the dryland, and the disposition of the many wooden posts or piles on the platform

27
Plan of the wooden posts at Alvastra, Sweden, revealed by early excavations of Frödin (main area uncovered) and Malmer (trenches at north). Among the abundant timber and hearths, some distinct alignments can be seen. From Browall 1986.

suggested that there had been a series of rooms or compartments marked out, perhaps to segregate and divide the people who lived on, or visited, the site (Browall 1986).

But what was the site? How old was it, how long had it lasted before being engulfed by peat, and why was it there? It was clearly not a pile dwelling in the then-accepted Alpine lake settlement model. The spring mire was the puzzle, as it made the site constantly wet and the immediate surrounds must have been a treacherous bog, if not a watery marsh. The archaeologists could only guess at the date of the platform and at its longevity, and the answers they came up with were 'Neolithic' and 'perhaps several centuries', but the explanations were difficult to sustain.

In 1976–80, Mats P Malmer carried out a set of excavations on peripheral parts of the site, in association with environmentalists and dendrochronologists. The posts and logs were sampled and sent for analysis. They were identified as oak, hazel, lime, alder, elm, poplar and willow, and all were from young trees; it was thought that dendrochronology would not work. However, young alder from a trackway (the Abbot's Way) in the Somerset Levels had been successfully analysed for tree-ring studies by Ruth Morgan, and so Tomas Bartholin at Alvastra persisted with his analyses. He worked on 200 posts, of mixed species, and with Malmer's careful plans he succeeded in the experiment of trying to work out an internal chronology (Bartholin 1978, 1987). This revolutionised the interpretation of the site. What follows is an abbreviated version of the results, and the important aspect of it all is how the excellent preservation of young wood allowed the analyses to succeed.

The first evidence for activity in the immediate area, on the dryland around the spring mire, was a clearance of the trees of the forest about 75 years before the platform was conceived. The forest trees of oak, lime and hazel were felled, but the cutters left the elm trees standing, only pruning the branches, probably to encourage the production of elm leaf fodder for their cattle; Billamboz has identified a similar likely harvest of oak leaves from the Hörnle I forests. Some wild apple trees were also left uncut, presumably for the fruit harvest. This clearance, with elm and apple still standing, was maintained for about 40 years, and then no further felling or prunings occurred, and the woodland began to regenerate. The forest thus created then consisted of old elm, old apple and relatively young oak, lime and hazel, with willow growing in the wet edges near the mire. This was the woodland which provided the material for the platform at Alvastra; so far, the tree-ring analyses had worked well. The next stage was to see if dendrochronological analyses could help in working out the internal chronology of the site.

As it appeared that almost all of the trees had come from the same forest, showing the same sequences of growth, most of the platform posts sampled could be matched. This meant that the internal development of the site could be deduced. The diagram shows the result (illus 28). In the autumn/winter of arbitrary year 0/1, the East and West sectors of the platform were laid out. One year later (year

WARP

WETLAND ARCHAEOLOGY RESEARCH PROJECT

Professor John Coles
Fursdon Mill Cottage
Thorverton
Devon
EX5 5JS

Telephone 01392 860125
Fax (44)01392 861095

Received from
MJ C Coffyns
the sum of $40.⁰⁰

For books

By Beben
Enlarging the Past

Dec 7/99

Jan Carter

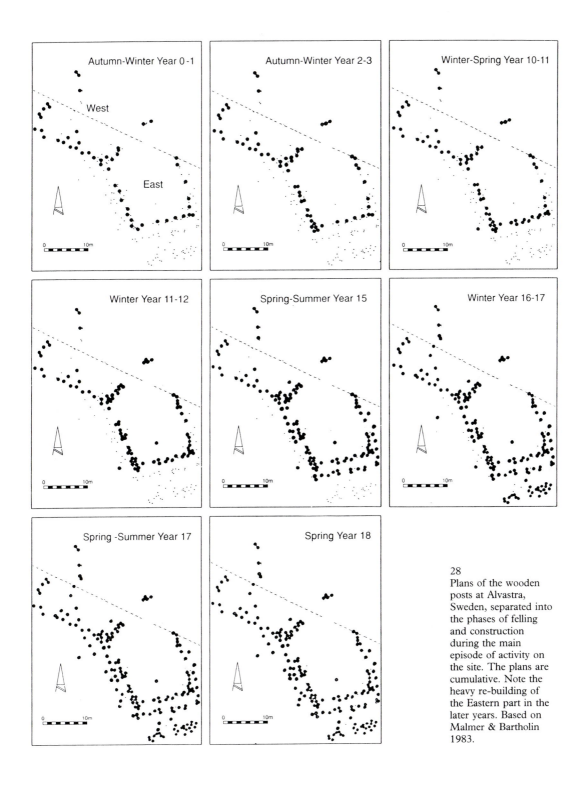

28
Plans of the wooden posts at Alvastra, Sweden, separated into the phases of felling and construction during the main episode of activity on the site. The plans are cumulative. Note the heavy re-building of the Eastern part in the later years. Based on Malmer & Bartholin 1983.

2/3), again in autumn/winter, more work was done on the East. Then there was a gap (see below) and in winter/spring of year 10/11, the East sector had more wood put in. In the winter of year 12, the East was rebuilt, and more wood went in in years 15, 16 and 17. In other words, the whole platform was built and renewed over only 18 years. Then there was a gap of 22 years after which a few pieces of wood were added, and now some human burials were placed on the site.

Within the 18 years of major platform construction, the tree-ring work on the willow species showed that the site had almost certainly been abandoned from time to time, and thickets of willow sprang up on and around the structure, mostly on the West sector, which was constantly being flooded or at least kept very wet beneath by the waters of the spring. This evidence of the willow trees disposed of any previous ideas of a settlement permanently occupied. The short life of the platform was also a revolutionary finding, although the wood sampled could not be used to provide absolute calendar dates. The radiocarbon dates for the site suggest an occupation *c* 3100 BC.

This brilliant set of analyses by Bartholin and Malmer provided new evidence for re-interpretations of Alvastra, particularly when allied to the environmental and other investigations (Browall 1986; Malmer 1986, 1991; Göransson 1995; During 1987). We now know that the site was very wet, placed deliberately by a spring that seems never to have stopped flowing. It was linked to the dryland, some 75m away, by a wooden trackway. Two main sectors, East and West, were laid out and 17 distinct rooms or compartments were built, with hearths, perhaps for individual families or other segments of Neolithic society. There were nine rooms in the East, eight in the West. The East sector was renewed often and its use was much more intensive and/or of longer duration than the West. The site was probably chosen because of its constant spring, its infertile land, and its inaccessibility. It could only be reached by a walkway through the mire, possibly obscured by vegetation or water. Around the mire was fertile dryland, and within an easy catchment there were a number of settlements and megalithic tombs. Surface survey as part of the Alvastra project has identified a number of Stone Age settlements very near the platform, both upland and lakeshore sites; these must have housed most of the people involved in the platform and its functions. One settlement within 200m of the mire was probably the 'mother' of the platform; it may have existed for a generation before the decision was taken to construct the platform. This platform soon became the focus for special gatherings of people from the neighbouring lands, who had established arable fields in the coppiced woods and whose sheep may have grazed around the platform during drier seasons.

From the platform there was a direct view to the granite and porphyry hill of Mt Omberg, 264m high (illus IIc); this may not seem much to Scottish hillwalkers but from the hill there are tremendous views down to the Alvastra site and well beyond, and from the platform looking west the hill ridge wholly dominates the scene. For one generation only (18 years), people came to the site; their arrival was probably seasonally determined. The various groups were strictly controlled, each of the 17 groups (families?) assigned to its own compartment (illus 29). Here hearths were built or renewed, fires were lit, a variety of animals drawn from a wide catchment was cooked and eaten, and during the short occupation some work in stone, bone and wood was carried out, and a large quantity of valuable

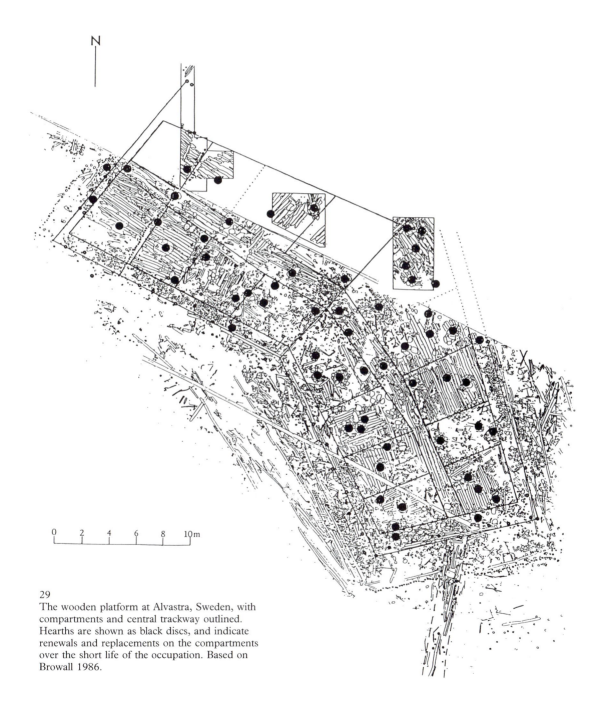

29
The wooden platform at Alvastra, Sweden, with compartments and central trackway outlined. Hearths are shown as black discs, and indicate renewals and replacements on the compartments over the short life of the occupation. Based on Browall 1986.

objects was deposited on the platform; stone battle axes, miniature axes of amber, flint and bone points, and fine pottery, were assigned to the ceremonies and abandoned to the forces of the mire when the groups left the site and returned to their homes. The East and West sectors may represent different social or economic populations; perhaps about 80-130 persons were involved at any one time (Browall 1986). After only 18 years of these activities, the practice was either discarded or was transferred to some other place. The platform was left, was overgrown and partly submerged by peat; then, still remembered, a small amount of renewal work took place and the platform received some burials. After that, nothing.

In a strange way, the sudden appearance and short life of the Alvastra platform is mirrored in the 20th century, 5000 years later. At the turn of the century, a railway passed by the platform; a station was built, together with a small hotel for tourists to Mount Omberg, and a small village emerged by the site. Today, railway, station, hotel and village are gone.

A CHALLENGE

The science of dendrochronology is not a new one, but its implications for European settlement archaeology have only been fully realised in the past few years. Our final example in this theme of Joining the Dots is a site wherein the application of dendrochronology has only now begun to yield results, and the powerful tool of internal tree-ring dating has yet to be applied to the entire site. The site is Biskupin, far larger and more massively built than Alvastra and indeed more substantial, profligate even, in the use of timbers throughout than any other prehistoric settlement in Europe (illus 30). Biskupin was discovered only in 1933 at a time when the level of the eponymous lake was particularly low and timbers were exposed to the gaze of the local schoolmaster (Rajewski 1970). The site was extensively excavated between 1934 and 1974, with serious interruptions and damage during the war years (Kostrzewski 1950). Parts of the site were reconstructed for public display and education, and Biskupin, a rather remote site well away from major centres of population, receives 200,000-300,000 visitors each year. The history of the site is itself long and fascinating, and it has required great determination and dedication on the part of the teams of archaeologists to maintain the ambitious programmes of work over the years, particularly in the past decade (Jaskanis 1991).

Biskupin fortified settlement, as it is called, was built on a low peninsula jutting into the lake of Biskupin sometime in the first millennium BC (Niewiarowski *et al* 1992). It was apparently destroyed and rebuilt at least once in its relatively short existence, and there is evidence that it underwent various episodes of damage from time to time, although these require to be worked out (Piotrowski 1995). The whole settlement was built of wood. The peninsula, almost two hectares in size, was enclosed by a rampart over 450m long and as much as 6m high. The rampart rested on an oak log foundation and was capped by a wooden palisade and had at least one tower gate. The rampart itself consisted of square-built oak frames filled with earth, and the entire structure probably required

30
Aerial view of the
fortified settlement
of Biskupin,
Poland, exposed
by massive
excavations in the
1930s. The
breakwater, box
rampart and
ringroad are
visible in the
lower left, with
house floors, stone
hearths and minor
streets in the
central area. The
photograph was
taken from a
balloon. Photo-
graph courtesy of
Biskupin
Department, State
Archaeological
Museum, Warsaw.

5,000–6,000 trees of substantial size, as well as vast quantities of wood for smaller fencing. The rampart was protected from storm-driven ice and water by 3–9 rows of oak and pine stakes driven into the lake shore at an angle of 45°, the 20,000 stakes probably representing the felling of 4,000 slender trees (illus 31). An oak causeway provided safe passage from the gate and alongside part of the rampart to the dryland some 250m away: it required perhaps 1,000 or more tree stems, 3-4m long.

Inside the rampart was a heavy ring road of oak and pine logs laid transversely, to form a 2–3m-wide road. From this, 11 streets ran in parallel across the oval site, creating a road system 1300m long and 2m wide; the number of logs required for this probably approached 15,000, representing a huge number of trees. The streets were lined with rows of terraced houses, or apartments, built of logs, each house measuring 9m x 8m in plan, standing 6m high with a pitched roof. Each had a door facing south, an entrance hall for storage and animal shelter in the severe winter months, and one main room with a 'family bed' in one corner and a central activity area with stone-built hearth. There may well have been an upper platform for storage or sleeping. It is estimated that a single house, and there were just over 100 of them, required 50–100 trees of oak and pine, the oak 50 year-old trees and the pine younger; thus, 5,000–10,000 trees had to be felled and cut to

31
Photograph of the breakwater poles (right), box rampart frames (centre) and ringroad (left) of the Biskupin settlement, protected in part by the 1930s water-logged condition of the site. Photograph courtesy of Biskupin Department, State Archaeological Museum, Warsaw.

shape to create the houses, with an unknown quantity for repair and renewal wood.

The total amount of wood required for this great fortress is difficult to calculate as there are many imponderables, but on any reckoning it is huge. The Biskupin builders were as voracious *mangeurs de bois* as their counterparts at Hörnle I. Large areas of forest must have been cleared, some perhaps clear-felled for pasture and arable cultivation, and others more selectively felled. Recent very important palaeoenvironmental work has indicated that at the time of construction of the settlement, the pollen of oak shows a slight increase rather than falling away dramatically. It has been suggested that selective felling took place, clearing out all the younger more slender trees, leaving a relatively few older trees to flower more extensively in the opened landscape. It may have been more complex than this, with much wood floated in from other forested areas linked to the Biskupin Lake by streams and smaller lakes. The pollen evidence suggests that the settlement may not have been constructed as one massive undertaking, but developed over a longer time of, say, 50 years or more. If the settlement existed for about 100–150 years, there would be time for deliberate planting and coppicing cycles to be established, to provide the essential repair material as well as any major renewal or expansion of the roads, rampart, causeway or houses. It may be that the environmental evidence, allied to tree-ring studies (see below), will show that the causeway in particular was a later event, and the breakwater as well, both stabilising elements in an increasingly delicate balance between water and the peninsula (Piotrowski & Zajaczkowski 1993).

The recent palaeoenvironmental investigations have done much to clarify the conditions under which the settlement was established and the reasons for its demise. The kame-derived deposits which formed the low peninsula into Lake Biskupin were only 1.0–1.5m above the lake levels at the time of occupation, and were capped by dried-out peaty soils. At the best of times, then, the settlement was never far above the waters and there is good evidence that during the occupation the lake levels were rising, causing some of the house floors to be raised 0.2–0.5m by extra layers of wood or earth.

The work of analysis of the 6 million objects recovered from the excavations still goes on, and relatively little of it concerns wooden artefacts or the wooden components of the fortress itself, although the variety of objects made of wood is extensive; disc wheels of carts and wagons, logboats, ards and other agricultural tools, gates and doors, ladders and bed-frames are among the more substantial items.

There is a very extensive list of animals kept and hunted, and plants cultivated and gathered. The environmental evidence points to a substantial increase in grassland and in fields of cereals at the time of the settlement. The land taken in for arable crops is estimated to be 250ha but other calculations suggest an area twice this; wheat, barley and millet were grown, as well as peas, beans, poppy, turnip and other plants. The land cleared and maintained for cattle, sheep and horse was probably very great, with much grazing on the many meadows fringing the lakes and streams, and hay-making. The long cold winters would necessitate the laying-in of good supplies for the animals, including humans. The wild animals hunted included deer, boar, bear, wolf, otter and beaver, wildfowl and fish, and among the plants gathered were hazelnuts, acorns and sorrel. The whole territory of the settlement must have been well-known, patrolled perhaps, and its seasonal and regular offerings anticipated and guarded.

The settlement itself has had only a very broad and simple phasing based on early stratigraphical observations. The early settlement was built mostly of oak and a later, smaller, settlement overlying the first was built of pine. But this simple phasing may well mask extensive repair, renewal and rebuilding on the site almost constantly, with old wood re-used, new wood brought in, and different species selected for the particular task; this is what we have seen on the other sites discussed in this chapter.

The dating of the Biskupin fortified settlement has always posed problems for central European archaeologists who have had to rely upon the typology of the artefacts and radiocarbon dates for structural elements not necessarily tied into the detailed sequence of building. When the site itself is the type-site for the whole region, typology can become tautology. It has generally been assumed that the main phases of occupation were of the Early Iron Age, and Biskupin fitted into a site territory conforming to an area of control of about 25 sq km, with a string of other sites to the north, on the lake and river catchments; Sobiejuchy is the nearest site and about three times as large but its preservation has not been as good as that of Biskupin.

What was an obvious need for Biskupin was for some attempt to be made to obtain dendrochronological precision for the site phases, and internal tree-ring analyses, and for a start at working over the site and pinpointing crucial overlaps and associations of structures. Despite earlier excavations, much wood remained in place, protected by soil, or had been left exposed for visitors to see in an eroded condition; there was no problem in finding samples (illus IId). In 1993, the first results of a sampling of timbers came from Tomasz Wazny, with a dendro-chronological date of 738 BC for a post from a main phase of building. A series of felling dates, 742–726 BC, emerged and must represent the first great episode of construction in oak (Wazny 1993). What is now required is a strategy to sample all the main terraces of houses, the cross streets, the ring road, the rampart, tower, breakwater and causeway. By so doing, the site's development might emerge and questions could be posed about a number of features that so far have resisted efforts to explain:

1 The origin of the settlement. Did Biskupin begin as a small tentative occupation, only later expanded into the massive fortified town? Or was it organised from the first as a major establishment, with a large labour force introduced to the area? If the latter, from where and how was this organised?

2 The development of the site (illus 32). How was the site laid out, as it gradually or rapidly turned from either a village or encampment to a heavily fortified town? When and how did renewals and renovations take place?. What was the effect of the underlying dampness of the low peninsula? It is remarkable that the extensive excavations of the site have failed to expose any substantially larger, more elaborate, or more isolated structures that might have housed the organiser (leader) of the population; a planned town of 500–1,000 people required some measure of control, but in this case the control may have been exercised from a discreet position on the site, or more probably from off the site. If the latter, from where? Similarly, the excavations have not revealed any unusually large structures, or central place, where communal acts might be performed and watched; other sites of the same period often have such places. A 'village square' of about 300 sq m lay just inside the main entrance and was probably an unloading area. Only 20% of the Biskupin settlement remains unexcavated; it is too much to ask that this may hold the answer to these questions of control, organization and performance.

32 Reconstruction view of the fortified settlement of Biskupin, based on earlier drawings from Rajewski. The uniformity of the layout is only one of the puzzles concerning this site. The causeway extended along the edge of the drier land off to the right, as the settlement was built on a peninsula rather than an island. Drawn by Mike Rouillard.

3 The episodes of destruction. How extensive were these? Perhaps there were accidental fires that damaged only parts of the site. A whole row of terrace houses would be vulnerable to a single accident on the windward side. Perhaps there was a huge conflagration and deliberate destruction. If so, by whom, and how was the site restored? How long would that take, from where came the new supplies of wood, pine instead of oak, and why would a site once shown to be

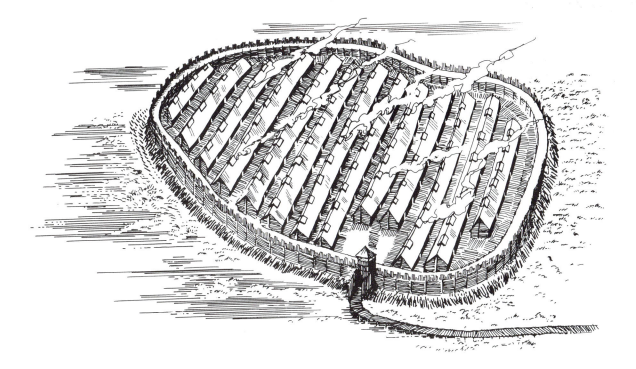

indefensible be rebuilt to a smaller and less fortified plan? Perhaps there was a replacement of population.

4 The end. What caused the settlement to be abandoned? Was it a final assault that exhausted the will of the defenders to persist in a hostile political environment? Was it an economic problem that had become unbearable, as land was exhausted, and supplies of wood became scarce? Or was it as simple and effective as a rise in the level of the lake, that brought water flooding in and made conditions hopeless for occupation? The environmental evidence is clearly in favour of an environmental catastrophe, with the ever-rising lake level overflowing the earthen banks and creeping into the streets and houses. In time, the whole peninsula was flooded, and lake sediments were laid down over the abandoned and collapsing structures. Yet there is evidence that a final occupation took place shortly after the collapse of the fortified settlement, leaving behind no defensive structures but clear signs of a determined effort to squat on the site and persist with a water-based economy. In a way, this is the most intriguing of the horizons of settlements. How soon after the major abandonment did it occur, and were the people involved the remnants of a scattered population, or an entirely new group of people? The entire episode of settlement on the peninsula was perhaps only 150 years, but this has never been more than a guess based on the typology of the material culture, and may well be found to be wildly out.

Some of the answers to these questions can be achieved by the full analysis of the excavation records, and study of the artefacts. Others, however – and we suspect the majority – can only be gained by a massive effort at tree-ring analyses, not to give absolute dates but to provide relative dating to the elements judged crucial in the stratigraphy and structure of the site. Joining the Dots, or some of the Dots, at Biskupin would not necessarily increase its popularity with the public, as that is already assured and enshrined in the emotion of the Polish people, but it would increase its significance for our knowledge of central European prehistory and hopefully would lead on to even wider recognition. To foreshadow Chapter 5, however, the efforts now being made at Biskupin to preserve the waterlogged structures and integrity of the site are crucial if we are ever going to be able to undertake the selective but nonetheless massive sampling project for dendro-chronology. There is no purpose in devising a great strategy to Join the Dots if the Dots gradually fade under the pressures of pollution and desiccation.

a The Sweet Track, Somerset Levels. View looking southwards near the southern terminal of the trackway. In the foreground, the substructure of the track is well-preserved, and several planks which formerly provided the raised walkway can be seen floated off to the left. Photograph Somerset Levels Project.

b Reconstruction of the Sweet Track in use in 3806 BC. Drawing by Edward Mortelmans.

c Alvastra, Sweden in 1995: view across the site, marked in part by red posts, to Mount Omberg with Lake Vättern on the other side of the ridge. Photograph John Coles.

d

e

d Biskupin, Poland, 1991: first sampling of the timbers of a roadway by Tomasz Wazny; these yielded the dendrochronological dates 742–726 BC for the first episode of building. Photograph John Coles.

e A small basin bog in Bohuslän, Sweden. The moss and cotton grass have carpeted the surface but beneath is the black water. Photograph John Coles.

f The clothes of the Huldremose woman from Denmark: woollen skirt, sheepskin cape and other items. Photograph in Silkeborg Museum by John Coles.

g

h

i

II

g Nydam valley, southern Jutland: looking down the narrow valley towards the 1994 excavations in the middle distance. The Iron Age platform is thought to have been more-or-less where the shrubby trees are on the left, and the lake covered much of the valley floor. Photograph Bryony Coles.

h Wooden vessels from Nydam.

i The Nydam head upon discovery. Carved from alderwood, the tang-like neck suggests that the head was once part of a larger object. It is now on display in the Viking Ship Museum, Roskilde. Photographs h) & i) courtesy of Flemming Rieck.

3

THE GOOD, THE BAD AND THE UGLY

There is always a strange fascination about peatbogs, marshes and swamps (illus IIe). They don't seem to be of this world – no dry ground for your feet, no place to build your house, no dryland to plough and plant, and your animals sink – just a dank, dark flatness that seems to threaten, unwelcoming to all. Such places are just the scenery needed for countless dreadful movies set in swamps, bogs and other 'great scrope of drowning places'. Who can forget such classics as *The Creature from the Black Lagoon, It Came from Beneath the Swamp,* or *Swamp Thing*? In fact, who can remember anything about them except for the blackness that soon swallowed most of the actors, forever. But it is easy to exaggerate, invent and imagine all sorts of lurid tales about the beings, spirits, elves and unfriendly forces that dwell in such places, and there are plenty of tales recorded by historians and churchmen about the superstitions and fears of those people who lived near and often worked in the bogland. Sometimes danger, real danger, has actually existed.

In the autumn of 1968, Abbé Jominet of Aulnois-sur-Seille, Lorraine, went fungus-collecting with his dog Blanchette. While walking through a woodland he . . .

'. . . came to a small clearing with grass and moss growing. The ground gave a little under my feet but as there had been rain I was not suspicious. Suddenly, as I stepped forward, my right leg sank up to my knee. I grasped a branch of a tree that was growing out over the edge of the clearing, but it gave way. I began to sink in the morass. I called for help but nobody heard me. I sent Blanchette away in the hope she could find someone. The cold dampness penetrated my clothes. I realised there was no escape. Half an hour, then an hour, passed, and the bog had buried me up to my shoulders. I could not utter a word, I was gasping. In the distance I heard my dog barking, it became louder. I saw her among the trees, behind her ran a man I did not know. I was by now up to my neck in the bog. The man pulled me free after a great effort'.

The historical records compiled by two of the pioneers of peatbog archaeology, Alfred Dieck and Hajo Hayen, reflect the fate of other real people who did not survive the encounter. In 1920 a man's body was found in north Germany, spread-eagled as if trying to swim out, his hands clutching tufts of heather. And in 1945 a body was discovered vertical in the peat, arms upraised and one leg inclined as if trying to climb out of the grasping bog.

For us, the fascination of these bogs comes not only from their atmosphere of mystery and danger, but also from the many records of ancient human bodies and other things preserved within the peats, and also of the events, harmless actions, that led to their sudden exposure, and of the frightened reactions of those who encountered them. In this chapter we will consider a range of objects found in these places.

BODIES

Real bodies have a special attraction for many people from all walks of life. Cremated remains are rarely of wide interest because they are so fragmentary, although they often yield surprising amounts of information. Skeletal remains are generally more interesting to the public, particularly if they (the skeletons) are old. Most people are very curious about real bodies, of flesh and blood, with eyeballs and brains. Human bodies can be preserved by near absolute dryness, or by sudden freezing, or by sudden cooling and waterlogging in special conditions, and it is with this last phenomenon that we are concerned.

The trail of discovery of these bodies goes back in north and west Europe over 500 years (Dieck 1965; Glob 1965; Hayen 1987). Peasants cutting peat in a north German bog in 1450 came upon a body, but their priest advised them to leave it alone – elves dwelt in the bog and it was wicked to take anything. As time went on, more and more bogs in the north were taken for turf-cutting, and the records of discoveries increased in quantity, although not often in quality. A find made 220 years ago on Fyn in southern Denmark was remarkably well-recorded because a local magistrate was called in to investigate (Glob 1965). The body found was a male, naked except for a sheepskin cape over the head; he had a reddish beard and cropped hair, and his throat had been cut. Gradually, over the decades, more and more tantalising records of bodies were made, in Denmark, north Germany, the Netherlands, Britain and Ireland, and some idea of their antiquity began to emerge. A little-known body from the Balderhaar bog in Lower Saxony was described in a letter of 1862:

> 'three children found the head of a dead person in a crumbling peat bank . . . the long red hair hung out of the wall . . . stones had been laid over the head . . . nothing else of the body remained . . . there was a heap of burnt bones with charred pieces of wood. Among these lay a rusted and charred brooch.' (A Dieck pers comm).

The depth at which the bodies lay in the peats, and the occasional object found with them, and the numerous isolated finds made at equal depths, all suggested a great antiquity for the bodies.

Alfred Dieck spent over 40 years amassing records of bodies and creating catalogues of the discoveries; his great work of 1965 *Die europäischen Moorleichenfunde* was augmented by papers produced for two decades more; our contact with him was in 1977. He was sometimes rather over-enthusiastic in accepting old records of uncertain quality (van der Sanden 1990; 1995) and extended his search for 'bog bodies' far and wide. His southernmost finds came from Crete; the report claimed that bodies accidentally discovered before 1783 had not decomposed, were considered therefore to be vampires and were dealt with accordingly, presumably with the usual Hollywood procedures. Dieck listed 1400 bog bodies, of which about 300 could be dated, from the Mesolithic to medieval times. Among his many lists he could point to about 200 separate heads or headless bodies. Over 1000 discoveries were undated, and barely a dozen or so of the bodies had been lifted from the peat and taken to a museum or other safe, or safer, place (see below). This was because many of the bodies were come upon suddenly, by a single or pair of peat-cutters, at work in the dark bog; their spades might cast up a hand or foot, or the peat section might expose a head, or half a head. But it is surely remarkable that the earliest photographs of bog bodies, still *in situ*, show more or less intact bodies, little damaged by the probing spades. The Rendswühren man of north Germany was the first to be photographed, in 1871, but his preservation was extraordinarily fortunate (illus 33). Found naked but with a wool rug and skin cape over his head, and a leather garter on one leg, he was exhibited on a cart at the nearby farm. He lost various bits of himself, as souvenirs, as well as parts of his rug, and was unceremoniously propped up against the barn for photographs to be taken. Today he rests more peacefully in the Schleswig Museum, and in a better state than many a body recovered more recently (see below).

None, however, has the impact of the most famous ancient face in the world, the posthumously-renowned Tollund man. His story is well-known and he can now

33
The bog body from Rendswühren, Germany, discovered in 1871 and somehow preserved by natural drying. His woollen rug lies over him. Photograph in Archäologisches Landesmuseum, Schleswig, by John Coles.

be seen, the real head on an artificial body, in a dramatic display in Silkeborg museum. His contemporary, the man from Grauballe not far away in central Jutland, is equally dramatic in his museum case at Moesgård, but the tranquillity of the Tollund face is a contrast to the rather startled grimace of Grauballe; no wonder, as the Grauballe throat had been cut from ear to ear, whereas Tollund man had only been strangled. Both of these famous bodies were of adult males, both naked, and both still had traces of their last meals (see below). A number of bog bodies are not naked, and some were dressed in elaborate, some in more simple, clothes; others had clothing piled nearby.

The most remarkable of the clothed bodies came from Huldremose in Jutland, with a subsequent history to match. In 1879 a peat-cutter was at work in the bog, and discovered a body about one metre deep in the peat. One hand was accidentally cut off, but otherwise the body was left untouched and the local teacher, a man deeply interested in archaeology, was called. He came at once and denied the onlookers any opportunity to take souvenirs. A local man had disappeared some years before and the police descended, put the body on a stretcher and carried it to a nearby barn where the body was undressed and cleaned; as it was clearly a woman, the police departed, leaving the head scalped due to their excess of enthusiasm. The district doctor took charge now and informed the Museum of Nordic Antiquities in Copenhagen that he had buried the corpse in the churchyard and that '. . . the clothing is now hanging to dry at my farm after having been cleaned. Everything is in good condition . . .' This was an exaggeration; some days later two boys found a knotted woollen string with two amber beads hanging on a wheelbarrow, and tried it on with disastrous consequences. The museum telegraphed back and requested the clothing and also the body, so an exhumation took place and the whole lot went off to Copenhagen by steamship. All of this was in 1879. By 1904 the museum was short of space and it wrote to the 'highly honourable Museum of Normal Anatomy' in the same city suggesting that the corpse be transferred; thus the University of Copenhagen came to possess a well-preserved naked body, with little or no information about it. The clothing remained in the Museum of Nordic Antiquities (now the National Museum) and became recognised as the finest set of Iron Age clothing ever discovered (Munksgaard 1974).

The woman had an outer cape made of several pieces of sheepskin in two colours, with the hair outside (illus IIf). It was lined with sheepskin on the neck, shoulders and sleeves, the hair inside, and beautifully sewn with fine stitches. This cape was closed at the neck, so that it had to be put on like a sweater. A separate inner cape of lambskin, hair inside, was well-worn unlike the almost-new outer cape. An ankle-length woollen skirt, very wide, and finely seamed with a feather stitch, was held in place by a leather thong with a leather button and loop, drawn through the warp threads of the skirt. A woollen scarf was worn over the shoulder and under the left arm, and fastened with a bone pin. The hair when found was held with a long woollen string also wound around the neck and the woman had a necklace of two amber beads (the wheelbarrow necklace). In the lining of the inner cape were various trinkets – two thongs, a horn comb, and a woven hairband.

But what of the body transferred to the University in 1904? It was soon lost in the archives until a search was made in 1978 when, behold, the corpse was found; it was not a member of staff after all. The body had dried, naturally, and had not apparently changed much since its first discovery in the peatbog when it was described as 'looking rather like a smoked ham and greatly wizened'. It is exactly the same today, although a little more flattened. The woman had broken her left thigh bone in life and walked with a limp. Her left arm was tied to her body with a leather strap. The right arm, having lost its hand in the 1879 discovery, had also been broken in antiquity and chopped by an axe that almost cut through the bone. This may have been the cause of her death. Her gut contained the remains of her last meal, a rye cereal bran with various wild seeds. This is not dissimilar to the vegetarian meals of the Tollund and Grauballe men, a barley gruel with a variety of wild seeds such as spurrey, camelina, clover, persicaria, pansy and mustard. Was this a starvation diet brought upon the communities by natural disaster or humanly-induced unrest, or was it a special pre-death meal, or was it the normal food of the people in the Iron Age? Certainly it does not sound very tasty, and those famous TV archaeologists Mortimer Wheeler and Glyn Daniel tested it in a well-publicised experiment. The gruel, made up of seeds obtained from a London birdfood shop and Kew Gardens, was thick and oily, greyish-purple in colour with orange and black flecks floating on the surface. Wheeler claimed that Tollund man had probably committed suicide if he had to eat this stuff every day, and he and Daniel required much Danish brandy to wash it all down; it was clearly a successful experiment. More recently it has been suggested that the stomach of Tollund man contained an ergot fungus from the crop gleanings on damp ground, and thus he was high on psychotropic drugs, hence his tranquil expression; this all may be mischievous gossip. But all of these well-preserved bodies have stories attached, and have inspired tales, poems, plays and other public activities, most about the peaceful fen, the dark deeds, the silence of death: 'Here was I drowned . . . where worms in darkness dwell and, through the walls, the waters of the bog seep in.' (C Hostrup *A Sparrow among Hawks*).

The bog bodies of Denmark are generally associated with the name of PV Glob whose book *The Bog People* (1969) is one of Europe's best-selling archaeological texts. This book first appeared in 1965, the same year as Alfred Dieck's more wide-ranging and less readable book was published. Since then the study has moved on, the discovery of bog bodies has slowed to a trickle, and effort has been concentrated more on scientific analyses, dating and preservation rather than social matters. Much of the new work is brought together in van der Sanden's book on the Dutch bog bodies (1990) and in Turner and Scaife's *Bog Bodies* (1995). By an exhaustive search of the archives, Dieck's quantification of bog bodies has been revised so that the totals from Denmark (*c* 500), Germany (*c* 900) and the Netherlands (55) represent all the bodies for which some sort of record exists. Some of the records consist of the actual surviving bodies or parts thereof, others seem reputable by virtue of a number of reports or scientific notes, and others are represented only by a single less satisfactory report. In addition, work on dating and on the provenances of bog body finds has shown that the practice of depositing human bodies in wetlands extended back into the Mesolithic and earlier Neolithic of north-western Europe. This important development in studies came from work on two skeletons from Bolkilde bog in Denmark (Bennike *et al* 1986); both bodies were male and had been stretched out on their backs. The older man had had a severe hip injury during his life and was probably permanently disabled. Fragments of cloth were nearby and a piece of rope lay beneath the neck of the older man. The skeletons were found in 1946, and were wholly overshadowed by 'real' bog bodies discovered in that year in the Børremose, and by a succession of bodies leading up to Tollund and Grauballe. Yet the radiocarbon dating of the Bolkilde bog finds, and other skeletal remains from northern bogs, extend the practice of disposal of humans, probably executed, back to the Mesolithic period (Bennike & Ebbesen 1986).

The dating of bog bodies has been further refined by the recent work. The Dutch evidence indicates no bodies of pre-Bronze Age date; most are of the closing centuries BC and 1st century AD. The Danish evidence points, as noted above, to a much longer span of time, with again a concentration in the later first millennium BC and early centuries AD. No German bog bodies have had radiocarbon dates applied to the human remains, but pollen evidence suggests that many are of the late Iron Age and Roman Iron Age, that is, the same general period of concentration as in the Netherlands and Denmark. The British and Irish evidence is not far removed from this range (see below). But it is useful to remember that human remains have been placed in rivers, lakes and peatbogs from very early times, and that these are almost always reduced to skeletons or isolated bones, rather than being preserved as classic skin and fleshy bog bodies with hair, clothing and the rest. The phenomenon of bog burial was long-lived and widespread, but we can still get the most useful information from those bodies, of the later periods, where preservation has been good.

BOGMOSS

The question of preservation has always intrigued us. How is it that a human body, or that of a dog, cow or sheep, can survive seemingly intact in a peatbog? What is it in the bogs that prevented or inhibited decay? Preservation of bodies, even that of Tollund and Grauballe men, was not 'perfect' and bone is often seriously degraded if not entirely absent; the skin and shoes were all that remained of the Damendorf man. The essential ingredients for preservation appear to have been that the bodies were put into the cold (less than 4° C), and were covered at once by water or wet peat so that maggots, foxes and other creatures could not attack them. Furthermore, the water or peat had little or no oxygen and was still, not flowing, and the bogmoss, the *Sphagnum* peat, folding itself around the body, contained the cell-wall polysaccharide Sphagnan which created a kind of tanning effect, turning the bodies leathery while at the same time converting to humic acid and thus dissolving the bones (Painter 1991). The peatbogs where bodies are found are not themselves acidic as Terence Painter has now demonstrated but nonetheless the preservation of bodies is extremely varied, from a bag of skin to a skeleton, with intermediates all along the way – skulls with hair, bones with cloth, heads with brains and eyeballs, a mere smear of decayed bone. Dieck records an extreme example of this. In Bavaria, 1955:

'a corpse was found in the so-called Black Bog. The body lay in a ditch, 2m wide and *c* 5m deep, floating face downwards. It was unclothed and very well preserved. Around the neck were the remains of a collar of the kind formerly worn by the 1945 German army, and on the feet were preserved the remains of army-issue socks' (A Dieck pers comm).

It may be hard to believe all of this, but Dieck says he saw it.

It seems clear that the specific conditions for survival in a peatbog – cold, still, mossy, and a pool or pit – all suggest that the bodies were not just dumped into any old pool or wet hole, where they would soon float to the surface, but were placed in deep watery hollows in the surface of the bog, or in old peat-cuttings also filled with water, or in hollows or trenches filled with a thick soup of water, peat lumps, floating vegetation and silty muds. In still water, the bodies would have to be held down by stakes or stones, and some are; in the soup, they would be stuck, in whatever positions were adopted – vertical, flat, bent as if prodded down – and some are. Some of the problems of dating of bog bodies, where the body dates do not match the peat wall dates, may reflect the bog pool and pit circumstances; this has been exposed by the difficulties of agreeing dates for the Lindow Moss bodies from Cheshire (see below).

The most famous staked body is that of Queen Gunhild, identified as such by some University professors in 1835 when she was discovered in a Jutland bog.

34
Queen Gunhild, actually a woman of unknown name, found in 1835 in Jutland, Denmark. Her oak coffin was provided by King Frederick VI and she lies in a side chapel of the church of St Nicolas in Vejle. Photograph John Coles.

The bride-to-be of King Eric Bloodaxe, she met a shameful end at the hands of his men and was put into 'a terrifyingly deep bog'. However, as usual with uncritical professorial opinions, this was wholly incorrect; the body was that of an unnamed woman, who, about 2000–1800 years ago, was placed in a hollow in the peat and held there by wooden hooks (branch and stem joints) over the knees and elbows, with horizontal pieces of wood across the chest and stomach also held by hooks. The woman had some woollen clothing, a leather cape and cap and seemingly had been pinned down in the bog to die by drowning; her facial expression was described 'as one of despair'. This discovery more than any other of the 19th century excited much interest and conjecture. King Frederick VI presented an oak coffin in which the Huldremose woman lies today in a side chapel in the church of St Nicolas in Vejle; beside her is Lt Col K de la Mare Aggersbøl who died in 1713. Unlike him, she can be seen and is in rather good condition, dark and wrinkled, but entirely naturally dried (illus 34). A little modern damage has occurred; the church is active, and at a recent confirmation service for some young boys, one of them was so pleased with himself that he went and shook Queen Gunhild's hand, which promptly came away from her arm. He put it back.

RESTLESS BODIES AND SOCIAL VICTIMS

One of the questions that has always created interest, and argument, is that of intention (Munksgaard 1984; van der Sanden 1995; Ebbesen 1986; Fischer 1980). Why are these bodies, in their hundreds and probably thousands, in the bogs? The tradition, as noted, extended back 4,000–5,000 years or more in the north and west of Europe, but it is a smaller group of bodies dated to the later 1st millennium BC and early centuries AD that is a major concern. The Danish, German and Dutch bodies that survive or have adequate records show signs of unnatural death, by strangling, hanging, stabbing, cutting, chopping, beheading, beating. Of the rather few bodies analysed, almost all are adult, many aged 20–35 years, and there are more males than females. But all these suggestions are no more than that, as no real catalogue exists and as so many bodies were lost and perhaps casually identified as conforming to the perceived pattern. The reasons why this particular group of bodies came to be deposited in the bogs, or in special small bogs, are not entirely clear and there are various possibilities advanced over the years.

Perhaps the bodies can be divided into two groups, the Restless Bodies and the Social Victims. The Restless Bodies are of those individuals who had violent or unnatural deaths (illus 35); they could be suicides, victims of an accident or unforeseen event, victims of a crime, or they could be criminals executed for serious offences or people killed for anti-social behaviour. The Roman writers, speaking of the unconquered people of the north, spoke of Germanic traditions of punishment for cowardice, treachery, robbery and adultery, but these writers were perhaps exaggerating or inventing anti-native propaganda for home con- sumption. Nonetheless, all the proposed Restless Bodies had unnatural deaths, whether deliberate or accidental, and these deaths created bodies not yet of the time to die, unsettled, unready, and of concern to the living. By abusing those to be killed, and those bodies newly killed, by disposing of them outside the areas of domesticity and ordinary living, by submerging them in water or the soupy peats, perhaps it was thought that these bodies would lie still and not disturb the survivors.

The Social Victims are, or were, in a different category, chosen to be sacrificed for the good of the society. They could be sacrificed in a time of crisis, of famine, pestilence, or impending attack, in order to gain extra strength for survival. They could be sacrificed in payment after the event, or for simple natural resources to continue to be available, like a spring of good water, or a good crop of wild foods. Or they might be killed in anticipation of these good results, or as regular seasonal celebratory offerings to the forces that drove the world and converted the seasons. In some cases, the death throes of those strangled or bled could be viewed and interpreted as divine signals or propaganda. In placating the supernatural powers, by offering their best, their most valued members, with fine clothing, sometimes with elaborate coiffures, and with prized possessions, perhaps the dark and light forces would not clash over the community. In this view, those members of the group chosen for the supreme moment were the elite, persons of rank who had not toiled in the fields or forests. Their skin was clear and clean, their fingernails unscratched, their bodies unbent by labour.

These different opinions taken of the bog bodies are not all exclusive, and some might be complementary in purpose and effect; a person accused of some misdemeanour might be 'saved', immobilised perhaps, for some seasonal or other votive offering. Hajo Hayen was one who suggested (1987) that no single explanation suited all the bodies, and he must have been right. If so, it will only

35
A restless body? The Windeby body from north Germany, found undamaged in a former bog pool and perhaps drowned there some 2,000 years ago. Body in Archäologisches Museum, Schleswig. Drawn by Mike Rouillard.

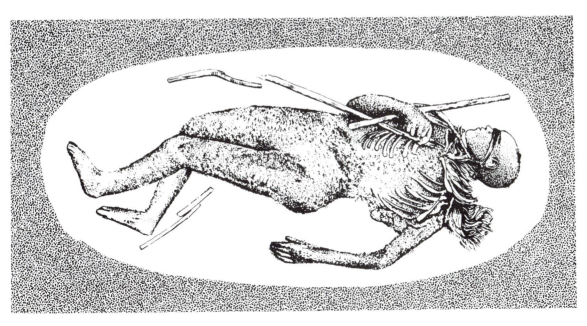

be a careful analysis of those records and those surviving bodies that will begin to disentangle the evidence, and perhaps to point to further and future enquiries. As an example, there are records of bodies with heads shaved on only one side, and bodies damaged on one side, and bodies lying on one side; are these all the same side, and if so, can this be reflected in deliberate damage to other objects placed in the bogs – wooden figures, pots, animals? What is common, if anything, in those bodies pinned to the bog, or placed in other contrived positions? What is the explanation for the content of the last meals of the people in relation to the normal diet of the community? And what were the conditions during the closing centuries BC that prompted a seeming explosion of bog deposition practices? The earlier bodies, now skeletons, in the bogs show the very long tradition of deposition, and continuity in practice may reflect a similarity of purpose. But the later Iron Age bodies are very much more abundant than those of other periods. In what way were environmental, economic and social conditions now more conducive or persuasive for the practice than previously or subsequently? What is common about the places of deposition of the bodies, the small pools, peat cuts, the size of bogs, the surroundings of dryland, the viewpoints for those assembled to see the activities? Only some of these questions have been asked of the evidence, and generally the excitement of the discovery, the rush of onlookers, and the need to extract the body in some urgency have led to loss of information.

BOG BODIES FROM BRITAIN AND IRELAND

The bog bodies of Denmark, Germany and the Netherlands have counterparts in Britain and Ireland, and the recent discoveries of human remains in Lindow Moss in Cheshire have prompted much research and thrown up many problems. In the pursuance of the evidence, the work of Rick Turner has been crucially important (1995a; 1995b). He it was who recognised the body of Lindow Man, or Lindow II as he is now listed. But the story begins earlier, in 1983, when the peat-cutters at Lindow found a human head in the factory sorting shed (illus 36); the police were called, as they were investigating the disappearance some years before of a woman. News of the discovery filtered to the woman's husband who, considering that his work of destroying the evidence had gone awry, confessed to the police that he had done her in and disposed of her in the moss. Alas for him, the head (Lindow I) was dated by radiocarbon to over 1700 years ago; he is now serving a life sentence. In 1984, the same factory machines yielded a foot, and Turner was called in, searched the peat cuts and found the upper half of a male body, Lindow II. This is the body so well conserved and now in the British Museum (Stead et al 1986). In 1987, the peat-cutting machines consumed part of another body (Lindow III) which was retrieved in over 70 small pieces; this too had been a male, and having been found near the original head, it is now considered likely that Lindow I and III are one and the same; the head was not a woman's, after all, and the confession was unjustified on that ground too. In 1988 the lower parts of a male body (Lindow IV) were found, having lain undetected in peat stacks since 1984, and these are believed to belong to Lindow II. So we have two adult male bog bodies, one killed by a blow to the head, strangled with a rope and throat cut (II and IV), the other beheaded (I and III) (Turner 1995c). The radiocarbon dates for these finds still create problems, but the bodies are likely to be of the early centuries AD, thus a bit later than the Danish-Dutch-German group of the late Iron Age. The Lindow men had eaten different last meals, Lindow II/IV a griddlecake or bread of wheat and barley, Lindow I/III some hazelnuts and cereals; both had intestinal worms (Holden 1995). The four pollen grains of mistletoe in Lindow II/IV gut have caused much Druidic comment, as has the somewhat enigmatic evidence that both men had body paint, adduced by electron probe X-ray microanalysis; this paint was probably a clay-based copper derivative, and the paint seems to be different on each man (Pyatt *et al* 1995). Some of these features and other elements of the evidence have persuaded two authorities to write a book about Lindow II, *The Life and Death of a Druid prince*; he is considered to be an Irish druid called Lovernius, sacrificed on 1 May AD 60. This is unbelievably amazing.

The Lindow discoveries have prompted a surge of research into the 'paper bodies' of Britain and Ireland: that is, bodies now lost but for which some record exists. The list of discoveries is impressive (based on Turner and Scaife 1995):

Bog bodies	England	Wales	Scotland	Ireland
Prehistoric	3	—	—	—
Neolithic	1	1	—	1
Bronze Age	22	—	—	1
Iron Age	3	1	—	2
Roman period	7	—	—	1
early medieval	2	—	—	1
medieval	—	—	?1	1
post-medieval	3	—	10	31
no date	55	5	6	51
	96	7	17	89

Of these 209 bodies from bogs or other wet places, most are now lost. A head from Worsley Moss, near Lindow Moss, was found in 1958 and is that of an adult male whose head was severed and who had possibly also been strangled; he is of the Roman period and could be exactly contemporary with one or other of the Lindow men. Most of the English bodies are from fenland peats and have been reduced to skeletons, and include remains of several bodies at Flag Fen, where a huge platform and alignment were created, in part at least, for the deposition of precious objects in water (Pryor 1991). The Irish evidence is better preserved, and includes a body from Gallagh, Co Galway, male in a leather cape with a 'band of sally (willow) rods' around the neck and dated to the late prehistoric period (Ó Floinn 1995). For Scotland, the records are clear – no prehistoric bog bodies have so far been identified and there is nothing certainly earlier than the 17th century AD. The best-known bodies are those of Gunnister on Shetland and Arnish Moor on Lewis, the first probably a traveller who lost his way and was

36
View from the peat factory (sorting shed) at Lindow Moss, Cheshire. Outside lie the heaps of cut and dried peat, with loads coming into the factory on small railway trucks. Within these peats were found the multiple fragments of Lindow III. Photograph John Coles, 1987.

buried where he fell, the second a person whose bones were reduced 'to a consistency of rubbery seaweed', and probably a murder victim. There must be every hope that a prehistoric bog body will one day emerge from the Scottish peats, but it will almost certainly appear under difficult circumstances of identification, recovery and interpretation. That seems to be the story of bog bodies from the first exposures 550 years ago.

OTHER OFFERINGS

Glob, in his survey of bog bodies, stressed that prehistoric peoples made a multiplicity of offerings and sacrifices, from the scraps of cloth and bowls of food and simple artefacts of the poor to the elaborate weapons, prestigious animals and jewellery of the rich. Finds of bog butter and ancient cheeses may be examples of food offerings, a wooden container and bow could be examples of relatively simple artefact offerings, and strange objects like the Torrs chamfrein (Atkinson & Piggott 1955) may represent a gift from the wealthy. With isolated finds, it will often be difficult to distinguish between the things that people put into the peaty wet for practical motives and those that they gave to the bog for an essentially religious or ritual motive.

Practical motives are not much discussed, nor will they be here except to note briefly what they might be. Wooden artefacts that are used seasonally may be immersed when not in use to keep them in good condition. Wood and antler may be soaked prior to working. Food can be buried for a while to mature: think of *gravlax*, the Swedish alternative to smoked salmon. Sometimes clothes or containers may be immersed for cleaning, although fast-flowing water may be preferred to a peaty bog in such a case. And just as valuables were buried by some people in dry ground for safe-keeping, so those who knew their wetland may have felt it offered an even safer place of concealment.

To set beside the single objects or small groups of objects which may have reached the wet for one of the above reasons or for some other mundane purpose, there are certain finds which by virtue of their character and location have always been interpreted by archaeologists as votive deposits, or at the very least as 'ritual'. One such discovery comes from north Wales, from the western edge of the island of Anglesey.

The story begins in 1942, when the Royal Air Force was building one of many war-time air-fields, this one on the sand dunes of what is now RAF Valley on the west coast of the island, at the southern end of the strait separating Anglesey from Holy Island. To stabilise the sand, peat was taken from several nearby boggy lakes; it was dug using a mechanical scoop, taken by lorry to the air-field site, and then it was spread using a harrow. The harrow, as harrows do, raked out the larger stones and bits of wood and other obstructions, and one day something stuck on its tines which turned out to be an iron chain (illus 37). Whether it was war-time shortages or a general approach of 'waste not want not' we do not know, but soon the chain was put to good use dragging out lorries that became stuck in the soft ground. When the harrow revealed further metal objects from the spread peat, and animal bone too, the Resident Engineer reported the finds to the National Museum of Wales. As a result, in 1943, Cyril Fox visited the air-field; his subsequent report was published in 1947.

During his visit, Fox talked to the men who had been digging the peat and he

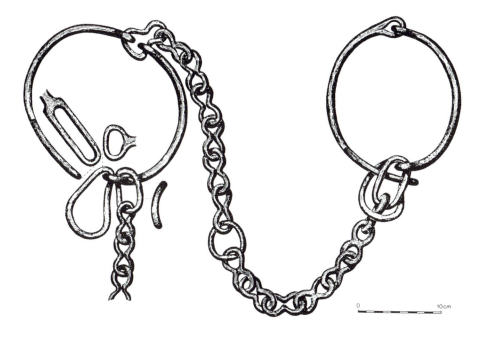

37
Iron chain found at Llyn Cerrig Bach on Anglesey, Wales. Dating to the later Iron Age, it is thought to have been used as a slave-chain and subsequently offered, along with many other artefacts, to the lake. From Fox 1947.

went to the places the peat had come from. The men thought the bone and metal had all come from a single source, and it was only here that Fox found any trace of such materials. The place was Llyn Cerrig Bach, and it has given its name to the considerable collection of objects, mainly metal, which were eventually brought together and studied by Fox.

The objects retrieved from the lake included wood and bronze as well as iron; Fox described them as largely 'masculine and military in character'. There were swords and spears and armour and a horn. There were harness pieces for chariot ponies and fittings for chariots. There was a second iron chain, both chains interpreted as slave-chains; the strength and durability of the one used on the air-field suggests that no prisoner could have broken these bonds. There were pieces of cauldron. There were iron currency bars. And there were the animal bones, mainly from cattle, some sheep, perhaps a single horse and pig and dog. We should note, however, that very little of the bone was retrieved and identified.

At the time of writing, the metalwork and the site are being re-investigated (P Macdonald pers comm). Doubtless new information will emerge concerning the typology, technology and dating of the artefacts, and perhaps further evidence concerning their provenance; this will be a welcome complement to Fox's war-time account, which provides the basis for the present description. For the time being, it seems that the metalwork belongs to the later Iron Age, somewhere between 200 BC and AD 50. It is probably drawn from a diversity of sources: Ireland, mainland Britain, the continent and perhaps locally from Anglesey. Little can be added to what is already known of the animal bone, since only eight pieces now survive.

The Llyn Cerrig Bach collection of metalwork and bone is interpreted as a votive offering, or series of offerings, for several reasons. First, there is the location. Fox described a rocky shelf beside the lake where the finds were made, an ideal place for people to stand as they cast sword or cauldron into the waters, and the only such natural platform in the vicinity. He noted, too, Anglesey's renown as a sacred island. To this we would add that the probable find spot lies near the outflow of a series of lakes and only about a kilometre from the sea. As for the objects, Fox pointed out that a number had been deliberately bent or broken or rendered in pieces, for example a bent sword and the bits of cauldron. Such treatment of things to be deposited in the wet was not uncommon, as we shall see. It is as though people were making doubly sure of the exclusion of their offerings from any normal use in the future. No longer functional, no longer 'living' perhaps, they were consigned to the boggy waters, irretrievable.

A NEW LAKE

A little later in time than Llyn Cerrig Bach but still within the centuries of bog body deposition, and over in that part of northwestern Europe where so many bodies have been found, people stood beside another boggy lake not far from the sea, and cast their broken or dismantled offerings into the waters. The lake is that of Nydam in southern Jutland or, more properly, we should say that it was a lake but is now a narrow peat-filled valley about 4km long and 500m wide, mostly given over to rough wet grassland grazing (illus IIg).

Nydam was discovered by peat cutters and explored by Conrad Engelhardt, an archaeologist in charge of the Royal Collection of Nordic Antiquities in Flensborg. He excavated at the site from 1859 and by 1863 he had found parts of at least three boats together with numerous artefacts of Iron Age date. By 1864, however, Germany and Denmark were at war, with Germany pushing northwards into Jutland and Nydam in the thick of the fighting. Some finds and records were taken to Copenhagen for safety, others now reside in Schleswig Museum including one of the boats. For over half a century, Nydam lay in German territory; in the 1890s there was some excavation in the valley by archaeologists from Kiel. In 1920, the present border between Denmark and Germany was agreed, with Nydam within the territory reverting to Denmark. In the meantime, that part of the valley where Engelhardt had worked had been bought by a Dane from Odense, who left it in his will to the Danish National Museum. In 1939, archaeologists from the Museum had a brief look at the site but it was not until the late 1980s, following a revival of local interest, that a concerted programme of investigation began, directed by Flemming Rieck from the Institute of Maritime Archaeology of the Danish National Museum (Crumlin-Pedersen & Rieck 1993).

The new investigations have demonstrated that, contrary to expectation, there is still much of interest in the Nydam peats. First, there is the record provided by the peat itself; palaeoenvironmental studies have shown that the Nydam valley was covered by lake-waters for much of the post-glacial period but, as with so many lakes, it gradually filled with peat and by the 1st millennium BC the lake had become a peatbog with alder trees. Some-

38
Nydam, southern Jutland. Wooden steering oar for a large boat. Photograph courtesy of Flemming Rieck.

thing then happened to dam the valley, and a new lake appeared which in turn gradually became peat-bound. The new lake, which may have existed from about AD 100, is known to have been used as a place for offerings from about AD 200; perhaps different and as yet unexplored areas of the lake were used in the preceding century. By AD 500, when the final offerings were made, water had once more given way to peat. Whether in AD 200 people knew of the lake's history, whether indeed people were responsible for damming the valley in AD 100, we cannot tell, but the location held a significance that was retained even as water became wetland and the final acts of deposition required a hole to be dug, a relatively mundane act perhaps beside the earlier watery ritual.

A little of that ritual can be reconstructed from

the evidence excavated. The artefacts lie in the peat as if they had all been thrown out over the lake waters from one place, probably a slightly raised, built platform, just on the edge of the lake. In the early years, a number of the artefacts were broken or dismantled before deposition; for example, shields are found as individual wooden slats, and in 1993 a very fine wooden steering oar was found (illus 38), a reminder of the boats in pieces that first brought the site to widespread archaeological notice. In later years, the artefacts seem to have been offered without breaking or damage beyond that sustained by use in warfare. Many of the items are reminiscent of warfare: shields, spears, swords, arrows for example. Others, such as knives or wooden bowls (illus IIh), are less obviously 'military and masculine in character', but still probably part of a soldier's personal equipment.

Preservation can be excellent, with fine detail like the thread binding feathers to an arrow shaft, but selective in that the feathers have gone. There is some difference in preservation from one part of the bog to another, with wood and metal in good condition in some places whereas in others the iron artefacts may be heavily corroded, or the wood may be damaged by drying out or by plant growth. It is possible, usually, to tell if damage has occurred before deposition or during the centuries of burial, and breakage of a spear-shaft due to peat cracking can be distinguished from deliberate breaking before the weapon was cast into the water. This is an important distinction to make when interpretation rests in part on the damage which people inflicted on their offerings before parting with them.

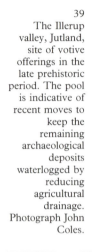

39
The Illerup valley, Jutland, site of votive offerings in the late prehistoric period. The pool is indicative of recent moves to keep the remaining archaeological deposits waterlogged by reducing agricultural drainage. Photograph John Coles.

The Nydam artefacts, boats included, are usually interpreted as war booty, a thank-offering from the victorious side following some prehistoric conflict. Similar collections from sites such as Thorsbjerg, Illerup (illus 39) and Hjortspring have been seen in the same light, extending the practice in time. Hjortspring, on the Danish island of Als, lies within 10km of Nydam and it too has yielded a boat, this one from a small peatbog which can only be reached by an overland route. The boat must have been carried, not floated, to its resting place alongside swords and shields and knives and chain-mail. Animal bone was found, horse and dog and sheep. Recent work on the Hjortspring finds, which were excavated in the 1920s, dates them to the later 4th century BC (Rieck 1994), definitely earlier than Nydam and probably a little earlier than Llyn Cerrig Bach.

Other places could be described, some earlier some later, with similarities of ritual and offering to those detailed here. Flag Fen and La Tène, mentioned elsewhere in this book, could be included, but this is not the place for a comprehensive survey and Richard Bradley has provided a recent discussion (1990). Instead, we will simply make further brief comments on location.

The three sites described above, Llyn Cerrig Bach and Nydam and Hjortspring, are all close to the sea but themselves freshwater, as was Flag Fen in the Bronze Age but never La Tène. In several cases, a site near the outflows of a lake had been chosen, La Tène and Llyn Cerrig Bach for instance, and Flag Fen has the makings of a similar location. Nydam was possibly a lake made by people, or at least a lake that came into being within folk memory of its first use for offerings (the name Nydam, new dam, refers however to a more recent blocking of the valley). A few other wet places of deposition are thought to be made or improved

40
Discovery of the Nydam head. Photograph courtesy of Flemming Rieck.

by those who would use them, for example the large artificial pond known as the King's Stables which forms one element in the great complex of Navan or Emain Macha, Ulster's ancient capital. Here deposition of animal bone, a human skull, broken clay moulds for casting bronze swords, took place probably in the earlier 1st millennium BC (Lynn 1977). Nearby Loughnashade received bone, including human skulls, and four splendid bronze horns dating to the 1st century BC and akin to the horn from Llyn Cerrig Bach (Warner 1986). We might ask why Loughnashade would not do for the earlier depositions, why the King's Stables pond, maybe 25m across and 3.5m deep, was laboriously dug out? The attachment to a particular location reminds us of the attachment to the Nydam offering place, even as conditions changed from open water to vegetated peatbog, a continuity of use that underlines the significance which such a place could hold for people. Wetlands, as we have stressed elsewhere, were not uniform, and an understanding of their different characters has much to contribute to the interpretation of what is found within them.

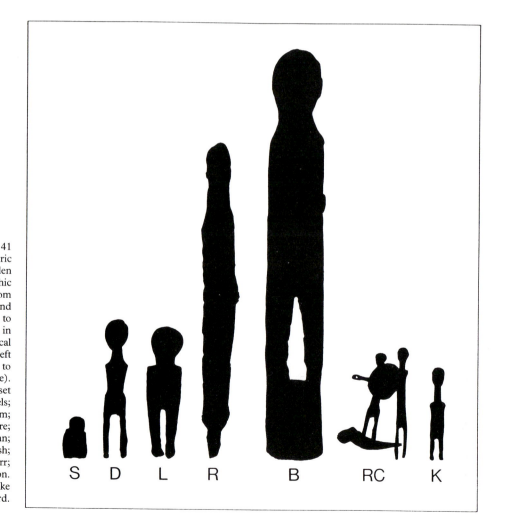

41 Prehistoric wooden anthropomorphic figures from Britain and Ireland, drawn to scale and in chronological sequence from left (Neolithic) to right (Iron Age). S: Somerset Levels; D: Dagenham; L: Lagore; R: Ralaghan; B: Ballachulish; RC: Roos Carr; K: Kingsteignton. Drawn by Mike Rouillard.

One recent discovery at Nydam has yet to be mentioned. In 1993 the excavators came upon a carved wooden head of a man, about 40cm long and made out of alderwood (illus 40; IIi). Themselves expert in boat archaeology and intent upon the retrieval of evidence for early boats, the excavators have said that, although the head might be a boat-fitting, it is not obviously so (Rieck 1993). Perhaps it belongs with another category of finds from the wetlands, the small but growing collection of wooden anthropomorphic figurines known from north-western Europe.

HUMAN EFFIGIES

The interpretation of these figures is as problematic and diverse as that of bog-bodies. One of the present authors has already aired her views in print (B Coles 1990, 1993) but this need not hinder some further description, comment and speculation arising from the bringing together of bodies, offerings and the human-like carvings. The only known prehistoric wooden figure from Scotland, from Ballachulish, is a key to the discussion.

The figures from Britain and Ireland range in date from the Neolithic to the Iron Age (illus 41). The small ashwood God Dolly from the Somerset Levels begins the sequence, followed by the Dagenham pinewood figure which is dated to the late Neolithic. An oakwood figure from Lagore crannog is Late Neolithic or Early Bronze Age (turn of 3rd–2nd millennium BC). A millennium then passes before the yew-wood Ralaghan carving, twice the size of its predecessors. Ballachulish is bigger again, and dated to the second quarter of the 1st millennium BC. Mid-millennium comes the group of relatively small figures from Roos Carr and their boat, and from the third quarter the determined-looking oakwood man from Kingsteignton. The Somerset God Dolly is dated by its close association with radiocarbon dated trackways; all of the others have themselves been sampled for radiocarbon dating.

Four other wooden carvings from Southern Britain may be relevant. One, from Ickham in Kent, is associated with late Roman material. Another, which may come from Strata Florida or Tregaron Bog in west Wales, has no secure provenance and no date, but displays a certain resemblance to Scandinavian figurines made of gold or bronze and dated to the Bronze Age (illus 42). Two others no longer exist, but the paper records indicate a possible prehistoric date; these are the wooden figures recorded from Oakhanger Moss in Cheshire and from the peats of Misson-Haxey near the Isle of Axholme. From central Ireland, we should include the head-like carving on the end of a pole found below the Iron Age Corlea 1 trackway recently excavated by Barry Raftery.

Northwestern Europe has a number of wooden figures, several of which are known to be of late 1st millennium AD date and one possibly Mesolithic, presenting a longer chronology than for Britain and Ireland. What is interesting is that several of those of probable Bronze Age or Iron Age date come from northern Germany and Denmark, the lands of bog-bodies and offerings. The kneeling or seated figure from Rude Eskildstrup, the phallic man from Broddenbjerg and the pair of tall slender figures from Aukamper Moor, Braak, may all be contemporaries of the human bodies found in bogs. The Nydam head, which lay with artefacts dated to about AD 350, would come near the end of the sequence.

COMING TOGETHER

It is difficult to know if the not dissimilar distributions of bog bodies and 'war-booty' type offerings and wooden carvings of humans reflect accurately the occurrence of human customs in the past. Obviously, the survival of the evidence is strongly governed by the distribution of wetlands and, as we have seen, the particular type of wetland may be important for one reason or another. Therefore, there may be no more link between the different categories of evidence than that provided by the availability of suitable environments for deposition and for subsequent preservation of the evidence.

One or two other common features can, however, be drawn out. Just as some of the 'war-booty' sites lie near the sea, so do several of the find-spots for wooden figures: Roos Carr, Dagenham and Kingsteignton were all found in estuarine contexts or in creeks and wetlands within the reach of tidal waters, whilst the Somerset Levels and Ballachulish were at the time of deposition little removed from the sea, as were the less-certainly relevant finds from Ickham and Misson-Haxey, Ickham on the Little Stour in north Kent and Misson-Haxey possibly near

42
Left a) Wooden figurine from Strata Florida, Wales; right b) gold figurine from Slipshavn, Fyn. The gold figurine, 67mm high, is dated to the 5th century AD. The wooden figurine, height 135mm, is an undated stray find which could be an ethnographic import of recent times but which, on stylistic grounds, could also be suggested to be indigenous and prehistoric. Photographs: a) Bryony Coles; b) from Kjaerum & Olsen, 1990, courtesy of National Museum of Denmark.

a   b

the meeting of the rivers Idle and Trent. Neither the exact findspots nor the ancient courses of the rivers are known for sure.

Strata Florida is the name of an abbey beside Afon Teifi in Wales, and also the name given to the nearest railway station which is on the northern edge of the Tregaron complex of raised bogs. It is possible that the wooden carving (illus 42a) came from the peat, discovered either during the building of the railway across the bog in the mid-19th century or in the course of peat cutting by hand. It was peat cutting on the raised bog that exposed a human body in 1891, or rather the tanned skin and bones of an apparently decapitated man. He was found quite near the railway station, maybe near the wooden figure. The human was reburied in nearby Ystrad churchyard and the carving became buried in the stores of Carmarthen museum.

Perhaps neither destination was entirely appropriate, if the body was that of a pre-Christian person whose end belongs to the Restless Bodies or Social Victims tradition and if the carving, stored on the grounds that it was ethnographic and probably North American, turns out to be the only surviving example of a prehistoric wooden figurine from Wales. In this scenario, one particular part of a large complex of raised bogs was perceived by Bronze or Iron Age peoples as the right place for the deposition of both a human body and a wooden representation of a human. An alternative scenario would have the human as a medieval Welshman who met an accidental death, and the carving a New World souvenir lost by some traveller or sailor when visiting the Cistercian ruins at Strata Florida. There is no evidence to prove that these Welsh examples belong to the present discussion, only suggestion in the description of the body and suggestion in the likeness of the carving to small bronze and gold figures known to be pre-historic in date, such as the gold figure from Slipshavn on the island of Fyn (illus 42b).

Another potential link between the deposition of human bodies and the deposition of goods is provided by the human bone sometimes found with the artefacts cast into lakes or pools or peaty bogs. This aspect is well covered in Bradley's survey and from the present discussion we should remember the human skulls found at the same time as the Loughnashade horns, and the human bone as well as varied metalwork from Flag Fen. The artefacts from both places include 'destroyed' pieces, and perhaps the humans had been treated in similar fashion. A further possible association is provided by Børremose, one of the largest raised bogs in northern Jutland and source of at least three bog bodies. Overlooking the bog is the findspot of one of the more famous of prehistoric European artefacts, the dismantled Gundestrup Cauldron.

At Rappendam near Jørlunde in Denmark a complex offering was found during World War II. There were eight groups of objects in the bog: the first to be found consisted of human and cattle bones and parts of a wagon, perhaps, it was thought, the remnants of a capsized vehicle, its draught animals and its driver. The human, at first considered to be a female, later corrected to a male, lay on his back with the knees bent; a plank of wood nearby is considered to have been the instrument used to despatch him with a blow to the back of the neck, the force of which pushed one cervical vertebra into the larynx. A few metres away from this deposit were other wagon pieces and cattle bones in three groups, and another two groups farther away. The Rappendam fen was formerly a narrow lake and it seems that these objects were tipped into the shallowing waters; 28 wheels, 13 hubs and other wagon parts were deposited, along with the human, perhaps over a short period of time before the character of the site had changed and the custom ended or was transferred elsewhere. With the evidence from other sites for vehicles and humans as components of deliberate bog depositions, and a wetland context at Rappendam that may have resembled Nydam, we tend to think this was not a prehistoric road accident but yet another extravagant offering.

There may be a significant contrast here between the two sites. The offerings at Nydam included boats, those at Rappendam were of wagon parts. Could these reflect the original condition of the wetlands, the one a lake, the other wet but terrestrial, at the time of their selection as places for these special deposits? Or did both originally have water of sufficient depth for material to be sunk? If so, how were the wooden components of boats and wagons held down beneath the surface?

43
Yew wood carving from Ralaghan, Ireland, dated to the Bronze Age. The figure is noticeably asymmetrical, in the treatment of the eyes, for example. It has been identified both as male and as female by different archaeologists. Photograph Seán Goddard.

Nydam introduces a link between wooden representations of humans and artefact offerings. The link is very direct and sure in this instance in that the carving was found during modern controlled excavation, lying with the artefacts in the peats of the former lake and probably thrown like them from the shoreline platform. What is less certain is whether the Nydam head belongs to traditions which have been tentatively identified with respect to the carvings. It has been noted that several of the carvings could be interpreted as either male or female, endowed with characteristics of both sex in the case of the God Dolly and deprived of unambiguous sexual features in the case of several others, such as Dagenham. There are exceptions: Kingsteignton is clearly, and only, male. Nydam, a head without a body, is described as bearded and therefore presumably male.

The second recurring characteristic of the carvings is a deliberate asymmetry of features, especially seen on the face and for the left eye. Ralaghan was carved to be asymmetrical from head to toe, with uneven eyes (illus 43). The Dagenham figure had a shallow left eye compared to its right eye, signifying that it was closed or weak or blind maybe. Similar treatment of the eyes was given to the Broddenbjerg man, in that his right eye is carved with a small socket whereas the left eye is almost blank, represented by no more than a faint line between eyebrow and flat cheek. The left eye and much of the left side of the Dagenham piece were damaged at some stage after carving and before the figure came to rest in the Thames-side marshes. Broddenbjerg is in too poor condition to be sure, but examination of the figure in Copenhagen suggests that the damage he has undergone is post-depositional and post-discovery rather than treatment meted out in antiquity. The Nydam head is not symmetrical, the right side of the face being narrower than the left, and slightly damaged about the jaw-line at some stage, but these features seem more accidental or incidental than deliberate. This head, the one carving from a secure and well-documented context, is not therefore a sure and certain addition to the group of figures which may emanate from a common ritual tradition.

A SCOTTISH BODY?

There remains Ballachulish, a large stern female (illus 44a). Recently re-examined and assessed for conservation by the National Museums of Scotland, Ballachulish is now known to be carved from alderwood, not oak as previously thought (Sheridan pers comm). Her femaleness is evident from the genitals rather than the breasts, the latter being small and high and no more developed than might be seen for either sex. They could be compared with the vestigial breasts of one of the two figures from Aukamper Moor, both tall and slender and one thought female and one male. Ballachulish has arms and hands outlined on her body, the hands with fingers spread across the stomach. Facial expression, breasts and hands are reminiscent of Scandinavian bronzes such as the small female from St Olof in southeast Scania (illus 44b). The bronzes are interpreted by some Scandinavian archaeologists as representations of a goddess of fertility and wealth, with stress on the second attribute.

The Ballachulish figure has another possible resemblance to a goddess of wealth. Her 'cross-sash' is still just visible, and so too is something held between her hands. From Poland, from late prehistoric contexts of the 1st millennium AD, there come the baba-stones, dumpy figures with something held between the hands which is interpreted as a drinking horn or a horn-of-plenty (Słupecki 1994), the latter an interpretation that again would link the Ballachulish figure to the Scandinavian representations of a possible goddess of fertility and wealth.

Other finds of possible prehistoric date have been made in Ballachulish Moss. The details are vague, but the records refer to casks of bog butter, wooden bowls, deer antler and cattle horns, flints, and probable burials in cists near the edge of the moor. Some of these items may have been in the nature of offerings.

Was the wooden figure itself an offering? The accounts of the discovery brought together by Christison (1881) indicate that the near life-size figure had been found face down at the base of the peat, possibly directly on the underlying gravel. Despite all that has happened to the image since discovery, it can be seen that the back is not significantly more weathered than the front, which suggests rapid burial. Indeed, the recent identification of the wood as alder (above) rather than oak makes this all the more necessary. Peat forms quickly at times, but not at the speed required to cover the wood before weathering. Therefore it seems probable that the image was placed face down in a pit, perhaps a prehistoric peat-digging.

a

44
a) The Ballachulish wooden figure, propped against a board for photography shortly after discovery in the late 19th century. The small breasts are just visible, with the cross-sash passing between them and over the right shoulder. The hands are splayed across the stomach, with something held in the right hand; b) small bronze figurine from St Olaf, Scania, displaying characteristics of face, breasts and hands similar to the Ballachulish carving. Photographs: a) courtesy of National Museum of Scotland; b) from Kjaerum & Olsen 1990, courtesy of National Museum of Denmark.

b

The late 19th-century accounts refer to stakes and wickerwork, which perhaps overlay the image and were intended to hold it down as the pit filled with water. In the descriptions of bog bodies above, we have noted some placed in pools or old peat cuts, we have noted some held down by stakes, and literary references to hurdles, and we have argued that some bog bodies were the bodies of Social Victims, people who were perhaps respected and favoured members of society and in all respects proper for sacrifice when the occasion demanded. Stern Ballachulish may have had a life of respect before becoming an offering that is the closest we have to a prehistoric bog body from Scotland.

4

WORTH A SPECIAL JOURNEY

Not all sites are equal in the importance attached to them by archaeologists, and this is as true for wet sites as it is for those that are dry. Certain wetland settlements have preserved such an abundance and variety of evidence (of structure, industry, economy and environment) that they continue to prompt new work. In this chapter we discuss two such settlements, and our title 'Worth a Special Journey' is deliberately taken from the Michelin guide to places to eat in France; by the end of the chapter the relevance of the choice will become clear.

What is it that makes a good wetland site for archaeology, and what does such a site bring to the study of the past that a good dryland site does not? We think that not everyone will agree with our assessment, but we suggest that wetland sites can provide the following:

1 Stratigraphy of living surfaces, one upon the other, like a tell, and not ploughed or eroded flat onto a single surface as on many European dry sites.
2 Wooden elements, posts, stakes, walls, roofing members, rather than dark stains in the soil representing unknowable types of wood.
3 Complete artefacts, tools, weapons and ornaments, with handles, glue and string, not just the stone or metal parts.
4 Objects made entirely of wood or other organic materials that have totally disappeared on dry sites.
5 Economic evidence, of plants such as leaves, stalks, seeds, roots and fruits, and delicate parts of animals, of fish and birds and small mammals, instead of only the sturdiest of animal bones.
6 Environmental evidence, of pollen, plant remains, beetles, spiders and other fragile and minuscule elements, as well as soils and charcoals that occur more widely.
7 Coherence of the package of evidence, all of it in a stratified understandable entirety, instead of fragments or collapsed layers of evidence.
8 Models of behaviour both individual and corporate, preserved in detail in place of the anonymous jumble of indistinguishable elements of society.

Not all wetland sites are as good as this, in fact rather few have all of these attributes, and not all dryland sites are as bad as we have painted, but some certainly are. The point of the declamation and accusation is that, where conditions are good and where archaeological work has been appropriate, wetland sites can reward us with information that we just cannot acquire from other sources, unless they be the strange icy heights of the mountains, the frozen steppes, or the arid deserts.

DATES AND WALNUTS

Our first choice of a wetland site well worth a Special Journey is of the early medieval period, from Lake Paladru in eastern France (illus IIIa). A legend, first recorded in the 16th century but known earlier, tells a story familiar to wetland archaeologists in many parts of Europe. Different versions have diverse embellishments, and one Paladru version runs something as follows:

'Here by the lake was once a prosperous village, somewhat given to boasting of its wealth and hospitality. One day, the Lord God wished to determine if the villagers were as hospitable in deed as they were in word. Disguising himself as a pilgrim, he walked into the village and sought shelter. One and all, rich and poor, the householders turned him away. Angry and indignant, God Almighty smote the village, which immediately sank and was overwhelmed by the waters of the lake'.

(Colardelle & Verdel 1993b, 79; trans, with a degree of licence, BJC)

The notion of a sunken village below the surface of Lake Paladru was reinforced by occasional finds of artefacts and settlement debris, brought up in fishermen's nets. By the mid-19th century a local historian had identified several sunken settlements around the shores of the lake, one of them near the present-day village of Ars and the subject of the legend. Ernest Chantre, an archaeologist from Lyon who had been inspired by discussion of the Neuchâtel pile-dwellings, began to excavate at the site of Grand Roseaux at the northern end of the lake. The material found was thought to be Iron Age, although Gabriel de Mortillet, a leading French prehistorian, declared that it must be Roman or later. His judgement was based not on the typology of the artefacts as one might expect, but on the identification of two different sorts of cherry and three sorts of plum.

In 1903 another sunken village was noted at the southern end of the lake, beside the present-day village of Charavines. In 1921 the lake level was exceptionally low, and Hippolyte Müller, an archaeologist from Grenoble, visited the site. He was able to study material revealed by a recently-cut ditch and he judged it to be of Carolingian age and contemporary with Grand Roseaux. Close along the shore to the west was a second site, and this one Müller identified as Neolithic on the basis of the flint typology.

Time passed, and the posts of the sunken village were a minor attraction for the growing holiday industry at Charavines. A camp site and bathing beach were popular enough to warrant a summer life-guard, who in his time off in 1971 explored the site and took his finds in to the museum in Grenoble. Soon he warned the regional archaeologists of a plan to develop the shore as a marina. The threat of development prompted the rescue excavation of both settlements at Charavines, and both turned out to be exceptional sites of their period. We have already described some of the results from the Neolithic site of Charavines-Les Baigneurs (B & J Coles 1989, 99–102) and a new and lavishly illustrated overview has now been provided by Aimé Bocquet, director of the excavations at Les Baigneurs, (1994). The present account is of the later site, known as Charavines-Colletière and excavated and published by Michel Colardelle and Eric Verdel (1993a, 1993b). Our description of the site relies heavily on their work, and much discussion in the course of a winter visit to the site; the interpretation is at times embellished by our own views.

It took about 25 years for Charavines-Colletière to be excavated, and the measured pace has contributed to the results. A part of the site is now protected, not excavated, for the archaeology aroused sufficient local and national interest, and tourist potential, that the marina plans were shelved. Where excavation did take place, the results from one season influenced the next, and the early demonstration of the site's significance brought in increasing funds and an impressive range of specialist investigations.

In general, excavation took place under water. Two divers worked turn and turn about for half a day, digging with their hands, followed by a second pair. Everything, including all the spoil, was taken back to dry land where a back-up team of 15–20 people processed the small finds and sieved the spoil (illus 45). All the sediment was washed through 8mm and 4mm mesh sieves, and one-tenth of it also went through 2mm sieves. Every bucket came from a known location on site; and all the material sieved out and sorted could be given a find-spot. The sort of material retrieved in this way included stone, baked clay, plant macro-remains, charcoal, faunal remains, coprolites and small artefacts. The impressive but laborious sieving programme was complemented by extensive coring, and sampling of a number of the posts.

45 Charavines-Colletière, France. Sorting through the material retrieved by sieving of the excavated deposits. Many small artefacts and much debris from meals were found in this way. Photograph Fouilles de Colletière.

The range of specialist studies included local geology and soils, and lake sediments. The cores provided samples for analysis of diatoms, pollen and microfauna as well as site stratigraphy. Sieving produced the material for study of plant macro-fossils, fish, bird and mammal remains, and some of the radiocarbon samples. Excavated wood and artefacts were studied in terms of technology and typology, and the wood also provided the samples for dendrochronology and for study of isotope variation and past climates. Allied research by historians was stimulated by the excavation, and has contributed to the understanding of the site. All in all, the criteria suggested above for what makes a good wetland site were met in just about every respect.

The dating of Charavines-Colletière places it in a period for which there was little known evidence in this part of eastern France when the excavation began in 1972. The first attempts to date the site by pottery typology suggested somewhere between the 7th and the 12th centuries AD, not Chantre's Iron Age but later, as de Mortillet and Müller had thought. Further artefacts were recovered, including metalwork; local typological studies were stimulated, the results narrowing the dating range of the lake-shore site to about AD 850 to 1050. The imprecision of the dating prompted recourse to radiocarbon, which was otherwise little used on medieval sites in the 1970s. Eight samples were taken and the results, averaged and calibrated, suggested occupation from about AD 995 to 1020. By the end of the excavation, 39 coins had been recovered, which belonged to the period from AD 993 to 1038 but numismatists were not too sure how long coins had remained in circulation at this time and therefore when they might have been used and lost by the site's inhabitants.

As Colletière was built of oak, samples were taken for dendrochronology. At first, there were major problems to overcome such as the lack of a regional master chronology; at the time, in the early 1970s, the nearest French tree-ring laboratory was in Normandy at Caen, and its work had little relevance to Paladru oak. Many of the Colletière posts had lost their bark and sapwood through erosion, and this also hindered progress. However, the excavations again stimulated the development of regional studies, in this case the building of an oak reference curve which has enabled the precise dating of the Colletière wood. We know now that the first felling episode began in AD 1003, the main felling was in AD 1007–1008, and no wood was felled for sure after AD 1040. What was this short-lived settlement, as briefly occupied as a Neolithic village? Who lived there and what had brought them to the lake shore?

Reference to the reconstruction drawing (illus 46) shows a compact group of three solid buildings within a fence, along with several sheds and workshops. These were all put up within a few years of each other. It has been suggested that the central main building, referred to as Building I, had a tower 14m high. Building III, to the left when viewed from the lake, lies in the unexcavated part of the site but it is known by the posts that protrude from the lake sediments. Building II, on the right within the excavated area, was rebuilt in the early 1020s, perhaps because it was the most affected by a slight rise in lake level and also due to a change of use. The central building appears to have been the wealthiest, and it had an attached stable and a porch or lean-to. Building II may have started out as a stable, but was used for human habitation following its rebuilding. There was a metal-working area just outside Building II, and a forge between the two buildings. The wooden fence or palisade probably encircled the settlement, with a simple water-gate and a more elaborate way-in on the landward site. The whole was set on a small rise just off dry land and separated from the shore by marsh.

The surroundings can be sketched in from pollen and sedimentary analyses. The region was densely forested, little touched by cultivation since the Roman period, although the inhabitants of a neighbouring valley may well have made use of the Paladru slopes. The tree cover was mostly deciduous, with some chestnut and walnut and box, indicative of reasonably warm conditions. Both pollen and sediments provide evidence for a slight fall in lake level and an increase in alder trees and reeds and other shore-line vegetation just before settlement began. While people lived at Colletière, a substantial part of the surrounding forest was cleared for grazing and for arable fields. When they left, the forest regained some but not all of its former ground.

The pollen evidence for farming is supported by the evidence from animal bones

46 Charavines-Colletière, a reconstruction drawing of the settlement and landscape *c* AD 1020, based on the excavated evidence and palaeo-environmental analyses. From Colardelle & Verdel 1993b.

and plant remains. People grew several different sorts of cereal. Rye was the most popular, probably well-suited to the local soils which today go by the evocative name of *Terres Froides*. But the soils were good enough to grow some wheat, perhaps for bread for the wealthy whilst the less well-off made do with rye-bread. Oats perhaps fed horses as well as people, and barley could have been intended for brewing. Millet, flax and hemp were grown, and possibly grapes.

The Colletière people ate a lot of pork. At least 353 pigs were killed and butchered, which thanks to the dendrochronological dating of the site duration could mean that about one pig a month was eaten for the three decades or so of occupation. At least 154 sheep or goats were eaten, along with a minimum of 31 cattle and 25 hens, the latter of course providing very much less meat than the cattle. These animal numbers, it should be noted, are probably well below the actual numbers consumed, because over half the bone recovered was too fragmented to identify. The inhabitants' meat intake was probably greater than one pig a month. The domestic animals would have been useful when alive, supplying milk and wool and eggs, as well as manure for the fields. Six horse bones, six dog bones and four cat bones were also recovered.

Wild foods were important, particularly plants and particularly during the early years of occupation. People collected acorns, either for flour for themselves or as pig-food. They collected beechnuts and hazelnuts, to eat or to press for oil, and the same could be done with the huge quantities of walnuts brought into the site (illus IIIb). Chestnuts were popular too. Fruits were abundant: cherries, strawberries and raspberries, sloes, hips and haws later on. There was some hunting of red and roe deer, hare and wild birds, but of little importance as a source of meat compared to the domestic animals.

Bones and scales of fish were recovered, the bone predominantly from perch and the scales from roach or dace or something similar. Without sieving, few if any scales would have been recovered, an illustration of potential bias in recovery following differential preservation, and a reminder that however careful an excavation the record is unlikely to be complete. The growth increments on the fish vertebrae indicate that at least 50% were caught in late winter or early spring. Maybe they were easy to spear as they came into the reeds to spawn, maybe they were a welcome food in an otherwise lean time, maybe they were a customary food in Lent, and quite possibly all these reasons and others too account for the seasonal surge in fish consumption. Apart from the fish, the lakeside setting does not seem to have had much influence on people's diet.

Something is known of food preparation. Cereals were threshed and cleaned indoors, ground to a coarse flour and then used for gruel, porridge, flat cakes or bread. Food was boiled either by setting a round-based clay pot in the embers of the central hearth, or by dropping hot stones into the cooking pot. Bread and flat cakes were baked in a clay oven. Shallow metal pans with a long handle would have done nicely for fried eggs, kidneys and other quick-cooking delicacies. Meat was more often boiled than roasted, bones were split for the marrow, and hams may have been smoked in the chimney-like hoods above the central hearths. Little evidence survives for how the fish were cooked, except that the roach or dace were de-scaled or skinned. The amount of rubbish that accumulated on the house floors, together with the evidence of hearths and ovens, and cooking and eating utensils, show that food was an indoor matter and not separated from other domestic activity.

Of the 9,700 mammal bones identified, only six were horse, yet the site has produced ample evidence for the importance of horses to the inhabitants. The annexe to the central building has been interpreted as a stable for horses because horse shoes were found there, and nails for the shoes and smithy tools, and pieces of harness. The clinching evidence for the presence of horses in the annexe came from a sample taken from its floor: it contained eggs of *Parascaris equorum*, an internal parasite that lives only in horses. The eggs would have reached the floor in the horses' droppings.

Turning to the artefacts from the site, the discrepancy between the number of horse bones and the importance of horses to the way of life of the people at Colletière is noteworthy. Many artefacts relate to horses, harness for the animals and equipment for their riders (illus IIIc, d). There are iron bits and bridle-fittings and wooden parts of saddles, sometimes decorated. The status of horses is indicated by the richest artefact from the site, which is a jewelled fitting for a bridle (illus IIIe). The riders wore spurs, and may have carried spears or javelins. and fighting axes and swords; cross-bows were popular, but these were not necessarily used from horse-back, neither were the ordinary bows and arrows. The horses are thought to have been robust and cob-sized at 14–15 hands. The impression is of a fighting company, mounted cavalrymen and foot-soldiers with cross-bows. It would be only slightly anachronistic to visualise the Colletière warriors as cousins to their Bayeux Tapestry counterparts, a little earlier in time and with regional differences in style but the same general idea.

These warriors were fishermen, farmers, loggers, carpenters and house-builders too, as we have seen, and some amongst them also had time to practice other skills. The site has produced good evidence for shoe-making (illus IIIf), and other leather-work such as the horse harness. Child- as well as adult-sized shoes have been found, indicating that children were around. The farrier was blacksmith too, working iron and producing domestic and agricultural tools as well as weapons. Many wooden artefacts were made, tubs and boxes and bowls, hafts and handles, ladles and spoons, fine wooden combs, linen-beaters and bobbins and much else besides (illus IIIg). There was, as we might expect, careful choice of wood species for some artefacts. The combs and spoons, for example, were made from boxwood, ash was used for axe-hafts and yew for bows. Wool, flax and hemp was home-produced, prepared and spun and woven into cloth or used for ropes and string.

There was time for amusement too. The wooden parts of several different musical instruments have survived (illus IIIh), not always easy to interpret but including percussion, woodwind and strings. There seems to have been a drum, probably flutes and oboes and a precursor of the bagpipes, and a viol or other stringed instrument. We don't know what tunes they played, but the variety of instruments suggests relatively sophisticated music. Board games were played, chess and backgammon, and dice were made from little cubes of hazelwood. Children, it seems, had less durable toys for none has been found apart from one small cross-bow, and were it not for the little shoes we might think the settlement was childless.

Apart from iron and salt, the inhabitants were essentially self-sufficient. Why then had they suddenly arrived on the lake-shore, who were they and where had they come from, to live in what was the middle of nowhere in AD 1003? The self-sufficiency and the warrior element led Colardelle and Verdel to suggest at first that Colletière was a settlement of warrior knights. By 1993, with the publication of the site monograph, Colletière was put forward as the dwelling of a fairly wealthy family with dependants and servants, three households in all (illus IIIi). It still could be seen as virtually self-sufficient and well-equipped for fighting and for defence, precursor in these respects of the castles that were soon to be built. Perhaps the lake-shore settlement was something in the nature of a frontier-post, staking a claim for one of the several competing political units in Burgundy at the turn of the millennium. Or maybe it made a secular claim to land that was, within 50 years, to be taken over by the new Carthusian order. These questions we can only ask because Colletière belongs to a time that is partly documented, but the nature of the documents is such that they do not provide answers to questions about this specific site. The archaeological evidence on the whole answers a different set of questions. Yet, taking the two together, Colletière can be tentatively fitted into the historical framework.

The territory that was to be occupied had interested few people since the Neolithic, and there is no archaeological evidence for settlement around Lake Paladru itself in the decades and centuries preceding the foundation of Colletière. Study of sediments, pollen and tree-rings, the latter for $0^{16} : 0^{18}$ ratios, indicates that the climate became drier and the level of the lake dropped by a metre or so in the second half of the 10th century AD, particularly in the last quarter. The exposed lakeshore was colonised by vegetation but was not yet thickly forested when, in AD 1003, the Colletière settlement was founded. In the same year, the settlement at the other end of the lake at Grand Roseaux was also founded, and probably a third settlement at Pré d'Ars; this we know from dendrochronology. The simultaneous appearance of two or three fortified settlements makes plausible the idea of a planned expansion to stake a claim to land. The excavation of Colletière coupled with limited dendrochronological work at Grand Roseaux and Pré d'Ars indicates that all three complexes were built rapidly, and that from the outset people knew what they wanted in terms of terrain, buildings and layout. This too reads like a planned colonisation, co-ordinated and purposeful.

The typology of the Colletière artefacts, in particular the pottery, suggests links to the northwest towards Lyon rather than southeastwards to Grenoble. Historical documents provide evidence for a large territory, the county of Sermorens, which

a

b

a Lake Paludru and its hinterland, looking down towards the modern village of Charavines. The Neolithic settlement lies to the right and the Medieval settlement of Charavines-Colletière lies just under water near the modern raised walkways leading back through the lake shore vegetation to dry land. Photograph courtesy of Michel Colardelle & Eric Verdel, Fouilles de Colletière.

b Some of the many nut-shells found at Charavines-Colletière, placed on a wooden dish from the site (not found together). Walnuts, hazelnuts and acorns are easily recognizable. Photograph Fouilles de Colletière.

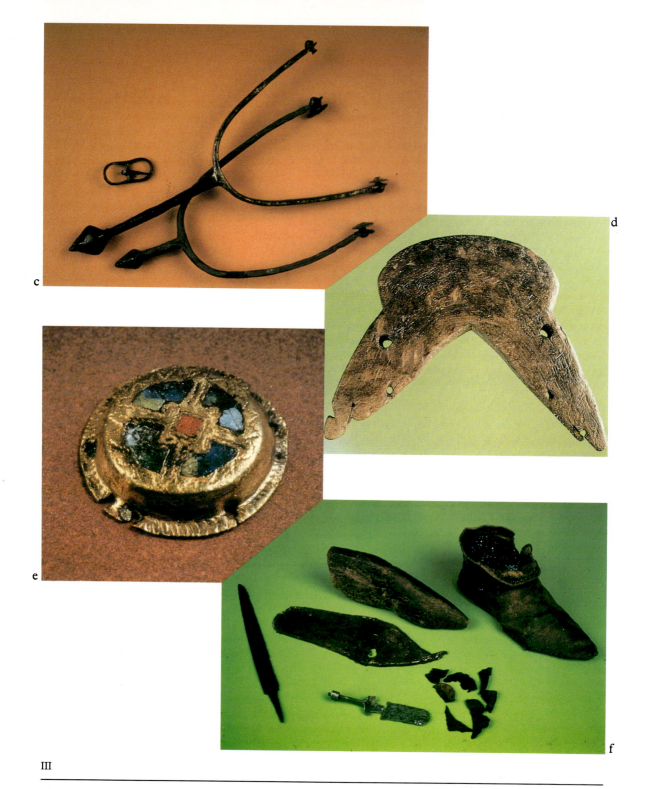

III

Charavines-Colletière.
Horse gear from the early 11th century AD: c iron spurs worn by a rider;
d part of a wooden frame for a saddle worn by a horse; e jewelled fitting for a horse bridle.
f A leather shoe and wooden shoe-last together with cobbler's tools, a sole and scraps of leather, all indicative of shoe-making
  on site.
All photographs Fouilles de Colletière.

g

h

i

III
_____

Charavines-Colletière.

g Tableware of the early 11th century AD: wooden utensils and plates and bowls with a spouted ceramic pot used for liquids – perhaps wine?

h Wind instruments of the early 11th century AD made from bone or wood; top right, a bone whistle; centre, a flute made from a bird long bone; bottom left, an elderwood flute.

Photographs Fouilles de Colletière.

i A reconstruction drawing of the interior of the central building. Structural evidence, artefacts, food debris and palaeo-environmental analyses have contributed to the picture of a wealthy household eating well, playing board games, listening to music and chucking their rubbish on the floor. From Colardelle & Verdel 1993b.

j

k

l

III

---

j The Glastonbury Lake Village, more or less as first seen by Arthur Bulleid in 1892, with the low mounds of the settlement faintly visible in the central field. Bulleid restored the mounds after excavation so the field today resembles that seen in 1892. Photograph Jim Hancock.

k Various beads of glass and teeth from the Glastonbury Lake Village.

l The Glastonbury bowl, found by Bulleid in 1895, and used constantly ever since as the logo of the Lake Village. It is 116mm diameter at the rim. For a picture of it in use, see illus 48. Photographs John Coles.

existed from the mid-9th to the early 12th century and which was claimed by two rivals, the bishop of Grenoble and the archbishop of Vienne, a town some 30km downstream of Lyon on the Rhône; Paladru is fairly central to the county. Together, these two lines of evidence imply that the fortified settlements of Lake Paladru were lived in by people who owed their allegiance to Vienne, and their arrival may have been part of the archbishop's strategy to strengthen his hold on Sermorens at the expense of his rival in Grenoble.

The scenario just outlined might take us back to the idea of a settlement of Warrior-Knights, but Colardelle and Verdel are convinced that Colletière was home to families, women and children as well as men. Despite the great range of evidence from the site, it is hard to say what pertains to men and what to women. Who, for example, caught and smoked or cooked the perch? Who played chess and who backgammon? Was the little cross-bow really a child's toy? It would be possible to reduce the population to unsexed adults, and therefore assumed male in most interpretations, except for one category of evidence preserved in the waterlogged deposits. The shoes, as we have already noted, include a sole which is thought to come from a child's shoe; this seems reasonable as it was only 16cm long. Two parts of uppers were also child-sized. Other soles range, in continental sizing, from 34 to 43, about what one might expect for adolescents and adults of both sexes.

The population of Colletière expanded, another pointer to family occupation perhaps. Building II, initially a stable, became a human dwelling soon after AD 1020. The people who worked and ate under this roof had slightly different habits to those in the central building. No venison came their way, but they consumed most of the wild birds, including duck and heron. They ate rather more beef and mutton and rather less pork than their neighbours in the main building. Most of the weapons, and most of the evidence for games and music, came from the central building, a distribution that could be a function of its longer life in two respects. Either lost chess pieces and broken spears and so forth had an extra 15 years to accumulate, or from AD 1020 onwards the Colletière people had fewer such things. The difference in food remains, though, is a straightforward reflection of a difference at the time of occupation.

Weapons and mounted warriors suggest warfare, but Colletière suffered no attack that left an archaeological trace. In AD 1040, or within a year or so, the apparently successful, well-fed and well-protected inhabitants abandoned their home. So too did the inhabitants of Grand Roseaux and Pré d'Ars, according to the limited dendrochronological investigation of those sites and the typology of the artefacts retrieved from them. The archaeological evidence points to abandonment in the face of rising lake levels, something that would have affected all three sites simultaneously. Certainly, once people had gone, water soon covered the site, otherwise the organic artefacts and much of the other organic evidence would never have survived. Much the same is argued for many prehistoric lakeshore sites. But for Colletière a written record provides a human background to the move. A monk living at Cluny, about as far to the north of Lyon as Paladru is to the south, recorded that the years AD 1033, 1034 and 1035 were exceptionally wet (Colardelle & Verdel 1993a), so wet that the fields could not be ploughed and sown, so wet that there was a dreadful famine throughout Burgundy and the starving peoples turned cannibal.

Colletière was not abandoned in a panic, and perhaps the lake fish helped to ease any famine. The lake itself, which is largely rain-fed, would have slowly risen during the three wet years. The gradual flooding of their houses would have been enough to shift people onto drier land and out of the wetland archaeological record. Within three generations, early in the 12th century AD, Paladru people were to appear in the historical record with small mottes or stone castles documented, one in each territory of the three former lake-side settlements.

Charavines-Colletière is well worth a Special Journey, both through the medium of Colardelle & Verdel's publications and in reality, as there is now a museum for the lakeside archaeology. Visitors have the bonus of two well-preserved and well-researched sites, one Neolithic and the other the medieval settlement that we have focused upon here. The setting is pleasant, the food excellent, and walnuts are still much enjoyed. The potential of Colletière is but outlined here. We have said little about the research on climate, or the typological and technological studies of artefacts, nor have we explored population numbers or done more than touch upon the relative importance of different foods. What matters is that the evidence can be set in a sure chronological framework, due to a combination of undisturbed stratigraphy and dendrochronological dates. All that is known from the site belongs to less than four decades, and much of it can be attributed to a particular decade. Change in one aspect can be checked against other variables, making the interpretation of cause and effect that bit more secure. And, as we have seen for other wetland sites, the combination of dendrochronology and typology provides a reference assemblage of closely-dated artefacts for determining the chronology of related dryland sites.

Asked to sum up the excellence of Colletière, we might point to the sudden irruption of people into a landscape that had been almost empty of human settlement for centuries. We would note that their pioneer character was under-lined by the abundance of forest foods gathered in early years, gradually giving way to cultivated sources as fields expanded and the woodland edge retreated, a small enough detail but one that relates to the lifetime of an individual. Perhaps the mothers of 1025, tied to hearth and home, hankered after the good old days when they set out to gather wild strawberries or raspberries and maybe they thought their own daughters should not do the same, since now things had changed and the forest edge was far off. A flight of fancy on our part and a reminder of how much is still to be learnt of the people who once lived here.

À LA CARTE

In choosing the Glastonbury Lake Village as one of our key wetland sites, well worth a Special Journey, we are aware that we are recycling a very old site. The

Lake Village of Somerset has been known for over 100 years and has been studied, and re-studied, by many people. It has received a number of reconstructions, from pile dwelling (cf Swiss lakeside sites) to palisaded town (cf Viking fortress), all of them based on preconceptions, misreadings or pure inventions. The site is here in this chapter because it demonstrates how good a wetland settlement can be, even if excavated long ago. The Lake Village has many of the virtues of a good wetland site – good potential for environmental and economic evidence, well-preserved structural and artefactual evidence – and it has the benefit of extensive, near-total excavation, a full publication written by the excavators (Bulleid & Gray 1911; 1917), and now in 1995 a set of new analyses and fieldwork (J Coles & Minnitt 1995). All these provide what we think is a good example of what a wetland settlement can do to enlarge the past, in this case the later Iron Age of Britain.

The Glastonbury Lake Village was discovered by Arthur Bulleid, a medical student, in March 1892: 'when driving across the moor from Glastonbury to Godney, a field was noticed to be covered with small mounds, an unusual feature in a neighbourhood where the configuration of the land is for miles at a dead level' (Bulleid 1911) (illus IIIj). Bulleid had been led to the search by reading about the Swiss Lake Dwellings, and he expected to find a pile dwelling settlement of the Neolithic or Bronze Age. Excavations were begun at once and soon

47
The excavations at the Glastonbury Lake Village in the 1890s, with a group of visitors inspecting the work. In the foreground is a mound with an upper hearth of Lias slabs left in place. Behind is the trench face left by the spading team. The white uprights outline several round houses as defined by Bulleid. Photograph by Arthur Bulleid.

demonstrated that the settlement was waterlogged with good preservation of wood, and was liberally sprinkled with artefacts of the Iron Age. Bulleid took advice from his local Antiquarian Society, who adopted and became owners of the site, and from an Expert Committee which included General Pitt-Rivers, Professor Boyd Dawkins, Sir John Evans and Dr Robert Munro. The work went on until 1898 and drew admiring throngs of visitors from all around the world, and the press who penned various serious and not-so-serious accounts of the site and its findings. One of the poems composed in honour of the site had 21 verses, of which we think only two bear repetition:

'Down in moor th'de zay   An' a vullige wur thur, th'de zay,
That lately th've a voun'   Back in th'wulden time,
Al'zorts, boans be th'scoor,   'Tis gro'd al'auver wi gras,
Vaur veet unner groun'.   An' now thur's skearce a zine'.

Among the discoveries were some burnt bread and fragments of pottery, which occasioned comment along the lines of the 'worthy warrior's wrathful reception of his spoiled meal'. Bulleid pressed on regardless of the playful remarks and doubtless basked in his early election to the Society of Antiquaries of London, an honour never achieved by Robert Munro. After an interval, 1898–1903, during which he qualified as a doctor and got married, work began again in 1904 and the excavation was completed in 1907. Bulleid was associated in the latter campaigns with Harold St George Gray, one of Pitt-Rivers' assistants and soon to become a major force in Somerset archaeology.

The site was excavated rather quickly when we reflect on its size, 8,800 sq m, and on the depth of deposits explored, well over one metre and often approaching two metres; it took Bulleid and Gray about nine man-weeks to dig each of the 90 mounds (illus 47) or clay patches, whereas 100 years later the authors excavated smaller mounds at another wet site in the area and took 60 man-weeks per mound; in other words, they worked about 10 times as fast as we did. They had labourers, we had students; they recovered far fewer artefacts, pro rata, than we did. Nonetheless, the work of Bulleid and Gray was exceptional for its time, and its value much enhanced by their publication of the results, in 1911 and 1917.

The Glastonbury Lake Village was a settlement of round houses with various open work areas, the whole surrounded by a palisade, with boats and a dock, and it was 'wealthy' in terms of the number and character of artefacts discovered in the clays and peats. These objects suggested to Bulleid and Gray that the settlement existed from 150 BC to AD 50. On the basis of the evidence, Bulleid commissioned some reconstruction paintings of the site and its ancient inhabitants (illus 48 and 53), and these appeared in *The Illustrated London News* for 1911. The originals were thereafter dispersed and it was only in 1990 that some were rediscovered, handed over to one of the authors in a plastic bag with the words 'Here are some old pictures that may be of interest'. They are now preserved in the County Museum, Taunton.

The two monographs on the Lake Village contained 29 chapters, 101 plates, 179 drawings and 724 pages, and they cost £2.2.0d. These books have provided material for various reinterpretations over the years, most of which can now be shown to be either illogical or nonsense, or both (J Coles & Minnitt 1995, chapter 7). They all suffered from the handicap of ignoring the vast bulk of unpublished material in the site notebooks, drawings, photographs and unstudied artefacts, and one in particular was very inventive.

In 1984 the authors carried out small excavations on the site to check its survival, to test Bulleid's records, and to obtain environmental information; having worked for 20 years already in the Somerset Levels we knew that the environmental record was a key to the site. In 1992, 100 years after the discovery, we published a small biography of Arthur Bulleid and a history of the Lake Village work (J Coles *et al* 1992), a book which benefited much from the contribution of one of Bulleid's daughters, Armynell Goodall. In 1993 and 1994 we began to assemble all the unpublished documents, letters, notebooks, photographs and drawings, we re-located the Black Book of Relics (the original listing of all the finds), and we assembled and assessed the bulk of artefacts from the site. All were scanned for new information and new ideas, and at the same time we 'excavated' Bulleid and Gray's two volumes, analysing their records. Our aim was simple: could we do more with the evidence than Bulleid and Gray had done, and could we do better than those who had already made the attempt? We concentrated on the structure of the site and its evolution, and on the environmental evidence and the economic base for the settlement. We hoped to explain what the site was, why it had existed, and how it had coped with its wet and potentially difficult environment.

The settlement as Bulleid found it in the grassy field consisted of about 75 low mounds composed of layers of clay brought to the site and laid down on a foundation of logs and brushwood. On some of these clay spreads, some circular in plan but often more irregular, were laid wooden floors or

48
A reconstruction of life in one of the big houses at the Glastonbury Lake Village, *c* 100 BC. The hunters have arrived with a swan. The workers glance up from their grindstones. The regal lady on the right offers the bronze bowl to the thirsty men. Drawn by A Forestier for *The Illustrated London News* 1911.

stone paving, and they formed the base of round houses, or sometimes unroofed shelters. Bulleid drew many sections as his labourers cut trenches through the mounds, and these show the multiple floors of clay and their mounded shapes. Bulleid also drew a master plan of the whole site at a scale of 1/96 (1/8 inch: 1 foot) and this shows the edges of the clay floors and the thousands of wooden posts and stakes that formed fences, divisions, and walls of houses and shelters. He thought that the Lake Village had consisted of about 70 round houses and he, a craftsman, made various models to demonstrate how crowded the settlement had been. We disagree with his view on this and consider that only 22 mounds ever had round houses (J Coles & Minnett 1995).

The clay floors or spreads forming each mound varied in extent and in thickness; mounds could have up to six, eight or even ten clay floors, and some mounds had 1.0–1.6m of stratified floors, marking repairs and renewals over time. The clay floors or spreads could be very large, extending over wide areas of the site and linking several mounds. This meant we could use Bulleid's excellent plans to create a matrix of joins and to try to work out the sequence of site development. Bulleid had never done this, a strange omission given his solid scientific background and his careful plans and sections. By using his notes as well, we could separate the various clay floors and structural elements on most mounds and create a series of phases, linking mound to mound. By doing this we have been able to develop a site sequence which, although imperfect due to gaps in Bulleid's records and incompetence on our part, gives an impression of a settlement from its initial establishment to its final abandonment. To understand this it is first necessary to examine the place selected by the settlers for their homes (illus 49).

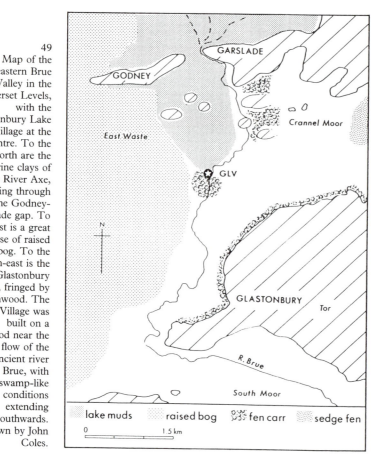

49
Map of the eastern Brue Valley in the Somerset Levels, with the Glastonbury Lake Village at the centre. To the north are the estuarine clays of the River Axe, squeezing through the Godney-Garslade gap. To the west is a great expanse of raised bog. To the south-east is the Glastonbury upland, fringed by fenwood. The Lake Village was built on a fen-wood near the flow of the ancient river Brue, with swamp-like conditions extending southwards. Drawn by John Coles.

In the closing centuries BC, the eastern end of

the valley of the lower River Brue was a mosaic of wetland and dryland. The swampy lowland was surrounded by the gently rising slopes of the Mendip foothills to the north, an eastern ridge and the Polden Hills to the south. The basin contained a number of low islands, some of rock and others of sand, that now rise 2-4m above the flats. The Brue, a very sluggish river, flowed from the south and drifted northward until finally escaping into the River Axe through the Bleadney Gap in the northern hills. This Gap had been partially blocked in the 1st millennium BC by a spread of estuarine clays squeezing through from the north, with a leading edge of freshwater muds. To the west was a huge domed raised bog, developed over 3,000 years, and creating its own barrier to the outward flow of water from the eastern end of the valley. The immediate area was a swamp, with reed-beds, sedge fen and open water in places, and patches of fen carr here and there. One of these carrs was selected for the settlement. It must have been very wet, yet with enough rooted trees to provide a base for the Lake Village.

The trees, willow and alder, were felled and the carr was cleared ready for the foundations of a huge crannog to be laid. Logs were felled on the dry slopes of the uplands and islands and floated in, and stone rubble and clay were quarried and brought to the site by raft or logboat; perhaps the logs formed rafts for the stone, the whole then turned into foundation material. Bracken, rush, reeds and any other debris were used to create a raised, uneasily firm surface for the actual settlement floors. The clay for these was also brought in by water, or just possibly by ox-drawn sledges over drier parts of the swamp, and by the end hundreds of tonnes had arrived on site. Quarries on the Glastonbury uplands were the source of the clay, as well as smaller more local areas where estuarine clays were exposed. The clays were spread by shovel and basket to form living and working surfaces, raised upon the foundations, and creating a small drier world amidst the great swamp. The clay spreads, often called floors, were the main structural feature surviving on the site for Bulleid to find and identify, and they provide us with the evidence for linking areas of the site and for its phasing (see below).

The floors were put to many uses on the site. Some were left as open spreads, for movement and other outside activities, others served as bases for windbreaks, sheds, animal pens or open-air hearths, and others formed the floors of round houses. All were enclosed, eventually, by a series of fences with various gates and entrances (illus 50). Over time, clay floors were renewed, replaced, and areas on the site altered in character and purpose; houses fell or were destroyed by fire, new ones were built, hearths were repaired or rebuilt, new areas of the original fen carr were taken into the settlement and clay spreads were extended or abandoned. The whole sequence of deposits speaks of change, and we can document over 80 substantial alterations to the mounds, from open clay floor to house or vice versa, or a new shape of a clay spread, or a restructuring of a building. Like almost every wetland settlement ever excavated, the sense of fluidity of the site is dominant.

The houses documented by Bulleid have come to be recognised as type-houses for the Iron Age of Britain. The walls were of stakes or thin posts driven through the edges of the clay floors into the foundation, and linked by woven rods or tied panels, the wall then packed with daub. The stakes were set 150-380mm apart to give a tight weave. Fallen wall panels survived on the site and were 2m high. The roofing timbers had also survived in some places as collapsed debris from burnt houses, or in the foundation dumps, but nowhere could Bulleid find any diagnostic joints or ties. Charred reed fragments were sometimes found, but rush or heather or straw might also have been used as thatch; all survived, in small patches, on the site. Entrances were made of heavy posts set 1.4–2.1m apart, and Bulleid found a narrow half-door of oak with pivots, like a saloon bar swing door, only 1.1m high and 0.45m wide. Perhaps it was a shutter for a window. Paved or timber-lined entrances, and parallel-laid timber floors were recorded; small porch-like entries, with outer paired posts were also noted. Central posts in some houses may have been for roofing support but some were probably a temporary constructional feature or marking post rather than an essential roof-supporting element. Houses were 5-8m in diameter and would not need a central post to support the roof. Nonetheless, even a small house required a considerable amount of raw materials, almost all of it imported to the site from distances of 500–1000m away, and brought in mostly by water.

Inside, fittings of the houses were not often noted, if they survived; the only exceptions were hearths, which were very numerous. Most were near the centre of the floor, and of baked clay (over 200) or gravel or rock (60). Most were raised above the floor clay, some with distinct rims, and almost all were circular. A few were rectangular and one of these was very substantial and had its surface marked with circle decoration; this was probably a table, not a hearth. Other than the

50
The Glastonbury Lake Village from the NE, outside the fence. Note the open areas on site with only a few round houses, some internal fencing, and piles of brushwood. A narrow clay-based walkway extends out into a reedy hide. Drawn by Jane Brayne.

hearths, internal fittings were sparse, with a few stone seats here and there, and no compartments were recorded, probably because of the method of excavation employed by Bulleid and Gray, but plenty of internal posts were found and it would only take two or three to hold a dividing wall of cloth, or skin, or a hurdle. The records made by Bulleid, particularly his plans, show a variety of other structures on the site, and contradict his own view that almost 70 mounds held round houses. The authors believe that far fewer mounds ever had houses, and never all at the same time (see below). Various stake and post settings, and the distribution of debris, and the clay spreads, suggest that rectangular sheds or barns once existed, as well as windbreaks and other open shelters. Short fence lines, pens and posts for temporary enclosures were all over the site, and tents may well have been used for seasonal or sporadic activities such as occasional visits of relatives or others from the uplands. Across the site were various pathways linking floors or leading onto other open spreads, and some dumps of wood or stone or clay can be identified, probably raw materials awaiting a purpose.

The whole settlement was ringed by fence posts except in a few places. Bulleid considered that the entire site was surrounded by 'a continuous line of posts' (1911) but this was not the case, as the records show at least 5 gaps and possibly 4 others, several marked by tree trunks or other timber lying across the entrances; no built gateways or other defensive structures were seen. There were short clay paths leading out from the settlement, beyond the fence, probably to allow people to squat amidst the fringing reeds in quiet contemplation. The height of the so-called palisade is uncertain, as the posts recorded by Bulleid were 1.5–4.3m long, sharpened at one end for driving or pushing into the underlying peats. Various lines of these posts existed, up to 4 lines in some places, and they probably had a dual function of holding in the clay floors and excluding unwanted outsiders. Some of the posts were joined at the tops by woven rods, and the authors think that the fence around the site was probably only one metre in height in most places.

The fluidity of the settlement has been indicated and is easy to explain. A wet subsurface deposit of peat holding a foundation of logs, clay, rubble and brushwood, itself weighted down by tonnes of clay and house timbers and roofing, is a recipe for slow collapse downwards and outwards. The clay floors can be shown to have squeezed outwards and pressed downwards, their original convex or flat contour becoming substantially concave as the central part, being the thickest and heaviest, slowly sank. Those clay floors within round houses were further distorted by the pressure imposed upon them by the walls. The subsequent dampness of the floors was addressed by renewal of the clays, rebuilding of the hearths, and strengthening of the floor edges by stakes. So the fact of a house having 8 floors and 9 hearths is not necessarily a reflection of its longevity as much as the inappropriate or unsuccessful efforts to stabilize it. Add to this the evidence that some houses burnt down and the problems of the inhabitants of the village are clear. Rain, floods, the churning action of animals and children on wet clays and peats, and normal domestic and industrial work must have often turned the living surfaces into quagmires; much of the site was covered with a black earth, a mixture of clay, peat, charcoal, and miscellaneous debris. At times the site was probably a real mess.

The authors' recent analysis of Bulleid's plans and texts suggest that the settlement went through a fairly rapid development. By, as it were, stopping the moving picture and freezing the frame at convenient points, we can identify four episodes in this evolution: Early, Middle, Late, Final.

The Early occupation took place on and near a small fen carr (illus 51). Felled wood and imported clay provided a base for a few clay floors and one house and several sheds were built in the north of the proposed settlement. About 25m to the south, another complex of clay floors and three houses was established, and a clay spread led off east to another house, perhaps a special structure. There

51
The Glastonbury Lake Village in an early phase of its existence, c 225 BC. Only a few houses were built, and slender fencing, as bulk materials arrived by boat and raft from the uplands. Drawn by Jane Brayne.

were two houses here but one soon burnt down and must have been replaced by the other. There were six post-and-stake settings nearby, and six houses were built in this Early phase; perhaps these settings were some sort of consecratory feature. A couple of clay dumps to the south probably represent landing places for the loads of material coming in from the south. Part of the settlement was fenced. We think there are four units of occupation in this phase, one north, two central, one east, and a population of about 50 persons, the pioneer settlers. The life of this Early settlement was perhaps 25–30 years, starting about 250 BC. During this short period the settlers got established, worked out sources of raw material, devised transport methods, acquired sufficient food supplies by import, barter and local gathering, and got used to living in the swamp. They must have been a hardy gang.

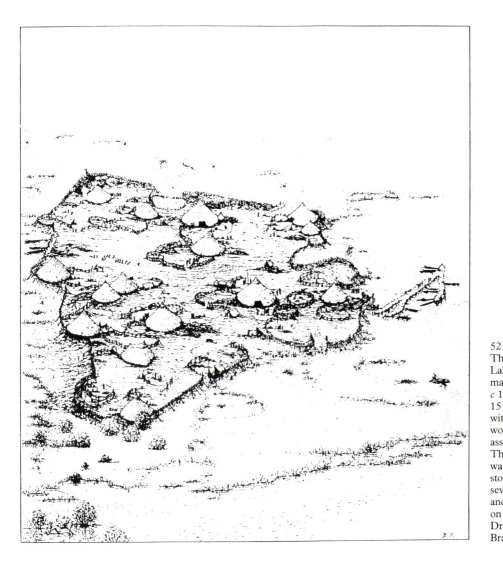

52
The Glastonbury Lake Village at its maximum extent c 100 BC. About 15 houses existed, with many open work areas and assembly points. The settlement was enclosed by a stout fence, with several entrances, and a boat dock on the east (right). Drawn by Jane Brayne.

Soon enough there was an expansion of occupation, with new arrivals to supplement the growing population of the Early settlement. The Middle phase is marked by a great increase in the physical structure of the site, with many new clay floors laid down on new foundations, 11 new houses built, various sheds and lines of posts, and a substantial fence constructed to enclose much of the site. An embankment was built on the east, for fishing as well as to receive supplies by raft or boat, but the wide-open western entry was still available. Three main areas were now built upon, and separate from one another, and a concentration of houses began to emerge in the southern part. We think that 10 units can be seen, a population of perhaps 125 persons, and this Middle phase represents about 50–60 years. This would be time enough for wider contacts to be made, for local supplies to be identified, for some internal organisation to become more firmly established, and for a general seasonal pattern of existence to be developed (see below).

The settlement continued to expand into a Late phase and its maximum extent (illus 52). Infilling of spaces and expansion to the east created a densely-packed settlement of at least 13 houses and various shelters, multiple unroofed clay floors, a near-complete fence with well-marked entrances, a strongly-built causeway on the east, sturdy log roadways at the south, and the emergence of a special structure near the south. This last, an oval house or enclosure, had a linking path to an open floor and an adjacent shed, and an internal clay table decorated with inscribed circles. There was a considerable amount of debris scattered in and around this complex and it may have been some sort of ceremonial or at least focal point for the settlement in this Late phase. We can identify about 14 units, and estimate a population of about 200 persons. The phase may have lasted for 75–90 years and a considerable amount of the artefacts recovered by Bulleid and Gray must be a part of this long occupation.

The range of artefacts (called Relics by Bulleid and Gray) recovered in the excavations is a sample, and a large one, of the material culture of the late Iron Age of southern Britain. The site yielded a larger number, and a greater variety, of objects than any other Iron Age site in Britain, it is said. Whether this is a reflection of the wealth of the inhabitants, or merely because so many small objects could get lost in the damp soils, is not certain and perhaps both factors help account for the abundance of Relics. These have been extensively and exhaustively presented in the Bulleid & Gray 1911–1917 monographs, some in our 1995 book and in other publications, and need not detain us for long. But they do show that there was some industrial activity going on at the site, and that some special objects were being brought in, probably acquired from neighbouring groups. Bulleid and Gray recovered several tonnes of pottery, most of it still unstudied, but some of it decorated and serving as the type series for late Iron Age wares. Bulleid made a special study of the decorated pottery and his drawings grace many a book. The distribution of pottery on the site can only be approximated as that was one area of recording where Bulleid and Gray fell well short of their usual capabilities. The coarser wares were certainly used, broken and discarded on site, but there is no firm evidence that they were made on site as no kilns were found, and no wasters either. The decorated wares have been the subject of several studies, and sources for the inclusions in the pottery suggest an origin in the Mendip Hills to the north, where some of the stones for querns were also quarried. There are a very few exotic potsherds, from cordoned bowls and painted pots, which are likely to have come from the continental side of the English Channel.

The site yielded considerable evidence for metalworking, with particular areas of concentration in the north-east and south. Iron smithing was probably undertaken, and the products left behind included just what we should expect of such a settlement: billhooks, sickles, knives and the like. Copper-alloys were melted and cast on the site and tin, lead and lead-tin alloys were employed. Bone and antler working was extensive, for weaving combs, toggles, points, hammers and other tools, many pieces decorated with dot-and-circle and geometric designs. Textile production was perhaps the major industry on the site, and spindle whorls, combs, bobbins, loom weights, points and needles were widely scattered and present in all phases of occupation. Spinning in particular seems to have been a common event, and combs for the making of braids, ribbons and narrow strips for halters, straps and belts were quite widely spread on the site. Loom weights for warp-weighted looms were more restricted, perhaps marking particular specialised places for this industry. Of textiles we have nothing, not, we think, because fragments had not survived but because Bulleid's team did not see them as the men spaded steadily along the trenches.

Another industry, in stone, produced various small tools such as hammers, polishers and spindle-whorls; flint was also collected from the uplands and roughly flaked to make unstandardised knives, points and scrapers. Because of the good preservation on site, wooden objects were recovered in abundance, surprising to many archaeologists of the time who were unaccustomed to thinking about such organic artefacts on their dry sites. Bulleid could not hope to conserve all the wooden objects, especially the larger pieces of structures or implements such as anvils or ladders. He reburied large amounts of wood in the hope that some future development would allow re-excavation and conservation; we have not yet reached that stage. But the smaller pieces were saved, and some survive today. Hammers, ladles, handles and bungs are among the more ordinary objects that were probably in everyday and common use. Wheel hubs, axles and spokes were being manufactured on site, probably a specialized activity, and a series of plain and decorated wooden vessels attest to considerable skill in carpentry and fine precision in engraving.

More individualistic and personal items such as beads (illus IIIk), armlets, finger rings, brooches and tweezers were found widely scattered on the site, but rather few in the Early phase. Almost all were probably imported to the site, and the glass beads show much variety in type and were clearly drawn from a number of sources; the mixture might suggest that the site had served as some kind of point of trade for groups from diverse places. Of weaponry and horse harness there was relatively little although cheek pieces are not uncommon, and there were various heaps of slingstones, probably for fowling and hunting small game.

Notwithstanding this, Boyd Dawkins, one of Bulleid's mentors, talked of a battle and a massacre on the site, much to Bulleid's annoyance. From around the fencing, however, and from within the settlement itself, came some adult skulls, several with sword cuts, which may point to some display of victims or other trophies. And the bone dice, so popular with the public imagination (illus 53), may strengthen the view of those who demand a hard-drinking hard-living warrior class on the site; there is really no justification for it, more's the pity. Bulleid and Gray eagerly sought the inhabitants of the settlement, of whatever class, but the cemetery, where some hundreds may lie buried, was never found; a few neonatal bodies were buried beneath the floors of some houses on the site. Probably cremation was practised, or the dead were put into the swamp waters, or were otherwise rendered invisible to Bulleid, and to us.

With all this evidence of wealth in material culture, in personal objects, in specialised industries, in importation of materials and artefacts, and in the organisation of the whole enterprise, we might have expected some evidence of authority, of a leader, to be found either in his or her house, or in some special equipment. There are places on the site where some extraordinary measures were taken, the consecratory posts of the Early phase, the decorated table in its elongated enclosure in the Late phase, but this is rather weak evidence for a major authority. Among the small artefacts, a baton of tin, with leaded bronze terminals, and, reputedly, gold leaf embellishment, was clearly unusually valuable. So too was the famous Glastonbury bowl (illus IIII), a sheet bronze container with rivet decoration, fondly considered by many visitors to Glastonbury town today to be the Holy Grail or at the very least to be associated with Arthur and his Queen.

53
Gambling at the Glastonbury Lake Village. Cock-fighting in the background. Most of the artefacts shown were not found on the site but the scene fired the imagination of many readers of *The Illustrated London News* 1911.

No such luck. These few artefacts and features of structural evidence are all that we have to signal the presence of the authority that had to be imposed from the start to get the settlement going and to keep it running. Even so, the evidence of the settlement itself in its Late phase, and the wide range and abundance of artefacts, suggest an occupation that was well-established and not under stress from natural or human sources. It was not to last.

The subsistence base of the settlement has always intrigued us, partly because of the wetland setting but mostly because Bulleid was successful in recognising and recovering a wide range of organic material. Furthermore, through his exalted committee of advisors, he was offered specialist identifications and reports by a panoply of scientists and other leading authorities. He did not have anyone to explore the landscape itself, however, although his own comments on the environment were supported by the later work of Sir Harry Godwin. It is only recently that a detailed environmental study has been done and the swamp-like conditions identified (Housley 1988, 1995).

In terms of subsistence, our concave landscape approach, reproduced here, tries to set out the variety of micro-environments that would have yielded particular supplies either seasonally or in some cases all-year-round (illus 54). The settlers could establish arable field and hoe plots on the low sandy islands to the north of the village, and find reed-beds and waters where wildfowl gathered, sluggish streams with eel and fish, plants along the margins, and use the water meadows and dry pastures of the Glastonbury upland, work the upslope coppice, and fell and hunt in the forests. All were within 1km of the settlement. Just to the west, the raised bog yielded its own seasonal harvest of berries and birds. Transport to and from these places was mostly by water, we think, and satellite farms were probably set up on the islands and uplands.

54
The concave landscape, with the Glastonbury Lake Village at its centre. From here, various areas could easily be reached and exploited. Drawn by Sue Rouillard.

The food remains found by Bulleid were very abundant, with wheelbarrow-loads of bones, grain and sloe stones. Wheat, barley, peas and beans were scattered

unmanaged woodland

coppice woodland

arable fields

hoe plots

pasture and
water meadows

reed beds

wildfowl

wild plants
at the margin

fish and eel

birds and berries on
the raised bog

about, and also 40 other plant species, including chickweed, goosefoot, parsnip, nettle, bulrush, buttercup, mustard, water lily, burreed and various berries and nuts. The bones of domestic and wild animals were abundant, especially sheep, and cattle, pig, horse and dog together with otter, beaver, deer and boar. Birds included various ducks, crane, swan, cormorant, geese, teal, heron, pelican and eagle. Fish bones of perch, shad, roach and trout were identified, and among the few boxes of human bones we have recently noted frog bones. Eel remains were not found but this is hardly remarkable given the likelihood of almost total consumption of the animal when properly cooked. The village dogs would have contributed to the loss of many bones, and their droppings, some preserved, might tell a story one day.

In the village there were many hearths and bake ovens, grinding stones, bowls and ladles and sieves, and bungs for leather bottles, all designed for the preparation and consumption of food. The authors have no recipes, but seasonal variety was probably a feature of the culinary skills of the cooks. We have experimented with some of the plant and animal remains recorded from the village, assumed that a few species not found by Bulleid were once there, extended the catchment into the not-distant estuarine waters of the Axe valley to the north, and supplemented the study by practical work in the Marais Poitevin in western France where wetland plants and animals are still harvested in traditional and seasonal ways. We have also consulted with Bernard Patarin, whose Marais food we always enjoy, and we present here a Glastonbury Lake Village menu which we recommend to our readers (illus 55).

The food remains from the Lake Village were often recovered under difficult circumstances in the excavations and it is not possible to assign any particular group, or diet, to any special place or phase of occupation. Nonetheless, the major episode of settlement, the 100 years or so of the Late phase, must have seen a good deal of the plant and animal foodstuffs brought to the site, dead or alive. For a time, probably in the late 2nd century BC, life may have been particularly easy, with an organised schedule of activities from coppicing and cropping, gathering and grazing, to fishing and fowling. Soon thereafter, conditions became more difficult.

The Final phase, insofar as we have been able to identify it, is a marked contrast to the major episode of settlement. The site underwent a profound change; it contracted, divided, shrank and lost its cohesion. Only a few houses were built, all of them replacements of previous houses and no new positions were chosen. Only in the east were new clay floors laid down and the fence maintained or reframed. The oval house with its decorated table was rebuilt to a more domestic purpose and the fencing around the site was fragmented. About five units can be identified, and an estimated population of about 50 may have persisted on the site for 25–30 years before abandonment. The appearance of this Final phase of settlement suggests that occupation had changed, from permanent to seasonal.

55 (*opposite*) The Glastonbury Lake Village Menu, devised and tested (mostly) by the authors.

What can have caused this to happen and why was the decision made to give up

MENU

Water cress soup made with duck stock, served with comfrey fritter

Sweet oar weed fried in nut oil and wild celery soup

Reed mace spikes and common mallow soup

Bean and duck egg salad with brooklime

Hazelnut cutlets with herb and kelp salad

Fish etc.

Tench cooked in crab apple juice with steamed laver

Smoked eel and wild celery

Pike steak and boiled marsh samphire

Terrine of eel and frogs' legs with nettle tips

Crayfish with herbs and waterlily tubers

Meat.

Filet of heron and stewed nettle with brooklime salad

Wild boar cooked with bog myrtle berries
and served with crab apple sauce and sea kale

Grouse or duck (in season) and raised bog cranberry sauce
with sea beet and crab apple pickle

Beaver tail roast with hazelnuts, peas and comfrey sauce

Saltmarsh lamb and sea purselane, with wild cabbage and meadowsweet

Roast swan with reed mace shoots and sea holly sweetmeats

Teal served with watercress and samphire

Sweet trolley.

Goat cream cheese and honey

Reedmace pancakes with honey or apple jelly

Raspberries with cheeses

Bilberry crumble

Tea or coffee.

Coffee: acorn, dandelion root, goosegrass

Tea: mint, limeflower, heather flower

(served with angelica crystallised fruits)

Drinks.

Beer: nettle, heather, bog myrtle, sweet gale, crab apple cider

Wine: birch sap, oak leaf, elderflower, blackberry

Afters.

fennel seed chews, willow bark aspirin, marshmallow chews

on the idea of a swamp village? Already in the closing period of the Late phase, when the settlement was at its maximum extent, some problems may have arisen for the people. Although the beginnings of these difficulties are hard to discern, we think that it was a combination of human and natural forces. The evidence from pollen, the enormous amounts of wood on site and the remains of arable crops and animals suggest that major clearances of the fertile upland slopes and islands had taken place, thereby accelerating the downward flush of rainwater in winters. There seems to have been a slow but inexorable rise in the water table, flooding the lowest parts of the swamp, the reed-beds, and the important grazing lands at the base of the slope (the water meadows).

In a flatland like the swamp of the village, any small but persistent change in water levels is crucial, either way. A rise of, say, 10cm would be a serious matter, just as we have seen at Colletière. When allied to seasonal fluctuations, winter flooding in particular, the effect could be disastrous at times, and very difficult at best. It is likely that the Final phase of occupation was mostly seasonal, with perhaps one or two families sticking on site over the winters, patching and repairing their houses, and taking to the boats on occasion. But most of those once interested in the site preferred to squat on the dry slopes of the islands or the uplands, returning to the site for the spring and summer harvests of wild plants and animals. It would only take one or two particularly bad years of flooding to finally overwhelm the site; the settlement had already lost its permanent status, and the final drift away of its people was probably imperceptible. Of course there may well have been social or political pressures to augment and accelerate the process of abandonment, but by 50 BC (not AD) we think it was complete, and the collapsing houses and fences were left to be ultimately wholly submerged by the waters.

Where the Glastonbury Lake Village enlarges our knowledge of the past is not in its undoubted wealth of artefacts. It is in part in its revelations about the variety of foods available, gathered, prepared and consumed on the site, an indication of how people in the prehistoric past may have exploited far more than we find on their desiccated sites. But the enlargement of our information comes also from the structure of the Lake Village, in the uneroded, unploughed clay floors, the heavy log foundations, the house-lines of real stakes and posts, the hearths with clay walls still surviving, the long rows of fence posts, the wattle-work and windbreaks. This structural evidence, recorded a century ago, allows us to rebuild the settlement so that our reconstruction views require few imaginative leaps and invented features – except for the people themselves who are individually unknown.

The settlement itself is thus not the real problem. The question for us is the setting. Why was it placed in a swamp? To exploit the wetland resources of the Brue valley did not require the settlement to be actually in the swamp. Here it was difficult to establish a site, to maintain it, and there was always the threat of a natural disaster. Yet there the Village was, and by no means impoverished. It was well-placed to exploit the wild resources of the wetland and to carry out its cropping and pasturing of the nearby islands and uplands. Was the village positioned here to be remote and inaccessible, for reasons of security? Was it a special site where industry or other services were carried out for the regional Iron Age centres on the uplands? Apart from the spinning and weaving tools there is little to suggest that specialists were at work – there is no glassworking, no smelting of metals, and the woodworking, although skilful, does not seem geared for mass-production. Was the village a seat of local power and prestige, its setting as much withdrawn as that of a hillfort? The site could have been defended but it was not: its many entrances and low fence provided no obstacle to visitors.

About 5km to the west, over part of the great raised bog, was another late Iron Age lowland occupation at Meare. Work here by Bulleid and Gray in a campaign lasting from 1910 to 1956, and subsequently re-assessed, points to a site that was used for seasonal gatherings for people from the settlements of the Durotriges and the Dobunni; Meare lies at the territorial boundary (Orme *et al* 1981; J Coles 1987). This marketplace came into existence several decades before the Glastonbury Lake Village was established. It is possible that the village in the swamp was set up as an offshoot and a response to the Meare gathering place. A group of minor specialists, perhaps, may have decided to establish a permanent settlement in the eastern valley of the Brue, having seen the richness of the untamed landscape. Here they could find peace, isolation, ample variety of resources, and they could avoid any tensions that may have been felt elsewhere on the more populated uplands. In all of this, however, there may have been something more, something special, about the village in the swamp. It was not hidden, and would be clearly visible by day and by night, its smoke and open fires advertising its presence to all who watched from the uplands and islands. So perhaps the village was also placed to attract and to draw in the strangers and the neighbours, to engage in friendly intercourse, to trade a little, to get news of the outside world, and to establish and confirm good relations. Even if these didn't work, the food was probably worth the Special Journey.

5

THE DISAPPEARANCE OF THE INVISIBLE

Wetland archaeology suffers, if that is the word, from its spectacular character. Drowned villages, waterlogged bodies, wooden carvings, textiles and leather shoes, burial platforms, huge trackways, and human brains – these are the things that make the headlines. But of course such sites and objects don't often spring from the ground, ready to be seen and readily identified. Behind most of the wetland discoveries of the past century lies the patient archaeologist, carrying out the work of detection and excavation, hoping to identify the slender signs, the telltale traces of ancient sites now submerged by water, silt, sand or peat. He or she may be lucky, or fully deserve the rewards of discovery, but wetland finds are almost always made by those wholly or partly uninterested in the past, the workers in the field carrying out their jobs of digging, draining or ploughing the wet soils in bog or fen. Their discoveries, often communicated by chance to the authorities, are the most at risk, by neglect, decay or subsequent physical destruction. In chapters 1–4 we have seen the results of chance discoveries as well as of planned surveys, and in this chapter we will examine a number of responses to the wetland challenges.

56 (*opposite*) The Brue Valley in the Somerset Levels: Mesolithic and Neolithic finds. Heavy circles: areas of major activity, clearances etc. Lighter and smaller circles: other areas of activity, less intense, less well-identified. Open squares: settlement, known and presumed. Each dot or triangle represents a single find or group of finds. This map had only a scatter of find spots before fieldwork began in 1965. Drawn by John Coles.

Sites and objects in wetlands have been preserved by being submerged or overwhelmed by water, peat, silt or other waterlogged deposits, so the archaeologist is faced with a fundamental problem – how to find the site before it is exposed by other agencies such as drainage, ditches, motorway construction, industrial development and peat quarrying (see below). This problem has no single solution but over the years some opinions have developed through experiences, both good and bad. Most wetland archaeologists will admit that after some years of experiment, trial and error, few sophisticated technical survey methods can be applied with confidence to a wetland. Various subsurface-seeing machines have been tried, and some may pick up an ancient channel cut into the bedrock, or a tree stump that is massive enough to trigger a response (Jørgensen & Sigurdsson 1991; Grøn 1995). Aerial photographs of wetlands can also be very helpful, particularly in a drying wetland as has been demonstrated in the Fenland of England, as well as in the clear cold Alpine waters. But in a wet wetland, such as a soggy peatbog, a buried structure may well be as wet and porous as the body of peat in which it lies. Of the hundreds of brushwood trackways we found in the Somerset Levels, few showed any more resistance to the peat-cutters' spades than did the drying peat. The discovery of such wet wooden structures in peat will depend upon archaeologists being there during their sudden exposure, or searching the cutting or scraping soon after, as has been well-demonstrated in the Irish bogs. The same is true for the Fenland of eastern England – a presence during or soon after dyke(ditch)-cleaning or a search after ploughing of the organic soils

is the most successful way to discover sites. In most areas where an archaeological presence can be maintained, the opportunity to interest, persuade and instruct the machine-drivers who cut, scrape, dig or plough the peat or other soils will also be very important. In the Somerset Levels, as in central Ireland, the workmen have often made the first observation of newly-exposed structures, and whether or not they tell us depends on their attitude, which has to be encouraged to be positive. There are various ways to achieve this, and whisky/whiskey is one that works.

Another approach that has been successful in the discovery of sites is prediction. By now, we know reasonably well where ancient sites, and what kind of ancient sites, are likely to be present in a wetland. Small islands, fen edges, small inlets, narrows, peninsulas, all may well have been attractive to early settlers and others passing through or stopping for some small purpose. Palaeoenvironmental evidence may help in identifying local possibilities. Patterned drilling or test-square excavation may be used to explore likely locations as has been extensively used in the Netherlands (Brandt *et al* 1987). Experience of a landscape, by repeated or continued presence, is the best guide to what may be possible, as we in the Somerset Levels and others in the Fens (Hall & Coles 1994) or the Dutch delta (Louwe Kooijmans 1985) have been able to demonstrate. In the mid-1970s we sent our field officers to search an area of the Levels that had no record of archaeological finds; we 'knew' there would be material there. This was the beginning of our discoveries of settlement scatters on the dryland, platforms on the edge, and trackways in the peat along the Polden slopes at Ashcott and Walton (illus 56) (B & J Coles 1986, 75).

Another problem often experienced by wetland archaeologists is to convince the landowner, or indeed the local or national authorities, that something actually exists in the wetland. In pasture, and in ploughland, there is rarely anything to see – no walls, floors, mounds – just a blandness, innocent and deceiving. It is both encouraging and dispiriting to be able to demonstrate the existence of an important structure *after* the event, once it has been chopped in two by a ditch, or has lost its surface by ploughing, or rests in small pieces in a peat stack, or has over a year or so been drained to uninspiring scraps. However, this does not mean that all wetland surveys are doomed to disappointment and we will now glance at several different responses to the opportunities offered us by the current interest in wetlands where commercial or other developments are taking place.

We should distinguish two different kinds of wetland survey, because each has entirely different aims and responses. One is the standard survey carried out in parallel with some immediate threat, like a motorway across a bog or silt, a factory erected on wet ground already used for dumping, or a peat quarry. The other is a longer-term operation, with research aims, although it may have some rescue element as well, where the whole wetland is being gradually drained or otherwise 'developed'. The threat here is just as severe, but its immediacy may not be so apparent. The first type of survey is often very much an emergency action, the second should be able to control its work in a more considered manner.

The first type generally has little time, depends on commercial operations for most of the exposures or openings, and consequently the response when structures are uncovered has often been one of panic measures entirely unsuited to the site and to archaeology. The measures unfortunately may include an instant decision to do nothing, as it is too late to do anything appropriate, or may be an equally rapid response involving unsuitable technology and wholly inadequate back-up facilities. Take a logboat, exposed in a drainage ditch freshly-cut. Detected by a watching brief, or by the machine-driver, it may reside for some time untouched and begin to decay at the face. It is very large, heavy, wet and fragile. Few responses under these unplanned circumstances are adequate. Reburial may not be possible, and may fail utterly as Barbara Purdy has demonstrated only too clearly. An international conference photo of 1986 in Florida shows about 24 specialists (Rhind lecturers included) viewing a fine logboat hauled out of the peat only a day before (Purdy 1988); the boat could not be treated at once so was sunk in a deep pool on the peat company's holdings. By 1990 the pool had been drained, apparently inadvertently, and the boat was reduced to splintered fragments, wholly destroyed (Purdy 1991). An obvious effect, this, but all had been in place for a successful rescue of the object – it was just too difficult, facilities didn't exist, people got distracted, it was forgotten and the drainage was totally unexpected; there is no blame attached, it was 'just one of those things'.

Where accident, neglect or ill-conceived response to discoveries can be avoided, the chance exists to undertake the controlled destruction of the site, by excavation. In some regions of the world, this is the normal line of action: in other places there is no line at all. But how much better to respond to the known potential of wetlands by surveys well in advance of instant destruction, in the sure knowledge that slower but severe damaging effects are being exerted on the sites still buried, unseen and unknown, in the wetland. To be able to predict, and to take action in advance, and to have a plan to identify sites and to put them in a context of landscape, and to have in place mechanisms for study and conservation, all can be shown to have revolutionized our knowledge of the past in the wetlands. The surveys in England and Ireland are the best examples known to us of advance planning, although these, too, have particular problems. To illustrate the responses to the Disappearance of the Invisible, we will look at four countries, each with its own problems and solutions.

A JAPANESE RESPONSE

Japan, as indicated in Chapter 1, has considerable areas of river basins and other wetlands mostly under cultivation or settlement. Ancient sites in the waterlogged peats and silts are difficult to locate and it is often through impending developments that preliminary surveys are made. There are good opportunities to discover ancient settlements in these modern operations – river channel and valley widening and deepening, factory or housing development, rice field and terrace establishment, motorway or railway construction. The 1952 law for the protection of cultural properties includes archaeological remains as well as architecture and art. As the law is now interpreted and applied, developers have accepted responsibility to fund excavations necessitated by their operations. A subsidy from the government takes account of small housing and agricultural work where the 1952 law does not apply (Matsui 1992). In addition, the Japanese have a strong tradition of respect for cultural and historic properties so that accidental discoveries are generally reported to the local authorities.

Surveys in wetlands, that is fieldwalking over an entire wetland to locate sites, to predict sites, and to conduct a landscape approach, are not often carried out and most of the wetland archaeology is site-orientated. However, there are exceptions to this and some excellent work in river valleys has been carried out, to locate sites in the whole wetland catchment and to pursue palaeoenvironmental assessments. In Japan, as elsewhere in the world, it is difficult to preserve wetland sites from development by taking them out of the operations and paying compensation; the Centre for Archaeological Operations at the Nara Cultural Properties Research Institute (Nabunken) is working to develop such strategies. The trouble with water in wetlands, and everywhere else, is that it has a tendency to seek to lie flat, so a single site cannot be just set aside while the rest of the wetland goes up or down, depending on flood or quarry.

In an area near Okayama, for example, a wide and long valley is being channelled for better river flow and other improvements; surveys in advance, using trenches and coring, showed that the valley had been occupied over its whole length, with hunter-gatherer sites, rice fields, barriers and stream channels, and later settlements all noted by the survey which was triggered by the imminent threats of dredging. The response to this very considerable archaeological yield is to excavate almost every site, an operation due to occupy a team for about 30 years. Conditions here, at the site of Hyakkengawa Sawada, were so good that 2,000-year-old rice fields had boundaries preserved as well as the individual roots and low shoots of each rice plant, like finding an Iron Age field here in Britain with the individual stalks of corn still in place. In the suburbs of Okayama itself, a smaller, more intensive, response to wetland survey was the same. The site for an office block was trenched to discover any structures and then a full-scale excavation was mounted to examine a settlement of c 100 BC. The site, Minamikita, lay on the edge of a stream with paddy fields laid out for rice cultivation (illus IVa). Wooden sluices and barriers constructed to control the water flow still survived, and vast quantities of discarded objects of bone, wood, stone, basketry and pottery were dumped in the ditches and middens. Pieces of wooden armour, musical instruments, handles, bowls and furniture were beautifully preserved, and much food debris too, including rice husks. The small army of excavators had two years to complete the work before the office block was constructed.

So the overall response to wetland opportunities in Japan today is to carry out surveys by ditch inspection, drilling, trenching and some pollen analysis in advance of development, to conduct full-scale excavation of sites located, to have watching briefs for all commercial operations, and to accept that only very rarely are sites preserved in place and development halted. Developers pay about

£200 million a year for archaeology in Japan and *c* 10,000 rescue excavations are carried out each year. The problems, as we have seen in chapter 1 as well, are that wetland sites yield enormous quantities of finds requiring storage, analysis and conservation, and the display of finds and publication of results involve additional funds that may overwhelm even the most generous of systems. The contribution of wetland archaeology in Japan to general studies has been very considerable and is widely acknowledged and supported; the subject is a part of mainstream archaeology and not considered to be freakish, irrelevant and too expensive to pursue. In these respects, there is a contrast with other parts of the world, especially America.

LOST OPPORTUNITIES

Wet site archaeology in the United States began in Florida as we have indicated in Chapter 1. Frank Cushing at Key Marco was the pioneer, and his tale of exploration was so tragic that, perhaps unconsciously, people tried to avoid becoming embroiled in all the complications. Glen Doran and Barbara Purdy both make the point that dry sites were the easier option, both in the field and in the conservation and storage of the artefacts (Doran 1992, Purdy 1991). The potential rewards of survey in wetlands were ignored for decades, and untold quantities of unique evidence must have been lost through the known draining, quarrying and despoiling of wetlands in Florida and elsewhere (illus 57). Considering the amount of debate and argument about the need to develop new ways to analyse archaeological evidence, and the need for multi-disciplinary projects, and the value of ethno-historical observations, it is extraordinary that for decades in America

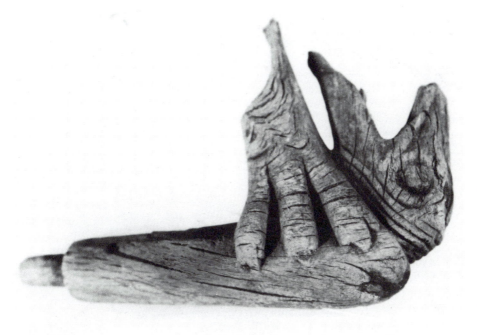

57
Wood carving of a turkey buzzard from Tick Island, Florida. The bird is shown prone as the talons of a raptor clutch it. This piece was probably the top of a staff, or base of a handle. It may be about 2,000 years old. Photograph from Barbara Purdy 1991.

there was hardly a single archaeologist who undertook, and published, research in wetlands or major wet sites. On the west coast of North America there were a few projects, and most notably, but late in this century, was the work at Ozette (Chapter 6 below) and a few other sites (Croes 1976). These demonstrated the huge amount of information that could be extracted from remains of wooden structures, plants, insects, cordage, basketry as well as objects of stone, bone and antler. They also showed that archaeologists could hardly cope with the volume and weight of material that had to be recovered from the sites. So the principles of wetland survey and of multi-disciplinary excavations, and acknowledgement of the requirements for conservation, analyses and publication were ignored by many and accepted by few.

Surveys of river systems, coastlines and marshlands were only initiated in the 1970s, and only in a very few places. The succeeding work and successes of Richard Daugherty and Dale Croes in Washington State and Barbara Purdy in Florida are good examples of the persistence and innovations that such operations require (Daugherty 1988; Croes 1992; Purdy 1991). Unlike Japan, the commercial development of wetlands does not carry with it the requirement, legal and/or traditional, to fund and support archaeological survey and excavation. Archaeo-logists must scramble for finance and it may not emerge in sufficient time or amount to undertake well-conceived and calmly-directed work under conditions of extreme urgency; the work of Glen Doran at the Windover burial swamp (Chapter 1 above) is a case where matters were resolved well, but there was many an anxious moment. Both Daugherty (1988) and Doran have documented the lack of involvement of North American archaeologists in wetland matters and the gradual decline of funding in general for research archaeology. Doran suggests that the National Science Foundation, principal source of grants for archaeology in the United States, provided an average grant of $50,000 in the late 1980s, and comments: 'What level of wet site investigations can be pursued with an average grant of $50,000? What wet site can be investigated in a single year? What wet site can be investigated without an interdisciplinary focus?' (Doran 1992, 127). We cannot but agree with his answer – not one.

The requirement is obvious. Taking Florida as our best example, as the central wetlands are drained to supply water to the burgeoning coastal resorts of Miami and the like, more and more sites protected for centuries by the peats and other waterlogged soils are drying out, or are being dredged out. A site at Belle Glade yielded an amazing number of carved wooden figures together with pottery, shell, bone and stone artefacts when it was partly excavated in the 1930s (Willey 1949); in 1980 test coring showed that '. . . the deposits and everything in them . . . were completely desiccated as a result of the drainage . . . the deposits had turned to dust' (Purdy 1991). A state-wide survey, followed by watching briefs, and strengthened by firm legislation is needed, together with development of facilities for storage, analysis and conservation. Some of this is in place here and there but it needs overall marshalling and direction. The sensational nature of the discoveries already made at sites such as Windover, Belle Glade and Fort Center (Sears 1982), and Ozette on the West Coast, must surely strengthen the hand of those in positions to press for a reappraisal of the word 'heritage' and an implementation of a resolve to protect it.

AN IRISH SOLUTION

Such resolve has been expressed and demonstrated in Ireland where a century or more of discoveries in the central boglands had created a crisis by the late 1980s. In earlier times, hand-cutting of peat had uncovered many significant finds – hoards of bronze implements, cauldrons, horns, gold ornaments, wooden tubs, human bodies (Chapter 3 above) – and archaeologists could cope with most of these as many needed little conservation. But in recent decades the milling of peat for power generation involved huge machines, rapid extraction, massive drains and an 'absence of presence' to retrieve the evidence. In 1984 one of the authors wrote a very depressing account of the state of wetland archaeology in Ireland, stating that: 'Ireland is the only country in Europe which has extensive wetlands, but which has no archaeological presence to deal specifically with them, and seemingly little interest to establish one. In the year 2000, it will all be gone, drained or quarried to extinction' (J Coles 1984). These comments did little to enhance whatever reputation we had at that time in Ireland.

In 1985, Barry Raftery, who had encouraged us to visit and assess the state of wetland archaeology, started survey and excavation in the central bogland, and demonstrated beyond question the abundance, character and significance of the bogland for wooden trackways and platforms dated from the 4th millennium BC to the 1st millennium AD (Raftery 1990). He concentrated on one massive roadway, at Corlea, Co Longford, dated by dendrochronology to 148 BC. We visited the excavation of part of this structure and saw what the peat milling had done to it in an adjacent area (illus 58). Subsequent to Raftery's examination of the Corlea road, public pressure in 1990 led to the withdrawal of threat by both peat milling and drainage operations for a short sector of the road, and the construction of a dedicated Visitor Centre where a conserved stretch can be openly viewed (see below). Furthermore, in 1991 the Irish government announced the formation of an Irish Archaeological Wetland Unit, with funding for five years. This put a professional survey team into the peatlands of central Ireland, working with the full co-operation of Bord na Móna (the Irish Turf Board) and with adequate facilities for some excavation, dating and the like.

The first report of the Unit provides an outline of the results (Moloney 1993a). From the area of bogland surveyed, there were 44 known sites prior to the arrival of the team of four; this total was raised to 1,282 by the survey. The Unit has estimated that the survey, if continued over all of Bord na Móna's land, would probably locate another 7,000 sites. This is mind-boggling stuff, and not only for the sites. 'No fewer than 12,000km were walked by the team, over bog which more often than not was heavy and glutinous and often in atrocious weather conditions' (Raftery 1993). A few of the structures discovered in the peat sections and surface exposures have been excavated, where there is no chance of preservation (Moloney 1993b). In addition, other Irish and Dutch agencies are

58
a) Corlea, Ireland,
in the midst of the
peat fields. One of
the authors stands
on an Iron Age
plank. Barry
Raftery stands
behind on the line
of the great Corlea
road, here totally
demolished by the
peat cutting
machines; b) the
Corlea road,
excavated by
Raftery, and dated
to 148 BC. Most of
the road is now
destroyed, but a
small part survives
in a protected area
(see illus 67).
Photograph
a) B Coles;
b) B Raftery.

now active in purchasing particular bogs for wildlife conservation and where ancient structures remain in these, there is a clear archaeological benefit. So here in Ireland, the implications of industry on wetland archaeology are being taken seriously, not by the legal or moral requirement for the developers to pay, but by public pressure and direct government action – to explore, discover and investigate in advance of damage – and where appropriate and possible to acquire, display and educate. Problems remain, in the need for continuation of funding, and in conservation and palaeoenvironmental work, but we can only applaud and envy the high-level interest and support given to wetland surveys in Ireland. There are lessons here for other countries.

THE ENGLISH SURVEYS

The Irish Archaeological Wetland Unit based its working practices on experience gained in the Somerset Levels in England. Here there had been some sort of archaeological presence since Arthur Bulleid's work at the Glastonbury Lake Village, and it is not often realised that Bulleid and his collaborator, Harold St George Gray, together put in over 80 years of work in the Levels. There were gaps here and there, and none more serious than when Bulleid finally stopped

a

b.

work in 1939, aged 74, although Gray staggered on until 1956 and an age of 81. Peat-cutting by hand of many parts of the bogland continued until the mid-1960s and only a few archaeologists took interest, with the botanist Harry Godwin providing an important link between the old and the new.

Godwin's work was influential in the design of archaeological surveys in the wetlands of England and his Somerset Levels work (Godwin 1981) was the starting point for our own project. Grahame Clark, still enthused by his Star Carr excavation and its reception by the archaeological world, was another who encouraged one of us to begin work on the Bronze Age trackways exposed by peat-cutting in 1963. From here the collaborative exercise with Alan Hibbert of the Botany School in Cambridge took off and sites were found, excavated, analysed and published (B & J Coles 1986); among them was the Sweet Track (Chapter 2 above) which inspired the offer in 1973 by central authorities to help fund a formal Somerset Levels Project. This allowed us to put field workers into the Levels for all the year, to follow the many machines then being used (illus 59), to contact the 20 or so peat producers, the many farmers and others, and to learn of discoveries being made at an increasing rate. Much useful work was done in the pubs of the area, where contact with the machine drivers was most easily made. It is hard to quantify the results of the Project in terms of sites found, but individual exposures of wooden structures recorded numbered in the thousands (J Coles 1989). Among the discoveries and excavations, our work on the Sweet Track, the Neolithic hurdles on Walton Heath, the massive Bronze Age oak roadway on Meare Heath and the immaculately-preserved hurdles in the same area, and the Iron Age bog occupations at Meare and the swamp village at Glastonbury (Chapter 4 above), were multi-disciplinary operations. The major contributions to their study came from full-time palaeoenvironmental work, innovative analyses of coleoptera, woodland management studies, and the

59
Field-walking in the Somerset Levels. The multiple machine-cut trenches, and stacked lumps of peat, may contain the chopped ends of wooden structures. Photo of one of the authors by the other.

development of tree-ring analyses on a variety of species (Morgan 1988). The Project operated for 15 years and its work is now carried on by the Somerset county authorities.

Partly as a result of the Somerset discoveries, Geoffrey Wainwright of the Inspectorate of Ancient Monuments recommended the establishment of another wetland project in 1981, in the Fenlands of eastern England. Here there had been a long history of discoveries, and Cambridge-based research driven by Grahame Clark and Harry Godwin in the 1930s, but matters had languished and the opening-up of the Fenland to enhanced drainage and deeper cultivation posed serious problems for the archaeological deposits known or suspected to be there (Godwin 1978). The shrinkage and wasting-away of the organic soils was astonishing, as we tried to explain:

> 'Today, much of the Fenland lies like one of its bog bodies, a desiccated corpse, a thin skin of peat stretched to breaking point over the skeleton in some places, the bare bones of bedrock exposed in others. Its arteries, that once carried life to those limbs and organs, are detached now, and the water is dragged hurriedly along channels now raised above the dried body' (J Coles 1991).

A Fenland field officer, David Hall, was already in place and his discoveries had begun to change previous ideas about ancient settlement of the Fenland, so by 1981 we were ready for a new assault on the problem. The logo chosen was *Solvitur Ambulando* and so it proved to be (illus 60).

The Fenland was originally a large valley floor through which flowed rivers that drained much of middle England. In time, due to fluctuations of sea-level, the

60
The logo of the Fenland Project, 1981–1988. Walking was the only method that could identify the slight traces of settlements, burial monuments, roadways, industrial sites, canals, field systems and other relics of the prehistoric and early historic periods.

Solvitur Ambulando

slow sinking of this part of eastern England, and natural plant succession, a large and complex series of deposits was laid down, of peats and silts, representing freshwater-based peat formations and sea-driven silts. For several thousand years, people had lived and worked, had died and been buried, on the varying fen-edges and islands exposed to different degrees as the wetlands expanded and contracted. Their settlements, clearings, industrial places and burial monuments had been submerged by peat or silt. Now the organic soils dry out and waste away, blowing in the wind, and the islands and edges emerge, as if rising up from the black fen. Shrinkage and deep ploughing in the silt fens are not as dramatic but nonetheless also expose ancient once-firm surfaces. For archaeologists it was an exhilarating experience to walk the fields, covering 60% of the Fenland, 360,000ha, noting sites marked by scatters of flints, stones, briquetage, potsherds and soil colours. It was also exhausting, and a 1770 poem about the Fens could as well describe the archaeologists:

> '. . . damp unhealthy moisture chills the air
> Thick stinking fogs and noxious vapours fall
> Agues and coughs are epidemical . . .
> Every face presented to our view
> Looks of a pallid and sallow hue'.
>
> (Anon 1770)

From a known base of *c* 450 sites, the total recorded by the end of the survey in 1988 was just over 2,500. The palaeoenvironmental surveys carried out in conjunction with the archaeological work allowed sites to be placed on a set of maps which showed the changing character of the Fenland from *c* 5,000 BC to the Saxon period and beyond. The sites identified ranged from the Mesolithic to *c* AD 1500. Among the major advances were the recognition of hundreds of Neolithic sites along the fen edges, the discovery of complete cemeteries of Bronze Age barrows untouched since overwhelmed by peat (illus 61), the recognition of Iron Age salt-making industry in the siltland, the mapping of Roman and other communication networks through the Fenland, and the documentation of Saxon settlement and episodes of early efforts to reclaim parts of the Fenland (Hall & Coles 1994).

Since the formal end of the survey of the Fens, we have taken about 150 of the sites that seemed to warrant further assessment, and compiled more detailed dossiers on these, noting their extent, character and potential for preservation. Then about 50 of these sites were selected for investigation by excavation, a few almost total examination but most merely sampled in order to define them more closely and produce ideas about their possible preservation (see below). Some of the excavations showed the good condition of some sites, waterlogged and sealed by silt or peat, and others pointed to the poor condition of other sites, drained or ploughed to mere shadows of their former existence. At Market Deeping in Lincolnshire, Tom Lane's work showed that a Romano-British occupation overlay a deeply-buried stream channel full of late Iron Age debris – wood, bone, antler, stone, metal and pottery, with some wooden structural pieces still in place.

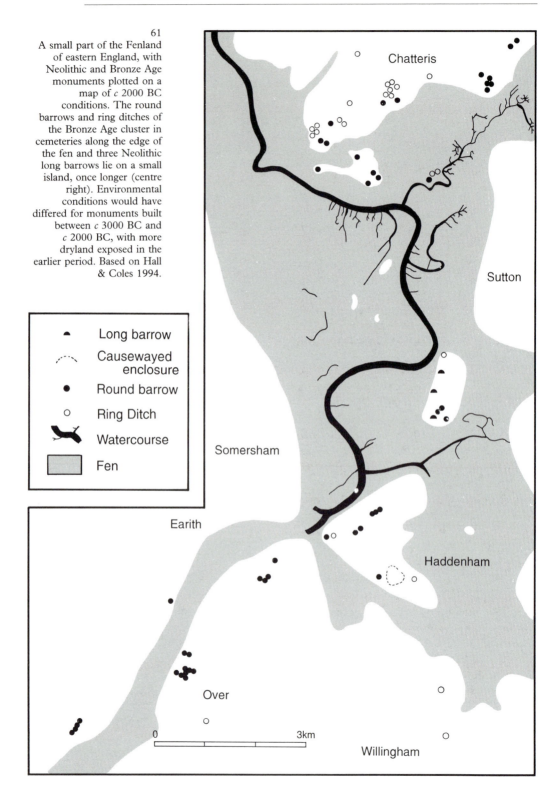

61
A small part of the Fenland of eastern England, with Neolithic and Bronze Age monuments plotted on a map of *c* 2000 BC conditions. The round barrows and ring ditches of the Bronze Age cluster in cemeteries along the edge of the fen and three Neolithic long barrows lie on a small island, once longer (centre right). Environmental conditions would have differed for monuments built between *c* 3000 BC and *c* 2000 BC, with more dryland exposed in the earlier period. Based on Hall & Coles 1994.

At nearby Dowsby, some Saxon potsherds in plough soil were explored by excavation, and a whole complex of Saxon pits, Iron Age ring gullies and enclosures, and postholes and pits of an Iron Age round house and also of a Neolithic structure were revealed. At Wardy Hill in Cambridgeshire, a large excavation by Chris Evans exposed an Iron Age camp, with banks (now ploughed flat), wet ditches, round houses and other structures for industry or occupation (Lane & Reeve 1996). These are only a sample of what there is, and what there was, in the Fens and now it is for English Heritage to develop strategies to help protect sites and landscapes from further deterioration.

The commitment of English Heritage to wetland archaeology has continued with a North West Wetland Survey (1990–1998) and a Humber Wetlands Project (1992–2001) (illus 62). These are building on the experience of the Fenland work in particular, and their results are and will continue to be significant in altering our preconceptions about wetlands as places to avoid, or to exploit in destructive

62
The English Heritage wetland survey areas.

ways. Already the known number of ancient sites in these areas has been increased significantly, and old sites re-defined and new sites assessed for their potential importance and future preservation (eg Middleton *et al* 1995; Van de Noort & Ellis 1995). It will be a test of the resolve of the archaeological community to protect significant wetlands, when practical as well as theoretical ways of preservation are put in place, in the Somerset Levels, the Fenland and the other major regions of English wetlands. It will be an experiment eagerly watched by other agencies around the world who are anxious and concerned, as we are here, to identify and protect elements of the past that will otherwise fade and disappear.

PROTECTING THE PAST

With the identification of well-preserved sites that warranted preservation *in situ*, such as Market Deeping in the Fens, with the prospect of more to come from the other English surveys, and in the knowledge that waterlogged sites have a habit of appearing unexpectedly (some of these are noted in Chapter 6), English Heritage in the early 1990s began to consider how best to protect wetland archaeological sites.

We had already gained experience in the Somerset Levels which suggested that the protection of archaeological sites in wetlands might be effected along the same lines as, and in conjunction with, the protection of wetlands for their wildlife value (J Coles 1986). In 1980 we had traced the Sweet Track along its full length, with key-hole excavations at intervals to examine the condition of the wood. We recorded the depth of peat over the trackway, very variable due to different histories of peat-cutting. We noted present land-use, whether pasture or peat-cutting or woodland. And we attempted to assess threats to the trackway's survival. About 500m of the southern half of the track lay under an area of light woodland and rough grazing, owned by the largest peat company at work in the Levels but leased to and managed by the Nature Conservancy Council (NCC, now English Nature). The trackway was in good condition here but two threats were identified: firstly the owners, Fisons, had long-standing permission to cut peat over the whole area, and secondly they were actively draining and cutting to the north, east and south of the nature reserve and the deeper the work the greater the water loss from the reserve.

We suspected that the trackway was being affected by the surrounding drainage, and several seasons of monitoring water-levels within the reserve proved this to be the case, particularly at times of dry weather. The NCC were also concerned at the effects of water loss on the fen woodland, and remnants of raised bog vegetation within the reserve, not to mention the wetland insect life. Together, English Heritage and the NCC made a successful application to the National Heritage Memorial Fund for a grant to buy the land of the reserve from Fisons and to protect it from further water-loss by sealing the exposed edges with a clay bund (bank). Fisons agreed to the proposal, and sold the land at an agricultural rather than peat-extraction valuation which made the price lower by a considerable amount.

For over ten years now the reserve, which is the Shapwick Heath National Nature Reserve, has been managed by English Nature to protect the Sweet Track and to protect and enhance the wetland flora and fauna (illus 63). Water has been pumped along the line of the trackway when necessary, and trees have been cleared from the immediate vicinity of the buried wooden structure. There have been some problems, for example a shortage of appropriate water supply on occasion when the reservoir of peat-drained water has failed, and water has then been pumped from an adjacent channel carrying water from the limestone uplands and the vicinity of Glastonbury. One task for management of the vegetation within

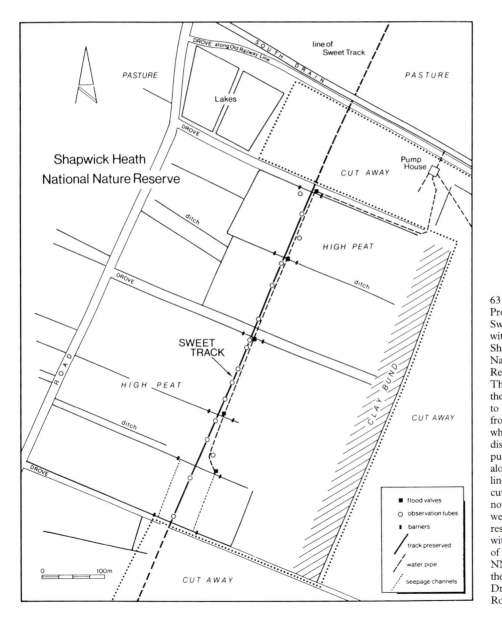

63
Protection of the Sweet Track within the Shapwick Heath National Nature Reserve, Somerset. The clay bund on the east was built to lessen water loss from the reserve, whilst the pipe distributes pumped water along the track line. The areas of cut-away peat are now managed as wetland nature reserves, along with the core area of the original NNR that contains the Sweet Track. Drawn by Sue Rouillard.

the reserve requires the hay meadows to be mown in the late summer, and to bring in the machinery to do this the water level has to be dropped; to avoid damage to the trackway, this has been done as infrequently and for as short a period as possible.

In 1995, after long negotiations with Fisons (now Levington Horticultural) and the acquisition for nature conservation of all of their peat-cutting land in the Levels, English Nature were able to extend the Shapwick Heath Reserve to the north, east and south. Management for wet habitats had begun some months previously, shutting off drainage pumps and blocking ditches to allow the natural re-wetting of the area. The heavy winter rains of 1994–95 were timely, and now the original core of the reserve with the buried Sweet Track is more-or-less surrounded on three sides by spreading reed-beds and a mosaic of open water and willow and birch vegetation, with countless birds, where once there was little but brown dusty peat fields. The transformation is remarkable, and it should help to ensure the long term protection of the Sweet Track in undisturbed and permanently water-logged conditions.

It is important to realise that the Sweet Track is not on display within the nature reserve, nor has it been excavated along this stretch apart from the key-hole sites mentioned earlier, and four similar openings due at the time of writing for a further check of the condition of the wood and initiation of an up-to-date monitoring system. The Neolithic wooden structure and the associated palaeoenvironmental record lie protected by a metre or so of peat, invisible to archaeologists and the general public alike. Wetland sites cannot be exposed for display or studied *in situ* without drastic consequences; from this situation there follow two necessary lines of action. One is to build reconstructions and make suitable displays about the buried evidence, a subject that we will return to in the next chapter. The other is to improve our means of protecting the invisible, and this is where one of the authors (BJC) was invited by English Heritage to carry out a survey of wetland management for nature conservation, in the hope of identifying solutions appropriate to wetland archaeology. The survey began in 1993, and the results were published in 1995. Many organisations contributed time and expertise, including Scottish Natural Heritage and the Scottish

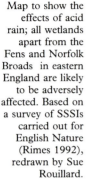

64
Map to show the effects of acid rain; all wetlands apart from the Fens and Norfolk Broads in eastern England are likely to be adversely affected. Based on a survey of SSSIs carried out for English Nature (Rimes 1992), redrawn by Sue Rouillard.

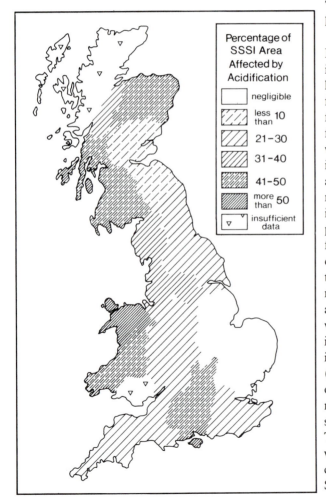

Percentage of SSSI Area Affected by Acidification

negligible
less than 10
21–30
31–40
41–50
more than 50
insufficient data

Wildlife Trust, and working with conservation officers and their colleagues has been an enlightening and rewarding experience. The survey (B Coles 1995) covered many different aspects of wetland management, and the present brief consideration is selective, focusing on some of the major threats to wetlands, on aspects of management which are particularly relevant to archaeology and on the significance of environmental legislation.

THREATS

Threats to wetlands include, paradoxically, rising sea-levels. The coastal wetlands of Scotland are less at risk, but in southern Britain many will be affected if sea-levels rise at the predicted rate. Salt-marsh will be eroded and submerged; wetlands further inland will be affected by tides, storms and perhaps salination of aquifers. The Fens, the Levels and the Humber wetlands, the Kent and Essex coast, the Solent and the Severn estuary, all of them archaeologically rich, are faced with a change in conditions that may well be detrimental to the buried archaeology. Little is known of the effects on waterlogged wood, or pollen grains, or other categories of evidence, when freshwater is replaced by salt. Sea defences may protect some areas, managed retreat will be the strategy for others, and in both cases an archaeological response may be required.

Acid rain is a recognised threat to our environment and one that, in Britain, we are all exposed to in some degree (illus 64). For wetlands, the extent of the threat depends on the amount of acid deposition and also on local geology and soils and the character of the wetland. In general terms, the areas of Britain worst affected are central-southern England, north and west Wales, and southwestern and eastern Scotland (Rimes 1992). If acid rain destroys the stability of a wetland ecosystem, archaeological features and palaeoenvironmental evidence may be lost as a consequence of chemical and physical changes, for example the erosion of blanket bog.

Development, drainage, extraction and afforestation all destroy wetlands, and these are threats familiar to archaeologists even if their impact is not always fully documented. The recent survey carried out for Historic Scotland by John Barber and Anne Crone has demonstrated that many of the known crannogs in southwest Scotland have decayed away. The disappearance of the invisible in this instance is attributed largely to agricultural drainage (Barber & Crone 1993), and in the light of Rimes' work mentioned above one might suspect that acid rain has been a contributing factor. The crannog survey is one of the few field studies of wetland archaeological loss, and similar programmes could be usefully carried out elsewhere.

Water abstraction from bore-holes, for domestic, agricultural and industrial supplies poses another serious threat to wetlands. Pumping from a bore-hole can lead to the de-watering of a wetland several kilometres distant, and abstraction will also affect the flow of rivers and place valley wetlands at risk of desiccation. Whatever records of the past are held in these wetlands will be detrimentally affected by the abstraction. In southeast Dorset, mapping of the known water-logged archaeological sites together with bore-holes and low-flow rivers illustrates the problem (illus 65); in this instance, remedial action by the National Rivers Authority to protect the environment may also help to protect whatever is left of the archaeology. In western France, in the Marais Poitevin, people have sought to impose a degree of control on water for many centuries (illus 66); a system of farming the low-lying land has evolved, based on drained marsh for cereal and grass cultivation, and wet marsh for pasture and timber-growing, with much exploitation of fish and other wildlife. There are good prospects for the survival of wetland wildlife alongside human exploitation. Now the traditional wet landscape and way of life are severely threatened by water abstraction to irrigate swathes of maize and sunflowers on the surrounding dry lands.

Lesser threats abound, and often dominate management strategy in the field at the level of the individual reserve. They include the vigorous tree-growth that on a drying reserve can threaten to overwhelm the vegetation typical of a raised bog

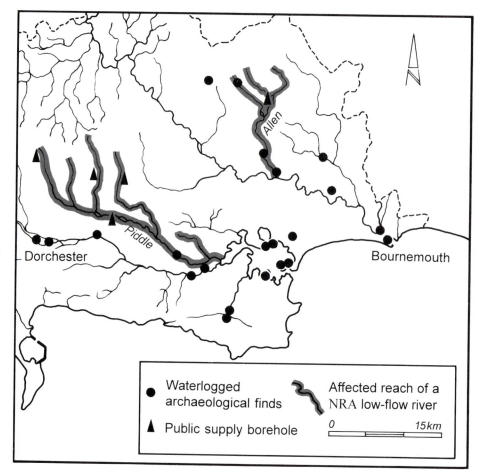

65
Rivers of southeast Dorset affected by water abstraction and the distribution of known waterlogged archaeological finds from the same region. It is likely that there are archaeological deposits at risk of desiccation along the valleys of the low-flow rivers. Drawn by Sue Rouillard.

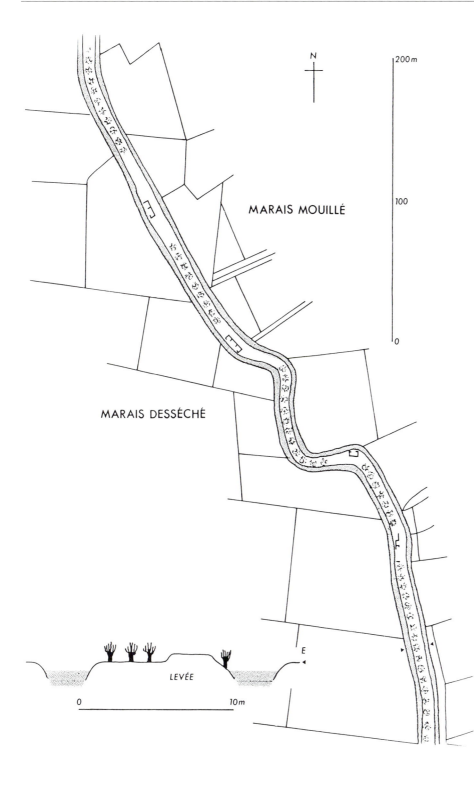

MARAIS MOUILLÉ

MARAIS DESSÉCHÉ

LEVÉE

0   10m

66
Part of the levée system west of Maillezais in the Marais Poitevin, France, constructed in the 16–19th centuries to separate wetlands designed for partial drainage and pasture (Marais Desséché) and those reserved for annual river inundation and wetland farming and forestry (Marais Mouillé). The levée is strengthened against the eastern floodwaters by its wide western berm. From the canals bordering the levée there run many small ditches. Most of the levée is assigned to ash pollard (tree-like symbol), with more or less regularly-spaced stone-built houses with garden plots and orchards of plum, pear, quince and walnut trees (open spaces on the levée). The occupants of these houses were responsible for the strengthening of the levée and maintenance of the system. This levée extends for over 3km. Map based on the authors' fieldwork in 1995.

or sedge fen. Pollution from a colony of gulls or excess phosphates from a local drain, the tramp of too many visitors on a popular reserve, poaching – all these things may cause deterioration of wildlife. Flooding, ironically, may threaten some wetlands because floodwaters can carry unwanted nutrients and pollutants. The effect of these and other local threats on the known or potential archaeology of a reserve will need to be assessed locally.

Measures taken in the field to mitigate threats, and to maintain different types of wetland ecosystem in a healthy state, are often steps appropriate to the care of buried and waterlogged archaeological deposits. For example, pollution from sewage and slurry can, in the short term, be treated by passing the polluted water through a reed filter-bed. By the time the water reaches the far end of such a system it has been cleaned of much of the unwanted material and it should be in a fit state to introduce onto a reserve or protected archaeological site (see B Coles 1995, 43-4, for description of an experimental filter-bed system).

An isolated, perched wetland reserve, such as the Shapwick Heath reserve before the recent re-wetting of its surrounds, may be bunded (ie sealed around the edges) to prevent water loss. The bund may be of peat or other local materials, and, in cases of severe water loss, a vertical polythene sheet may be inserted in the bund

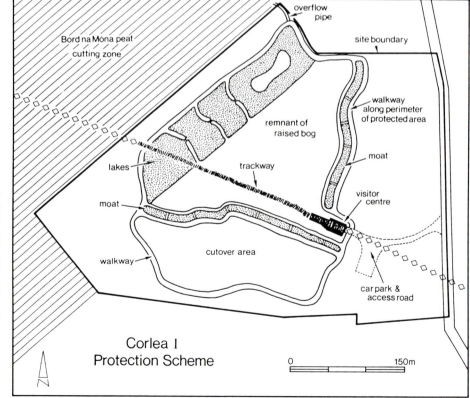

67
Corlea, Ireland: bunding of an undisturbed part of the raised bog to protect the Iron Age trackway that runs through it. A vertical plastic sheet is buried in the peat bank around the perimeter. Drawn by Sue Rouillard based on information from O'Donnell 1993.

to ensure a good seal of the edges of the reserve. A perched archaeological site can be treated in the same way. In all cases, the design of a bund will need to be adapted to the character of the wetland to be protected. The details of the bund around Wicken Fen in Cambridgeshire, for example, differ from those around the Corlea protected area in central Ireland (illus 67), not so much because the first is a nature reserve and the second holds a buried, waterlogged Iron Age wooden trackway, but because the one is a fen and the other a raised bog. In some cases, it may be appropriate to combine bund and moat as at Wicken Fen (illus IVb), and this can have the added advantage of visitor control.

There are many examples of wetland creation in Britain, making a wildlife reserve out of old gravel workings for example. These reserves can rapidly develop a high conservation value. Anglian Water's reservoir at Rutland Water, which came into being in 1975, is already designated as a Ramsar Site, meaning that it is a site of international significance for birds. It is also designated as an SSSI and SPA (Site of Special Scientific Interest and Special Protection Area). There is no way in which we can create and enhance evidence for the past in similar fashion from scratch. Organic archaeology doesn't grow.

What may be possible is the development of a wetland wildlife interest on or alongside an area protected for its archaeology. This is a different situation to that illustrated by the Sweet Track and the Shapwick Heath National Nature Reserve, which was important for both archaeology and wildlife from the outset. But in some places where a waterlogged archaeological site is known, it can be managed in such a way that the local wildlife is enhanced. For example, management of Stonea Camp in Cambridgeshire is designed to increase the wetland flora and fauna of an otherwise rather bleak part of the Fens, as a by-product of the protection of the waterlogged Iron Age defences of the Camp. At Chalain in eastern France, measures taken to protect a Neolithic lakeside settlement from erosion, pollution and de-watering have already benefited the local wetland ecosystem, and in doing so have enhanced the lake and its surrounds for visitors in the long-term.

In Chapter 2, we mentioned that steps were now being taken to protect the site of Biskupin in Poland. The strategy being adopted is of considerable interest for its simplicity and effectiveness, and it seems probable that it will benefit the ecology of the present day wetlands around the lake as well as ensuring the better preservation of the prehistoric site. As we have seen, wood has survived in many parts of the Biskupin settlement, a little of it exposed and air-dried for several decades, some of it excavated and reburied in the 1930-60s, and some of it never excavated. But in recent years, water levels in the lake system have been falling and at the same time levels of pollution have increased. The wetlands fringing the lake have suffered, and become impoverished, or they have been drained and converted to farm land. The site has faced the same threat of seasonally fluctuating water levels as the Sweet Track. All of this was evident during our visit in 1991 when we were asked to give opinions and offer advice. In 1992, after careful negotiation with lake-side land owners and users and with local elected bodies, a weir was built across the outflow stream from Lake Biskupinskie (illus 68). As a result, there has been less severe fluctuation in the level of the lake, the site is wetter than before and so too are the meadows and wetlands fringing the lakes. The necessary engineering works were small and simple: the weir. The coffer dam that was built around the site in the 1930s so that water could be pumped out to allow excavation now serves to retain water should it need to be pumped in (Piotrowski & Zajączkowski 1993). The people whose land has been affected by the raised water levels have been compensated, not by cash payments for which the Polish government has no fund, but by a reduction in their taxes, which is said to be generally appreciated.

The scheme will help to reduce pollution levels in the lake, because the increase in wetland fringe will buffer the lake waters from air-borne pollutants and will act to a certain extent as a reed filter-bed cleaning the run-off from agricultural land.

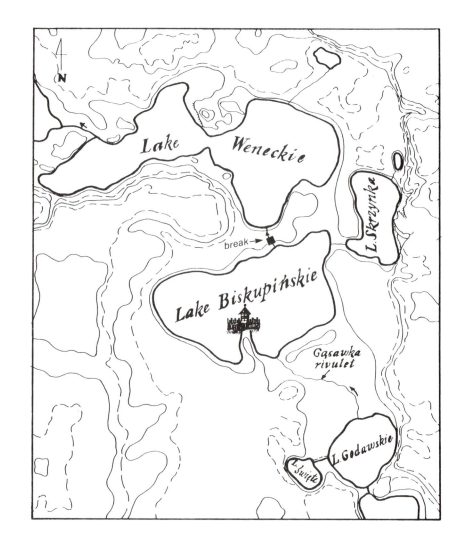

68
Lake Biskupinskie, showing the prehistoric settlement on its peninsula with, to the north, the location of the small barrier built across the stream flowing out of the lake. This barrier has been all the engineering work needed to raise the level of the lake sufficiently to keep the remaining archaeological deposits waterlogged. Based on Piotrowski & Zajączkowski 1993.

The lake ecosystem will benefit, another bonus for wildlife from the measures taken to protect an archaeological site. The problem of regional pollution still remains to be tackled; local awareness of the general environmental benefits of the Biskupin scheme, together with the national appreciation of the site, may help to stimulate action in this respect.

In cases such as Stonea, Chalain and Biskupin, where a wildlife interest has developed following archaeological protection, the archaeologists concerned for the site may in the future be able to draw on support from wildlife organisations. In a political climate where conservation is to be valued, the combination of wildlife and archaeological interest must be an asset.

Mention of Ramsar Sites and other designations raises the subject of legislation, and not so much legislation to protect archaeology as environmental legislation. Why? Partly because current archaeological legislation does not protect wetland sites from the effects of surrounding drainage, a problem which applies in several countries of continental Europe as well as in Britain; but mainly because legislation enacted to protect the environment can have a direct bearing on archaeology. Changes in legislation and changes in how it is implemented are fairly frequent, and what is written now may soon be out-of-date in some respects, but the basic importance of environmental legislation should be apparent. In some ways, the differences between what happens in England and what happens in Scotland can be used to make the point, in theory at least.

In 1989, the water industry was privatised in England and Wales, but not in Scotland. The National Rivers Authority (NRA) which was then set up, operated in England and Wales but not in Scotland where River Purification Boards were appointed with some but by no means all the same responsibilities. One of the aims of the NRA has been to 'conserve and enhance wildlife, landscape and archaeological features' (National Rivers Authority 1993). In theory, it could refuse to grant a license to abstract water if it could be demonstrated that the abstraction would de-water a valued archaeological site, even if that site was several kilometres from the proposed bore-hole. Alternatively, restrictions could be placed on the abstraction, as has been done recently to protect an SSSI in Shropshire. The NRA is shortly to be merged into a new Environment Agency, where it will play the lead rôle. When the relevant draft legislation was issued for consultation, it was seen to give the new agency reduced powers of conservation; fortunately, the resulting protests and representations have led to a strengthening in this respect. To become aware that the NRA could protect wetland archaeological sites, and then to see that rôle about to disappear, underlined the potential significance of developments in this area for wetland archaeology. The underlying reason, here and with other legislation, is that protection of wetland sites is most effective where there is appropriate control of the rest of the catchment, and if wetland archaeology is written into catchment management plans along with other environmental concerns, its future will be better assured than by any purely archaeological legislation.

A designation that can be applied throughout the United Kingdom is that of Environmentally Sensitive Area (ESA) (illus 69). ESAs are farmland, which includes wetland areas such as wet grassland but excludes uncultivated areas such as a raised bog, and entry into the scheme is voluntary. Each ESA has its own management prescription, normally designed to lessen or remove the pressures of intensive farming and to encourage the preservation and enhancement of habitats and landscape features that flourished under traditional farming régimes. The cultural as well as the natural heritage is taken into consideration, and the significance of the buried and invisible heritage has been recognised. In the ESA that we know best, the Somerset Levels and Moors, farmers may now receive £400 or more per hectare per year for managing their land with raised water levels and low intensity grazing, just the sort of régime that allowed the Glastonbury Lake Village to survive for 2,000 years.

It will be to the long term benefit of archaeology if ESA recognition of the cultural heritage is welcomed, and strengthened by the representations of archaeologists at every opportunity for consultation. An encouraging development of 1995 is the appointment by ADAS of archaeologists for the ESAs, as yet only a few and only on short-term contracts, but a very promising move and one that we wish other statutory bodies, including the new Environment Agency and English Nature, would follow.

Another development of interest was the appearance in June 1994 of *Water Level Management Plans: a procedural guide for operating authorities*. We mention this here because the guide stresses the significance of wetland archaeology, as a quote from the Introduction will illustrate:

> Wetland areas are also important, both as components of the historic landscape and for the wealth of well-preserved archaeological remains which they contain. Water level management which takes account of the vulnerability, fragility and non-renewable nature of these remains is therefore very important
> (MAFF 1994, 2)

69 (*opposite*) Environmentally Sensitive Areas in Scotland, Northern Ireland, Wales and England, based on information provided by ADAS. A number of the designated areas are predominantly or partly wetland.

The guide was issued by MAFF together with the Welsh Office, the Association of Drainage Authorities, English Nature and the National Rivers Authority, a gathering of organisations with little representation of Scotland or Northern Ireland. The potential benefits of Water Level Management Plans may therefore not apply outside England and Wales, a reminder that archaeologists need to research the environmental legislation applicable to their own patch as well as knowing what goes on at United Kingdom and European Union levels. They will also need to appreciate the difference between the enactment of legislation and issuing of guidelines, and implementation. In theory, Water Level Management Plans are a great boon for the protection of wetland archaeology in England and Wales. In practice, we have still to see how they will be implemented once they are drawn up, and a cynic might expect Internal Drainage Boards to pay as little attention to the Plans as they are said to have done to the earlier *Conservation Guidelines for Drainage Authorities* (MAFF 1991). What matters here, as with

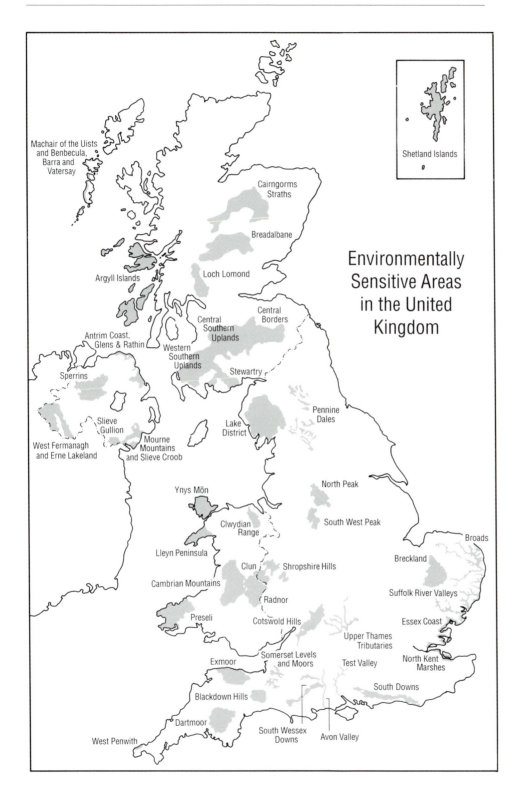

Environmentally Sensitive Areas in the United Kingdom

Shetland Islands

Machair of the Uists and Benbecula, Barra and Vatersay

Argyll Islands

Antrim Coast, Glens & Rathin

Sperrins

West Fermanagh and Erne Lakeland

Slieve Gullion

Mourne Mountains and Slieve Croob

Cairngorms Straths

Breadalbane

Loch Lomond

Central Southern Uplands

Central Borders

Western Southern Uplands

Stewartry

Pennine Dales

Lake District

Ynys Môn

Clwydian Range

Lleyn Peninsula

Clun

Cambrian Mountains

Radnor

Preseli

Cotswold Hills

North Peak

South West Peak

Shropshire Hills

Broads

Breckland

Suffolk River Valleys

Essex Coast

Upper Thames Tributaries

North Kent Marshes

Somerset Levels and Moors

Exmoor

Test Valley

South Downs

Blackdown Hills

Dartmoor

West Penwith

South Wessex Downs

Avon Valley

ESAs, is for archaeology to be well-represented at times of consultation and public discussion.

Representation is a crucial matter if wetland archaeology, indeed all archaeology, is to receive adequate care and protection. In this respect, as with management in the field, we can learn from, and join forces with, wildlife organisations whose experience and influence may well be greater than that of their archaeological equivalents. In Somerset, for example, the Royal Society for the Protection of Birds (RSPB) has bought land on West Sedgemoor, a wetland of high conservation value. Some £5 million had been spent on land acquisition and capital works by 1994, and, as a land-owner within the ESA, the RSPB both qualified for grants for the capital works and for the annual payments for farming with raised water levels. They also were in a position to influence the original prescription for the ESA, and to contribute to periodic reviews.

In Scotland in 1993 the Scottish Wildlife Trust (SWT) received £338,000 from the European Union for a two-year project, the Scottish Raised Bog Conservation Project. They have consulted archaeologists at various stages of the project, and the draft *Conservation Strategy*, issued for discussion at a conference held in Edinburgh in 1995, notes at the outset the value of the environmental and cultural archive held in raised bogs. But the main thrust of the project, and the document, is the conservation of active raised bog, naturally so since those were the terms of the grant and the recipients are a wildlife trust. The relevance to our present discussion is two-fold. First, the SWT seized the European opportunity, applied for funding, and was successful. Secondly, a strong theme at the 1995 conference was the significance of the archive for the development of sound conservation strategies: in order to manage raised bogs today, we need to know more of their past history, in general terms and in terms of the individual bog to be managed. We need to know how they reacted to climate change and to different levels of human impact, and to what extent the present aspects that we value are the outcome of long-term human activity. Here was a good example of how archaeologists and palaeoenvironmentalists could make a positive contribution to conservation, and at the same time a reminder to conservationists that they themselves needed the invisible archive as well as the visible living bog.

The Scottish Wildlife Trust has some 10,000 members, the Society of Antiquaries of Scotland has 3,000. In England, the difference can be much more marked. The Devon Wildlife Trust, for example, has 6,000 members to the Devon Archaeology Society's 800. More subscriptions mean a greater likelihood of paid staff with time to apply for grants, to attend public enquiries and consultations, to publicise and agitate and push their cause. More members make it that bit more likely that the wildlife organisations will receive legacies, as the Devon Wildlife Trust did recently with a £2 million gift. For archaeologists, one good investment of their more limited resources will be to educate conservationists as to the value of the cultural and palaeoenvironmental record, both in general terms and for the specific needs of conservation. Wetland archaeology, with its close links between the natural and the cultural, and its exceptional preservation, can provide the bridge.

If we can work jointly, whether at the level of lobbying for improved legislation or whether in the field for the management of a particular wetland, we are more likely to succeed in protecting our invisible heritage from decay, destruction and disappearance.

We know already that somewhere like Flanders Moss has archaeological potential in addition to its wildlife value (Clarke 1995). We can predict that damaged and threatened areas like Ballachulish Moss will, if properly managed, retain their important palaeoenvironmental record alongside an enhancement of flora and fauna appropriate to the Moss. At Ballachulish, any remaining cultural evidence is of course invisible but we know that up to one metre of peat remains, that the lower levels are still waterlogged (Pollard 1993), and that the Ballachulish figure was recorded as coming from the base of the peats, lying on gravel. Other archaeological evidence from the Moss and its immediate surrounds was reported in the later 19th century (Christison 1881), and it may be that Ballachulish, like

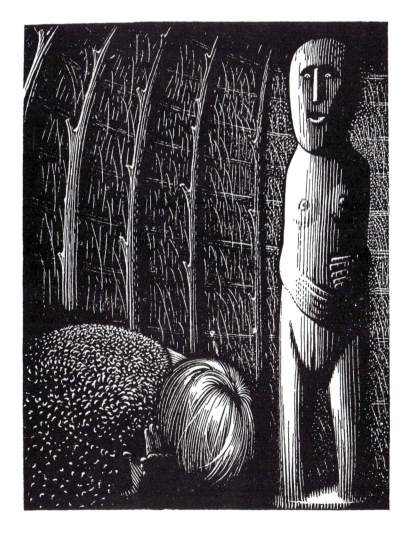

70
The Ballachulish figure: a reconstruction by Keith Henderson. From Piggott & Henderson 1958.

Llyn Cerrig Bach and Nydam, was one of those places just up from the sea that attracted prehistoric peoples and their offerings for several centuries or more. The archaeological potential of the Moss must still be high, well worth a concerted attempt to save it from disappearance.

Ballachulish Moss raises a final point for this chapter, one that we have mentioned before and will discuss more fully in the final chapter. Visitors to the Moss have little that is archaeological to see and few will appreciate the significance of such an area unless some display is provided. At the same time, the wetland evidence lends itself to the making of reconstructions which can be displayed, whilst management of the environment to enhance wildlife can provide residents and visitors alike with a further interest. Ideally, management would be designed to provide the best possible conditions for the survival of buried archaeological and palaeoenvironmental evidence, with the development, if possible, of flora and fauna appropriate to the past history of the location, the whole overlooked by a life-sized alderwood carving of the 'shape so indelicate' whose survival brought archaeological fame to Ballachulish Moss (illus 70).

a

b

IV

a Minamikita, at Osaka, Japan. A settlement of *c* 100 BC lies on the edge of a stream which was channelled and controlled by sluices and barriers to irrigate rice paddy fields. The excavation of such a clay-sealed waterlogged site involves much on-site conservation, here being applied by saucepan. The condition of organic artefacts was exceptionally fine. Photograph John Coles.

b Wicken Fen, England. The fenland nature reserve, owned and managed by the National Trust, is protected from water loss by a vertical plastic sheet buried in the outer bank beyond the moat. The thorn scrub growing behind the bank masks a drop of several metres to the arable fields below. The drop is due to shrinkage and wasting of the organic soils following drainage. Photograph Bryony Coles.

IV

Erkelenz-Kückhoven, Germany.

c A Neolithic wooden mattock. The handle was made from willow and the blade, which is seen edge-on and slightly damaged in this view, was made from maplewood.

d A modern replica made by Jürgen Weiner to illustrate the likely manner of use. Photographs courtesy of Jürgen Weiner and Rheinisches Amt für Bodendenkmalpflege Bonn.

e One of the Neolithic bark bags *in situ*. The bag has tipped over on its side with one of the string-bound lower corners up in the air and the other to the right on the ground. The rim or opening is to the lower left. Length from base to rim *c* 26cm. The binding is made from lime-bast string and the bark, as yet unidentified, may be oak. Photograph courtesy of Jürgen Weiner and A Thünker, Bonn.

f A modern birchbark pail from Ontario, Canada, with about the same 2-litre capacity as the Neolithic container. Photograph John Coles.

g

h

IV

g Excavation floor at Ozette, Washington State. The wooden artefacts exposed here include a seal-killing club, a loom frame piece, and several paddles. Photograph courtesy of Richard Daugherty.

h Three club heads from Ozette. Left and right, seal and fish killing clubs. Centre, an unworn owl-head club, possibly a shaman's club. Photograph courtesy of Richard Daugherty.

i

j

IV

i The *Pfahlbauland* island, at Zürich, Switzerland. The reconstructed Early Bronze Age village presents a united front to the approaching log boat enthusiasts. Photograph John Coles.

j Working with a loom at the Pfahlbauland exhibition 1990. Notice the interested throng of children watching one of the authors. Photograph by the other author.

6

EXPECT THE UNEXPECTED

From all that has gone before, it will be apparent that the wetlands of the world have continued to yield new and often surprising information about the past. Since 1853 when the enormous range of artefacts began to be hauled from the lakes of Switzerland, and since the startling exposures of human bodies were made in the peatbogs of northern Europe, wetlands have continued to produce archaeological evidence unobtainable from any other environment save the most extreme. By 1900, the information coming from wet sites was of such a quality that it promised to rephrase, if not rewrite, our prehistories. Yet the promise was never fully realised due to a combination of factors, among them the working-out of the upper levels of peatbogs, the gradual decline of hand-cutting of peat, the erosive character of water in some Alpine lakes, the silting of other bodies of water, the construction of massive docks, railways and roadways along lake shores and in river valleys, the use of some wetlands for dumping, the denomination of others as wildlife reserves, and the development of other areas of archaeological research that seemed more attractive at the time, and less bother.

The main reason why the flow of discoveries slowed was the mechanisation of many operations that had previously been done by hand; unseeing machines do not compare with the slower handwork of men, ditching, cleaning, digging, channelling, felling, ploughing by horse, and the multitude of tasks once accomplished by people who had time to be observant. Unseen by all was the gradual disintegration of archaeological material beneath the ground, by the ever-increasing drainage of wetlands and the taking-in of new land for cultivation. Where wetlands continued to be used in traditional ways, the yield of finds continued to surprise – there was a spate of bog bodies uncovered in the 1940s and 1950s, for example. In addition, new ways of exposing wetland sites were devised, such as aerial photography through the cold clear waters of Alpine Europe, showing the palisades and rows of house posts of former lakeshore settlements. But gradually the rate of discoveries began to slow, and deterioration, seen and unseen, became a dominant factor. By the 1970s this loss of archaeological potential was acknowledged in a few places but was overlooked in the development of new ways to look at old evidence – dendrochronology and tree-ring studies, macroscopic analyses of plant and insect remains, studies of sea-level fluctuations and their impacts, use-wear studies on well-preserved tools, analysis of food residues, more sophisticated work on animal bones, experimental work on structures and other artefacts, calibration of radiocarbon dates, and a host of other chemical, physical and biological techniques. All of these allowed wetland archaeologists to look again at their evidence and to define it anew. Unexpected or otherwise surprising results emerged, as we have tried to show in the preceding chapters, among them the short-lived nature of ancient settlements, the variety of plants and animals exploited in wetlands around the world, the extraordinary survival of evidence of textiles, brains, chewing gum and other substances from a variety of sites, and the precision with which ancient settlements and cemeteries can now be defined.

Yet now in all this there may be a sense of *déjà vu*, a feeling that we know these things, they are now predictable, and thus a disappointment when a wetland site does not turn up immaculately-preserved evidence. Often now a newly-exposed site will not have its wooden components surviving well, or its surface will have been ploughed, or it will have been chopped apart by some previous operation, or it will have decayed away and be reduced to a dryland site where only inorganics survive along with the stains of a once vibrant occupation. What would we now give for an opportunity to excavate Robenhausen, or Key Marco, or Glastonbury, or Lochlee or Ballachulish? We might well do better than those who did their best at the time (we could hardly do worse than poor Frank Cushing), but could we afford it? Whatever these theoretical questions suggest to us as individuals, we suspect that many authorities would turn away in horror at the prospect of an unending demand for support, and equally at the alternative prospect of ensuring the survival of such sites in pristine condition for the next 100 years. We will comment further on this at the end of this chapter.

In this last chapter, we could attempt to draw together the themes of the previous five, in order to emphasise the diverse ways in which wetland archaeology enlarges the past. We will not do so directly, but hope to achieve the same effect by highlighting some of the unexpected discoveries of recent years. There is a tendency sometimes to publicise archaeological finds as 'the oldest', 'the biggest', 'the best-preserved' examples of particular categories of evidence, and wetland archaeology does of course lend itself to this, especially in terms of best-preserved. More important, however, is the capacity of wetlands and waterlogged deposits to offer a different quality or character of evidence, not 'more of the same' but a new dimension.

UNEXPECTED PLACES

We start with a site that was altogether unexpected, Monte Verde in southern Chile, 15,000km south of the Bering Strait, which is still considered to be the point of entry of humans into the New World (Moss & Erlandson 1995, 10). The site lies about 25km from the shores of the Pacific Ocean in a densely forested area. The river Maullín flows south and west to the sea and one of its tributaries, a small creek, has created over time a series of gravel and sand terraces, with deposits of peat forming in abandoned creek channels. In 1976 the stream altered its course, cutting into the deposits and exposing some bones, stone and wood. Investigations of this unusual assemblage began at once, led by Tom Dillehay, and soon the dates of 12,500–12,800 radiocarbon years before present confirmed the archaeological evidence of a Stone Age settlement. That it was in southern

Chile opened a new debate on the arrival of modern humans in the New World (Dillehay 1988; 1989; 1996).

The settlement had been established on the banks of the ancient stream (illus 71). The settlers constructed at least 12 small houses with tree stems and branches for framing. The houses were rectangular, and some were joined to make a terraced row. The posts and slender poles forming the frameworks had traces of animal skin (probably mastodont) still attached. Inside each hut was a clay-lined pit for a hearth, and at least two large communal hearths were outside. Grinding stones and wooden mauls were used to prepare the plant foods; berries, nuts and roots survived in and around the hearths. Animals captured or scavenged included mastodon, a palaeocamelid (llama), and small rodents and amphibians. As the houses were covered by mastodont skin, and the remains of at least seven mastodons have been found, it is likely that this species was being hunted. Coprolites of unidentified animals, and human coprolites in shallow pits, will inform us about the diet. A human footprint in a clay patch around one of the large hearths is more of a curiosity.

Stone, bone and wood were used to make tools, including rough stone bifaces, bone points and wooden digging sticks. Some of the stone was not local, and ovoid pebbles may have been bolas stones. Pollen, plant remains and beetle

71
Sketch plan of the settlement at Monte Verde in coastal Chile. The small creek flows to the west, and the settlement was placed on a low sandbank (shown white), with a communal structure (to left) away from the living quarters. Only part of the site has been excavated. Behind the site was a wetland, with higher gravel terrace and forest beyond. The occupation is about 12,500 years old (radiocarbon years). Plan based on Dillehay 1984.

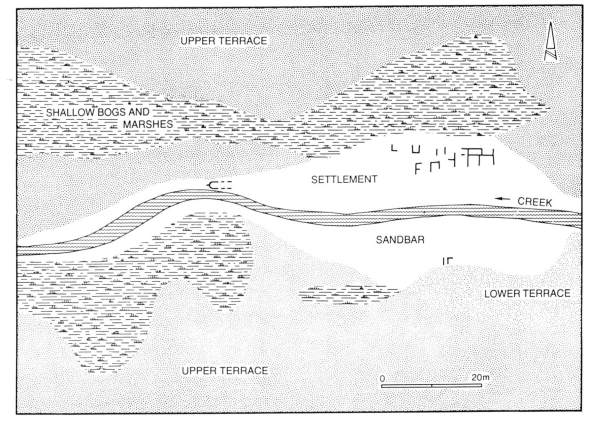

UPPER TERRACE

SHALLOW BOGS AND MARSHES

SETTLEMENT

CREEK

SANDBAR

LOWER TERRACE

UPPER TERRACE

0   20m

evidence show that the area was forested and that the river delta and nearby swamps were exploited. All of the woods identified suggest high humidity in the forested areas. A catchment extending as far as 30km or so is suggested on the basis of coastal resources brought to the site. The range of plants collected suggests that the settlement was a permanent one and not seasonal. Non-edible plants, some suitable as medicinal herbs, were also gathered. All of this suggests a measure of organisation, and set apart from the houses, on a low ovoid sandbank, was a horseshoe-shaped structure of posts and gravel base, probably skin-covered, with a hearth at the opening and traces of a wooden platform or plaza. Small hearths were inside the structure and on the plaza. Fragments of bulrush reed, found today 30km away, animal hide, and chewed leaves of a medicinal plant suggest some sort of special purpose here on the site. A spread of wood, hearths, mastodont bones, stone and wooden tools lay behind the structure.

The evidence from Monte Verde will take some time to analyse, in part due to the wide variety of resources used and surviving, and in part due to the unanticipated character of the site. Sites of this age in the Americas are generally restricted to stone and bone objects and archaeologists are often unprepared for the multi-disciplinary work required by a wet site. Of wide interest is the evidence for an early settlement of 11–12 houses, perhaps occupied by 25–35 persons, with a non-domestic structure set apart, communal and individual hearths, specialised activity areas, and a wide zone of exploitation concentrating upon aquatic areas such as swamps, marshes and estuaries. Because the peat covered the site soon

72
Excavations at Huseby Klev, western Sweden, 1994. The portable cabins lie near an Iron Age site. Between the cabins and the deep excavation are the water-sieving machines and tanks. Under the tarpaulins was the early settlement of *c* 8000–7700 BC, well-sealed by flooding clays. Photograph John Coles.

after its abandonment, perhaps its water base causing the withdrawal of the people, the preservation of the evidence is exceptionally good. Had normal processes of decay been at work, the site would have been interpreted as a temporary kill-site; in fact, it was so interpreted before the organic evidence was found in bulk and *in situ*. Unexpected in place, date, condition and character, Monte Verde has substantially re-shaped models of the early penetration of human groups into the Americas, indicates a greater awareness and early exploitation of natural resources than previously thought likely, and opens new debate on the development of early social structures that could only previously be proposed on theoretical grounds.

Another hunter-gatherer site, closer to home, was equally unexpected. In 1991 the Central Board of National Antiquities in Sweden organised the excavation of a late prehistoric settlement on the west coast of the island of Orust in western Sweden (Nordqvist 1994; 1995). The isostatic uplift of the land here is still proceeding, and ancient coastal sites are now well inland in places. Beneath and behind the Iron Age settlement, in a small infilled basin, the excavators at Huseby Klev found a small midden and occupation place that pre-dated the expected site by over 6,000 years (illus 72). The hunter-gatherer settlement of *c* 8,000–7,700 BC had been at the head of an inlet of the sea, soon flooded by the rising sea level of early post-glacial times and sealed by clays, then uplifted by the rising land which outstripped the high sea level. The site was well-preserved by the wet clay seal, and the entire excavated deposit was water-sieved to recover small bones, fish scales and seeds. Fish and sea mammals such as dolphin and seal were being caught, and bone fish-hooks and a resin-glued bone point, antler axes and adzes, amber (the earliest in northern Europe?), and stone tools marked the activity areas on the site. The camp had apparently been divided into areas for working of flint, for butchery of animals, and for woodworking. Aurochs, boar, red and roe deer and seabirds like the great auk were hunted, and wild apples, hazelnuts and other plant foods collected. Human bones also survived in the wet-sealed deposits. Lumps of resin, chewed by a 6–14 year-old person (illus 73), may have been prepared ready for gluing points to shafts unless it was done purely for the taste; the lumps have been commemorated by the book title of a popular report on the site: *Världens Äldsta Tuggummi?* (Hernek & Nordqvist 1995). Some resin was also found smeared on slats of wood, like boat caulking. The fingerprints of the worker

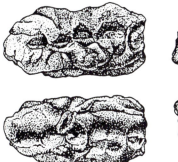
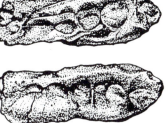

73
The world's oldest chewing gum? Two lumps of resin from Huseby Klev. The pieces have been masticated by a young person; a limb bone found on the site might just be the gum chewer's. Life size. Drawn by Anders Andersson.

were clearly visible. We know little about plank or skin boats of this age in northern Europe, if the slats do indeed represent such a craft; or the resin may have sealed a wooden box. Whatever the final interpretations made of this site at Huseby Klev, it points to the existence of unanticipated sites along the western coasts of Europe, uplifted by land movements but perhaps, as here, protected by a micro-environment of clays; the potential of western Scotland for comparable positions seems clear, and if a date of *c* 8,000 BC for human occupation of western Sweden is now assured, what are the prospects for Scottish archaeology?

THE WATER HOLE

The Mesolithic settlement at Huseby Klev was totally unexpected. So too was one element from an Early Neolithic site in Germany. Up on a loess-covered gravel plateau, it was not an environment for wetlanders, and the prehistoric settlement being excavated belonged to a tradition better known for its postholes than for any posts.

The location is between the Rhine and the Meuse-Maas, not far from the German, Dutch and Belgian border, on the German side and to the northwest of Cologne. This is an area of open-cast brown coal mining, horrific to see as the whole landscape is chewed up regardless of topography and the life on the surface, and spat out behind to be reconstituted but hardly reinstated. Where there is no open-cast there may be gravel extraction, smaller in scale but still a process that causes complete destruction of the landscape where it occurs. Both open-cast and gravel extraction are preceded by archaeological survey, with excavation of selected sites. In the late 1980s, just outside the village of Erkelenz-Kückhoven,

74
Erkelenz-
Kückhoven,
Germany:
excavation of a
Neolithic
settlement in
advance of gravel
quarrying.
Postholes are
indicated by white
markers.
Photograph
courtesy of Jürgen
Weiner.

a prehistoric settlement was selected for excavation because it overlay gravels that would be quarried away in the near future. The director of excavations was Jürgen Weiner, and his interim publications provide the basis for what follows, amplified by an excellent guided tour and much fruitful discussion when we visited him in the autumn of 1992, as well as subsequent correspondence (Weiner 1992a; 1992b; 1992c; 1994).

The settlement proved to be an early Neolithic Linearbandkeramik (LBK) village, situated on a loess-covered plateau about 2–3km from a watercourse flowing into the river Rur, a tributary of the Maas. LBK sites are traditionally seen as settlements of the first farming peoples to spread into the region, bringing with them domestic animals and cultivated plants and cultural traditions that had spread rapidly along the Danube and the Rhine from an ancestry in southeastern Europe. Erkelenz-Kückhoven was typical in many respects, with rows of postholes outlining long rectangular houses (illus 74), but there was one oddity apparent from the moment of its discovery. LBK settlements are normally closely related to watercourses, but this one was up on a plateau and, as stated, 2-3km from the nearest stream.

The pottery from the site belonged to an LBK variety strongly distributed along the Meuse; pottery typology together with radiocarbon dates placed the village in the centuries from 5300 BC to 4900 BC. There had been maybe 65 houses in all, with ten or so standing and in use at any one time. The village had been a substantial and well-established settlement, but what had it done for water? When the LBK people first moved onto the plateau, it was well-forested and some

75
Erkelenz-Kückhoven, Germany: excavation at a level several metres below the Neolithic settlement with the dark stain of the well-shaft and the first black timbers of the well-frames apparent just to the left of the archaeologists. Photograph courtesy of Jürgen Weiner.

76
Erkelenz-
Kückhoven,
Germany: split oak
planks making
box-frames to line
the Neolithic
well-shaft. The
first, outer, frame is
dated to 5090 BC
and the second,
inner, frame to
c 5065 BC. (The
third and final
frame *c* 5050 BC,
is hidden within
the second one).
Note the simple
but effective
interlocking of the
planks at the
corners; the joins
along the sides of
the planks were
caulked with moss.
Photograph
courtesy of Jürgen
Weiner.

scholars have suggested that there may have been a small stream. Forest clearance followed by centuries and millennia of cultivation will have altered the local hydrology, but still one might expect some trace of a local stream, and there was none. The question of how the village had been supplied with water remained unanswered.

In the autumn of 1990, a large grey area on the site was examined by the archaeologists. It appeared to be a huge pit, but no bottom was found. The gravel workers decided to remove the grey soily fill, which was of no value to them, and about 7m below the ground surface of the Neolithic village they came upon wood. One piece was taken to Weiner, who recognised that it bore the marks of being worked with a stone blade. The wood was immediately sampled for radiocarbon dating, and the result was a date in the LBK period, contemporary with the Neolithic settlement.

Following this discovery, the archaeological team resumed excavation of the grey

pit (illus 75). Very soon they found timbers *in situ* making a solid wooden box frame. The excavation continued until April 1992, by which time the approaching quarry face made further work difficult if not dangerous. The remaining structure was lifted *en bloc*, all 60 tonnes of it, and taken to a nearby motorway maintenance area where it could be excavated under shelter and in relative peace. The excavation was completed in December 1994; post-excavation work continues at the time of writing.

The Kückhoven wood had come from a timber-lined well-shaft which had been sunk to 15m below the Neolithic ground surface. For the bottom 8m, waterlogging had led to good preservation of the timber, together with a quantity of contemporary settlement débris including artefacts. There were in fact three well-linings, one inside the other (illus 76); they were built of solid oak planks and it has been possible to sort out the sequence of building by dendrochronological dating. The preliminary interpretation of events is as follows.

Late in 5090 BC, oak trees were felled and then split into planks about 3m long, 40cm wide and varying from 7–30cm thick. A thick plank would weigh 150–200kg. The planks were used to make a square, log-cabin-like construction (Frame 1) which was built up from the bottom of a deep cylindrical shaft with a cone-shaped top that had been dug into the compacted gravels of the plateau. Thick planks were used at the base of the frame, becoming progressively thinner towards the top. The surviving top, 7m below ground surface, represents about the mid-point of the original Neolithic well, which may or may not have been lined in similar fashion all the way to the ground surface. At the top, there was probably some sort of superstructure and windlass arrangement, parts of which later fell into the well and became preserved.

It is thought that the well-shaft was sunk until it just reached the water-table. Notches along the bottom edge of the lowermost four planks were probably cut to let in water. At some stage, maybe immediately or more likely after a few years when the well ran dry, a smaller pit was dug in the well base and lined with a fairly crudely-made frame. At this point or shortly after, the superstructure collapsed and some of the upper part of Frame 1 shifted. The well went out of use, and people used it as a rubbish dump; some of the material which went down the shaft at this stage may have been the debris of a burnt house. There is no precise dating of these events, except to say that they happened following the building of Frame 1 in 5089 BC and before the building of Frame 2.

By 5065 BC, it seems that the local water-table had risen again. A new box-frame was built, similar to the first but smaller and set within it. It reached down to the accumulated rubbish, but was apparently not dug into it. Within 15 years, the well had run dry again, and by 5050 BC Frame 3 was built. For this, people dug down below the bottom of Frame 2 and into the rubbish filling the bottom of Frame 1, causing partial collapse of Frame 2 which was then wedged up. Having dug the new shaft, it was lined with planks in the usual manner, up through Frame 2. The new timber lining was only 75cm square, and once it had been

77
Erkelenz-
Kückhoven,
Germany: part of
a Neolithic
oakwood rake.
About half of the
original rake-head
survives; the
complete object
would have had
six tines, *c* 10cm
long, and each
one carefully
rounded in
section. Half of
the shaft-hole for
the wooden
handle can be
seen towards the
top of the
righthand
(broken) edge of
the surviving
head. Photograph
courtesy of
Jürgen Weiner.

built up from the bottom there can hardly have been room for an adult to work within the shaft, which may partly explain why this was the last re-vamping of the well. If Frame 3 remained in use for a similar length of time to its predecessors, the well went out of use sometime between 5040 BC and 5000 BC at the latest. The bottom 8m lay waterlogged and undisturbed for the next 7,000 years.

Three deep timber frames built in the space of 40 years suggest that the LBK people may have had a similar attitude to the use of wood as other Neolithic peoples discussed in earlier chapters. Their willingness to dig for water, to live where it was not readily available on the surface, also has implications for our understanding of their use of the landscape, population densities and territories. It will be of great interest, in due course, to have the information about the character of forest exploited, earlier fellings, climatic variations and so forth which must be contained in the Kückhoven tree-rings. There may be, in that record, some answer to questions about rainfall and water tables in the centuries from the foundation of the village *c* 5300 BC to the year 5090 BC when the first oaks were felled for making the well-lining. There may be evidence for earlier felling episodes, reflecting phases of house-building and perhaps earlier wells. The Kückhoven oak planks also provide the earliest record of Neolithic wood-working

technology in Europe, a millennium earlier than the wood which has been studied from the circum-Alpine region and a marked contrast to what little is known of contemporary Mesolithic traditions of wood-use.

A range of wooden tools underlines the agricultural character of the village. Stone axe blades found on many dryland sites lead us to speculate about forest clearance for fields, but there is little in the dryland artefact record that relates to the subsequent cultivation of the ground and our knowledge for northwestern Europe depends heavily on the rare plough and spade marks preserved below earthworks together with identification of plough-soils and weeds of cultivation. From down the Kückhoven well come the wooden tools used by LBK farmers in the 51st century BC, 200 years after their great-grandparents had settled in the area, and therefore the tools of an established community rather than pioneer cultivators. Picks, mattocks, hoes, spades, rakes and their equivalents imply regular physical labour and varied tasks, obviously changing with the seasons from soil preparation through sowing and weeding to harvest, and also probably adapted to the cultivation of different types of crops. It is too early to be sure which tools were used for what purpose; replication and use together with analysis of wear-marks and residues may give some idea of precise function in due course.

The tools include a one-piece maplewood spade, found between Frames 2 and 3 with a broken blade and perhaps used in 5050 BC to dig out the shaft for Frame 3. The blade is about 25cm long and the handle, which appears to be complete or nearly so, about 60cm long. A second maplewood spade has a longer blade, more like an oar, and its overall length is slightly greater. A mattock or hoe-like implement has a broad flat maplewood blade with a straight working edge and a hole near the top for the willow-wood handle (illus IVc, d). The blade is 17–18cm long, thick at the top for weight and for strength at the point of hafting, narrow at the cutting edge. A composite rake-like implement of similar size to the mattock was made from oakwood. Three tines survive and there were probably originally six, 10cm long and carefully rounded (illus 77). Possibly this was used to prepare a good tilth for sowing. An implement not unlike a single-piece wooden pick, except that the handle is at a right angle rather than an acute angle to the rounded working end, may have served as a handled dibber to make holes for sowing. A second single-piece pick-like implement has its handle at an acute angle to the business end and it may indeed have been used as a pick or hoe; it was made from maplewood, a fairly common choice for the tools.

Many pieces of string and rope were found in the well-filling; preliminary identifications suggest that they were made from lime-bast. There is an interesting contrast here with the Mesolithic use of willow-bast for cordage, particularly as we know that the Kückhoven people used willow-wood in their tool-making and that willow-bast string-makers such as the Ertebølle people at Tybrind Vig were using lime trees to make their dug-out canoes (Andersen 1985). Admittedly, the earliest levels at Tybrind Vig are some five centuries later than Kückhoven, but a general comparison has some logic, because one of the Kückhoven finds may be an import from southern Scandinavia. Three fragments of worked elmwood, identified as worked only when sorting through the little bits and pieces of wood in the laboratory, belong to a bow-stave of Scandinavian Mesolithic type which has its closest parallel in one of the elmwood bows from Tybrind Vig (Weiner 1994). It may have come from a group of people living in the southern part of the Ertebølle range, via the Maas, exchanged perhaps for one of the polished stone axe-blades of LBK type which have been found on Ertebølle sites. Further research is clearly needed on well-dated Mesolithic organic materials, for the contrast between Mesolithic and LBK cordage to be confirmed along with the likely import of the bow.

One category of artefact from the well has no parallel, being completely new to the repertoire of prehistoric material culture from Europe. It is a bark bag or pail; 20 or so were found, including three right at the base of the well. The bags seem to be made of a folded-over sheet of bark, possibly oak bark, which was very carefully bound at the lower corners with lime-bast string leading into an irregular net covering over the body of the bag (illus IVe, f). The finished object was slightly taller than it was wide and tapered from base to rim, being about 23cm across at the base, 17cm at the rim, and 26cm tall. It is thought that the bags might have been used to haul water from the well; experiment by the authors with a paper replica indicates a working capacity of about two litres.

Kückhoven is full of the unexpected, and there will probably be more to come when studies of the timber structures and their fills have been completed. At this stage, it is hard to say what will contribute most to our better understanding of the period and the people. It may be the range of organic material culture with its emphasis on working the soil. It may be the direct evidence for the construction methods used by the earliest farmers in northwestern Europe. It may be the record of human impact on the forests. But what was completely unexpected was the survival for seven thousand years of a waterlogged feature on an apparently well-drained gravel plateau. And, according to Weiner, this was not the first well nor was Kückhoven the only LBK village on the plateau. Kückhoven has another significance, in that its inhabitants were in no way wetlanders and its range of evidence should allay the suspicions of some archaeologists about the relevance of wetland sites to the wider (ie drier) world. Bark and string and wooden tools were as common on the gravel plateau as around the lakes, and timber was used at the same profligate rate.

AN URBAN BOAT

In this book we have concentrated on those types of wetlands with which we are most familiar, and we have not often mentioned boats except in passing. But no discussion of the unexpected nature of wetland archaeology would be complete without a comment on the discovery of a Bronze Age boat in the middle of Dover, Kent (Parfitt & Fenwick 1993). In late 1992 a new ground-water pumping station was being built at the corner of Townwall Street and Bench Street; 6m below the level of the pavement and just below OD, timbers appeared at the bottom of a large pit. Rapid investigation showed them to be part of a large plank-built vessel, soon dated to *c* 1350 BC. Six days were given by the contractors to excavate and remove the wood, which was identified as the mid-portion of the boat. In view of its importance, a further eight days was then allowed to expose and remove one of the ends of the boat; the other end was left to its unknown fate beneath the streets of Dover. The boat had to be cut into pieces for the removal operations and it is to be studied, conserved and re-assembled. Its condition, with huge cleated planks linked by transverse boards, and yew withy stitches for the curved planks, is reminiscent of the well-known Ferriby boats but 'significantly different' (Parfitt & Fenwick 1993, 78). The recent discoveries of Bronze Age boat planks along the Severn estuary in south Wales (Parry & McGrail 1991; Bell 1993) added to the Dover boat and Humber boats (Wright 1990) now suggest that not only logboats might be expected to turn up, unexpectedly, along the Forth, or Tay, or Clyde if developmental work can be observed. Rivers and firths like these have varied their banks over the past several thousand years, and their tributaries are also likely to have provided access inland for ancient craft. From Scotland there are hundreds of logboats known to exist or to have existed; why not a planked boat or a dockyard of the Iron Age or Bronze Age?

MUD SLIDES

For shoreline and coastal archaeology, apart from submerged boats and crannogs, and uplifted ancient settlements, there may be more awaiting the vigilant archaeologist, who may have to be patient to be presented with opportunities. None more so than the prehistorians on the west coast of North America who anticipated much from a site but who were then overwhelmed by the information contained within it. The site is Ozette on Cape Alava on the Pacific coast of Washington State in America (illus 78). Here a narrow beach extends from a rocky shelf exposed at low tide only 75m back into a sharply rising hillside which has an upper terrace as well. There are several offshore islands which help protect the beach from storms, the beach itself rising only 1–5m above the high tides. The area has been occupied for over 2,000 years and all of the evidence logically points to an economy based heavily on maritime resources. In the recent past, the Indians of Ozette Village hunted whale, hair seal, sea otter and sea lions, bottom feeders such as red snapper and ling cod, shellfish, and the Ozette river yielded salmon. Forest elk and deer were hunted, and a variety of wild plants gathered including salmon berries and salal berries. The Ozette Indians were moved from

78
Cape Alava and Cannonball Island, Washington State. View to the south, with the Ozette site on the coastline (left), the Pacific Ocean lapping the shore. Photograph courtesy of Richard Daugherty.

this rich environment in the 1920s when the government decreed that the children had to attend agency schools, so the site was only seasonally visited thereafter.

In the mid-1960s, an excavation was made into the occupation deposits on the beach, and showed that relatively recent house floors and cultural debris were well-preserved, with an earliest settlement dated to *c* 2,000 years ago. In early 1970, a severe storm swept in over the rocky shelf and cut into the midden, collapsing the deposits and effectively dumping planks, baskets, mats, arrows and stakes onto the beach. The Makah people requested assistance in rescuing the evidence left by their ancestors, and Richard Daugherty started a salvage excavation which went on continuously from 1970 to 1981. Much of the work was done using hoses and sprays (illus 79), and the technique worked well (Daugherty 1988; Gleeson & Grosso 1976).

79
All-weather excavations with water hoses at Ozette, the eroding waves not far away. Photograph courtesy of Richard Daugherty.

The earliest settlement in the area fully excavated was dated to *c* AD 1250; this was extinguished by an enormous mud slide from the hillslope (Unit VI) which sealed the occupation deposit. Thereafter, an extensive settlement (Unit V) was developed on the site, beginning as early as AD 1440. Between 300 and 400 years ago it, too, was flattened by a mud slide (Unit IV). On top of this mud, the survivors settled once again, stubbornness being one of their characteristics. By then, contact with European traders (from AD 1775) brought imports of glass and pottery; the earliest of these historic period villages (Unit III) suffered the same fate as the pre-contact settlements but the occupation was re-established once more and lasted up to recent times.

The major settlement phase excavated was Unit V, sealed by the clay in a single moment of time, cutting off the processes of decay and preserving all kinds of organic as well as inorganic material. The remains of eight houses survived in places as low plank walls, with house posts and roofing timbers strewn about; the houses were up to 21 x 11.5m in size. They had been constructed on artificially-levelled platforms on the beach, and one at least had been abandoned because of the amount of hillslope water that flowed across the floor. The whole area excavated was essentially made up of occupation debris and midden, with the narrow spaces between the houses full of refuse (Samuels 1994). Over 400,000 bones of mammals, fish and birds were recovered, and over 300,000 shells and 448,943 seeds; all have been studied and Daugherty asks the pertinent question: 'How much is enough?' Sampling strategies for wetland sites are a subject that needs exploration. Some at least of the occupants were well-off; the whale meat and blubber represented by the bones in Unit V totals over 800 tonnes. The 13 dogs found wholly submerged by the mud must have had a good time of it, while alive.

The interiors of the houses also had much debris, mostly from the production and processing work going on just before the first, and last, warning of the oncoming mud (illus IVg). The excavations yielded over 50,000 artefacts, and about two-thirds were of organic non-bone materials: 1,330 baskets, 1,466 mats, 142 hats, 137 cradles, 115 bows, 1,534 arrowshafts and 5,189 wooden arrow-points, 124 harpoon shafts, hundreds of bentwood fish-hooks, 1,001 wooden boxes and pieces, 361 canoe paddles, 97 carved figures and clubs, and one full-size carved effigy of a whale fin inlaid with over 700 sea otter teeth. Hundreds of composite tools of bone and wood, wood and stone, wood and metal (non-European iron), bone and shell etc were recovered, many in the process of manufacture. Needless to say, the conservation of all this material has been, and is, a severe problem. The site is now properly commemorated by a fine museum and the bulk of the artefacts are 'on hold' in a new storage facility (Daugherty 1988 and pers comm). The similarity of problems and responses between the Ozette and Torihama sites (Chapter 1) will be obvious.

As a footnote to the Ozette story, which incidentally still needs the full telling (Daugherty 1988, 27), it is probably worth noting here that wetland archaeologists often face interpretive problems unusual for drylanders to encounter. A water-logged site where organic preservation is good will yield entirely new kinds of evidence, new foodstuffs, new structures, new objects, that are incomprehensible at first sight, and sometimes forever. Most of us know about stone tools like flint axes, scrapers, arrowheads and the like – and we know (or think we know) what they were used for. These things are commonly found and commonly studied; of course, many are so lacking their organic context that we will never interpret them. Other objects, of wood and bone, although more rarely seen are understandable, we think – like a bow, a paddle, a club (illus IVh). But wetland archaeologists sometimes hold in their cold hands objects of wood or bone or sinew or bark that they have never seen before, and often they haven't a clue either what it is or how the thing worked in the past.

From a hunting-fishing site of c 800 BC on the Hoko river, very near the Ozette settlement, the excavators recovered many pieces of cordage, fish-hooks and bones of flatfish like halibut, rockfish and cod (Croes 1992). The hooks were made of bone and bent wood and it seemed obvious that line-fishing was practised. With the help of the local Makah Indians, replicas were made and an expedition set out by canoe to fish. Not a single catch was made – what had gone wrong? After a small adjustment to the way by which the line was attached to the hook, a return trial was necessary. To save time and effort, the nearest source of water and fish was approached – Seattle Aquarium. Here the fishing re-commenced in the aquarium tanks and, doubtless to the complete astonishment of visitors, fish could not resist the hooks; as Croes said: 'We could catch anything in the Aquarium'. Problem solved.

MORE PUZZLING THINGS

Not all such matters are solved so easily. Wetland archaeologists, from the times of Keller, Munro, Bulleid and Cushing up to the present day have been puzzled by artefacts, mostly of wood, that have no parallel in contemporary society, and ethno-historical searches do not always yield convincing analogous objects. Any major wetland sites with a variety of organic artefacts will turn up these enigmas; the Swiss Alpine Bronze Age settlements have many curved sticks, knobbed pieces, discs, carved slats, and often fragments of larger objects. These provide an amusing problem for idle archaeologists who propose labels that have no parameters other than that of size: boomerangs, killing clubs, amulets and moon symbols, authoritarian emblems, parts of elaborate equipment, all are possible but wholly unproven. The wetland archaeologist should really be as well read in ethnography as in archaeology and be prepared to experiment, and even so must accept the inevitable uncertainties of identifications (illus 80).

In a perverse sort of way, one of Britain's most spectacular sites today was a find wholly unexpected in its character but the result of a well-organised campaign. In Chapter 5, we debated the virtues and problems of wetland survey, and pointed to the well-tried and tiring technique of ditch- or dyke-walking, looking at sections cut through peats and clays by machines designed to extract material fast. In the Somerset Levels, one of us (JMC) began to search the trench faces in 1963, and by 1983 had walked maybe 1000–2000 km, had spent a lot of time in pubs and in the peat companies' offices, and had worn out 14 exhaust systems on several cars. By then, the two of us and our Field Officers had made hundreds of discoveries. David Hall in the Fens 1976–1988 walked far more, found more, and lost fewer cars; and Francis Pryor on a dyke survey walked many kilometres, found much clay, silt and peat in the sections, some barrows truncated by the machines, and in late 1982 tripped over a piece of wood that turned out to mark

80
Problems of identification, courtesy of the Charavines-Colletière team. From Colardelle & Verdel 1993b.

the site of Flag Fen. The story of this site, up to 1990, has been well told by Pryor (1991; 1992) and we await further revelations of this extraordinary place, an enormous platform of wood, with collapsed structures and internal divisions, set in a watery landscape with a long alignment of posts stretching from dryland across and through the platform to another dryland, and the scene for deposition of offerings for several hundred years (see Chapter 3). This is surely a site that matches the excitement of Biskupin, Nydam, Ozette, Glastonbury and other major prehistoric settlements, with the added benefit, if benefit it be, of a character not yet fully explored. And all unexpected? Yes and no. Why else would an archaeologist have been there in the dark fen in late November except in anticipation of a discovery?

At least Flag Fen was found in untroubled times when a response could be prepared and carried out successfully. Not so for another sensational find. According to Alfred Dieck who made an exhaustive study of bog finds for many years, an unique discovery was made in Zealand just as the Second World War was coming to an end. A German soldier was digging a slit-trench when he cut into a series of logs set at an angle in the peat, to cover a sledge made out of wood and strips of bast. The sledge was 1.3m long with a plaited upright endpiece and the front was curved up and strengthened by strips of bast glued onto the frame. The base of the sledge had no runners, but a strip of birch fibre 40cm wide provided the smooth sliding surface, like a toboggan. On the sledge were a pot with a pointed base, stuck in a small heap of sand, an antler axe with wooden haft, a stone axe, a bone or antler fish-hook, and various flint and bone tools were in the pot; ochre was spread over some of the objects. Dieck considered this to be an Ertebølle votive offering. What happened next is painfully clear. The sledge and its contents were lifted from the peat, placed on a lorry which set off for the National Museum in Copenhagen. It collided with another vehicle, caught fire and was consumed in flames. An apocryphal story? No one knows.

SEEING AND BELIEVING

One of the main difficulties that wetland archaeology has always faced is the fragility of much of the evidence. The visitors to a castle, a stone circle, a hillfort or a cairn can see the monument, can walk around it, and can go and inspect the pottery, stone tools, metal objects and bones in a local or national museum. They can gain some idea and appreciation of space, bulk and context of the monument. A waterlogged site and its contents will not survive such exposure; the posts and timbers of a settlement will crack and warp, the wooden tools will distort, the textiles will crumble away, the fish scales and seeds will dry and decay, and any fleshy parts of animals (brains, skin, intestines) will disintegrate. So sites where preservation has been extremely good have to be dismantled, and the sites thereby destroyed, if there is no chance of reburial and of an appropriate water regime being installed. Either way, the sites will be lost to view – destroyed or buried. And objects from the sites have to be removed to conservation tanks from where they may emerge months later, looking good, or maybe not so good, and many objects cannot be conserved because of cost. So visitors who rightly expect to be able to see these unusually detailed monuments and objects are often disappointed. In the Somerset Levels, we regularly had visitors who came expecting to see the Sweet Track, even to walk upon it, but their hopes for the former were often dashed (unless excavations were going on), and as for the latter – not a chance. And yet time and again, wetland discoveries become instantly popular with the public, and they remain so if the right conditions are met.

Biskupin in Poland, with its on-site museum, its exposed (and badly decayed) posts, and its splendid reconstructions, draws about 200,000 visitors a year, although the site is well away from any major centre of population. The very small Visitor Centre in Somerset, with its Iron Age houses and prehistoric track reconstructions, draws 10,000–15,000 visitors. The more elaborate and permanent peat and archaeology centres in north Germany and the Netherlands attract 20,000 or more. Many tens of thousands go to see Lindow Man in the British Museum, and the new Flag Fen centre near Peterborough will undoubtedly draw many thousands to its open, and well-sprayed, excavations and its fine displays. The archaeological park at Hauterive-Champréveyres on Lake Neuchâtel attracted 10,000 people on its Opening Day in September 1995. The Corlea Visitor Centre in Ireland has already begun to attract many people to a place well off the normal tourist track. The crannog now under construction on Loch Tay (by the Scottish Trust for Underwater Archaeology) is an ambitious exercise and should prove to be attractive to many visitors who cannot fail to be astonished at the concept of living on a pile-dwelling. There can be no doubt that wetland archaeology has an appeal to many people – the discoveries have an immediacy about them, and a freshness that provides a link to us today. That wood looks as if it was chopped only yesterday, that basket woven last week, that grain cooked and burnt last night, that figure carved only last year, and that human killed within the viewer's lifetime. The problem for us is to demonstrate this link, to show that people in the past were like us, and were not wholly anonymous and their work reduced by time to mere bumps in the land, stains in the soil, bones and stones.

Wetland archaeology had its unexpected beginning in the lakes of Switzerland, and so it was entirely appropriate that the Swiss took up the challenge to interest and involve the public in a way not before attempted. The aims of the experiment were simple and clear – could serious archaeology be presented in such a way as to interest, and educate, a wide spectrum of the public? The various opinion polls pointed to the fact that some people often visited museums and exhibitions, and knew of and supported the aims of archaeology, but many people and whole segments of society seemed to have little or no interest in the past. Could the achievements of wetland archaeology be used to alter this situation? If not in Switzerland, where else could it succeed, other than Japan? The opinions were not favourable; the public knew little about the recent discoveries, school books were out-dated, and traditional views about the past were still widespread: 'Prehistoric man is popularly presented as a dishevelled cretin brandishing a club' (Ruoff 1992) (see illus 3 on page 2).

In 1988 the Society for Swiss Underwater Archaeology began to plan an exhibition to counter this view. The idea grew to include not only displays of recent discoveries and techniques, but also live experiments and demonstrations of various crafts, and reconstruction of a prehistoric settlement. To attract the public, the plan had to be expansive and therefore expensive, and in order to achieve this it was estimated that the exhibition had to draw about 400,000 visitors in the six months it was open. Such a visitor figure seemed wildly optimistic to all, but once into the project there was no stopping its progress. The City of Zürich allowed the exhibition to develop on a lakeside park near a prehistoric lake-dwelling, and 20,000 sq m were made available, including a small island (illus 81).

The area of *Pfahlbauland*, as it was called, was divided into three. On the island was to be the reconstructed village. On the mainland were three large halls for displays, audiovisual shows, and a linked workshop area for demonstrations and visitor participation. Outside the halls was space, for walking, viewing the island, paddling across to the island, eating and engaging in some outdoor activities (see below). We visited *Pfahlbauland* three times, and marvelled at a number of events.

The island village was based on the excavated evidence from an Early Bronze Age settlement recently examined in Zürich. The evidence was particularly detailed, with foundation timbers, corner and centre posts, a ridge pole and other elements surviving. So the reconstructions were considered to be as 'real' as possible. Eleven buildings were put up, a complete settlement, and in the work of building it became clear that each of the several rows of houses must have had a common roof, as there was not enough space between the individual houses for it to be any other way. The effect was that the village consisted of long houses, each however with two or three separate dwellings (illus IVi). The evidence of many excavations pointed to the houses of the Neolithic and Bronze Age as 'pile-dwellings' in structure, but in some the piles were set upon the dry lakeshore, in others the piles were on the very edge of the lake and thus seasonally flooded, and in others the whole settlement was built in the shallow waters of the lake. The romantic views of the Pile-Dwellers, snug and comfortably isolated from the world by deep water, were in need of some revision and the *Pfahlbauland* village helped in this. The first village built on the island was authentically done, with appropriate

81
Pfahlbauland, Zürich, 1990. The prehistoric village is on the small island. On the shore lie exhibition halls and work areas, assembly points and restaurant. Photograph courtesy of Ulrich Ruoff, from Ruoff 1992.

Bronze Age technology and materials. Two weeks after opening the exhibition, the project team was relaxing in the lake-village restaurant, gazing across the water to the village where a TV crew were at work during a storm. Then a dramatic glow appeared on the nearest row of houses, perhaps some special TV effect; it was not, the roof was on fire. A battle ensued, the team fighting the fire from inside and outside the houses. The fire brigade arrived and settled the matter, but it was clear that a prehistoric fire would have burnt the houses to the ground. One week later, an arson attack succeeded in the total destruction of the whole village. A rapid excavation was carried out to identify how the various pieces of equipment and materials in the house had survived the conflagration. Then the rebuilding commenced, paid for by an insurance company anxious to avoid having to pay for too many days of lost income due to the damage. Why did the Bronze Age people build their houses so close together when fire was such a risk? We don't know. Were there Bronze Age insurance companies? That would seem unlikely.

On the mainland, the exhibition halls were thematic: agriculture, landscape, and animals. Each had displays of finds, photographs and drawings, models and demonstration area where material could be handled. For example, corn could be threshed, pounded and ground into flour, then made into bread and baked in an oven for the visitor to take away and break his or her teeth on. Other workshops were more serious in design and intent, and the team's specialists not only instructed visitors in materials and technologies but also carried out detailed studies on woodworking, bronze casting, pottery making, spinning and weaving (illus IVj), boneworking, stone grinding and copper beating. Some of this experimental work was very impressive in its results, one of the main conclusions being that a simplicity of technique can only succeed when matched by exquisite

82
Working with stone at *Pfahlbauland*: father, mother and child intent upon their manual activities. Photograph John Coles.

timing of operations. Most of these materials could also be tested by the public (illus 82) and we noticed time and again the procedure: father telling child how to do it, mother watching patiently, child tries it, father instructs, father infiltrates, takes over completely, child watches, mother watches, father makes a mess of it. But all the time, the demonstrators were pelted with questions that were direct and simple, and not couched in scientific jargon or niceties. Those with whom we spoke admitted they were often baffled by their own lack of knowledge, or inadequacy of expression, in fielding such blunt questions. Of course, dealing with the three Swiss languages, as well as English, is a test for most of us even when we know the answers.

The animals on site – cows, bulls, goats, sheep and pigs – were kept on the island, beside the village and created a kind of farmyard atmosphere, but were a bit confined and played only a small part in the exhibition other than one bull who generally agreed to pull a wooden cart around the mainland site, delivering children here and there. More times, however, it was the fathers who stood between the poles. One cart, entirely of wood, rumbled its way back and forth with no major repairs for the whole six months (illus 83). Another less serious element on site was archery, held in a small well-fenced enclosure with targets of straw animals – deer, aurochs, pig – and copies of ancient bows drawn by children only, guided by members of the team; this was a very popular attraction.

83
Transport through *Pfahlbauland* in a wooden cart, with spirits undampened by rain. Photograph John Coles.

The project staff consisted of the original team members (all senior specialists) and other professionals and students. The student members who worked on the logboats that carried the public to and from the island seemed to us to operate some kind of selection process. Visitors, generally a family, wanting to get to the island by authentic boat (there was also a footbridge), could take one of several logboats and, suitably life-jacketed, paddle across. One or two of the boats did not settle into the water very well, and, being narrow, were rather unstable. We were told that such wobbly boats were generally reserved for the gnomes of Zürich, gentlemen in dark suits and their equivalently-togged guests, who set out confidently enough but who occasionally came to grief. A set of clothes driers was installed on shore but little was done to revive their dampened spirits.

Such people, and there were very few who fell in so dramatically, may not have paid return visits to the exhibition, but many others did. By the end, 380,000 visitors had come, including hordes of children, groups never before seen near a museum of any sort, and many families accustomed to a cultural diet of TV only. From what we could see and hear, everyone was enjoying the smells and tastes as well, and the children were being instructed and persuaded about 'heritage' in many of its aspects. The fact that *Pfahlbauland* lasted only six months prevented any possibility of over-kill or repetitive boredom, the wearing-out of the displays, the deterioration of the houses and the land, and any potential loss of enthusiasm on the part of the staff.

The overall message for us was threefold: 1) the archaeologists learned much from repetition and refinement of their experiments, and also by having to respond to hundreds of questions from the most simple to the most complicated; 2) the public learned how archaeologists work, and why we think that heritage matters are important; 3) the children learned that entertainment and education can come from the doing and not just the watching.

This example of wetland demonstration is not in itself unique, as other centres try to display and demonstrate the virtues of their own sites. Where *Pfahlbauland* seemed to clear new ground was in its determination to avoid some of the traps – no souvenir shops or other commercial enterprises unless directly connected to the project, and nothing out-of-keeping with the lake-dwelling concept; no representation of the ancient 'truths' without clear definition of the parameters of information; no exaggeration of the lakeside idyll nor of any prehistoric war-fare; full and frank exposure of archaeology as a discipline, a science and a humanity.

FINAL THOUGHTS

If nothing else has emerged from this book it must surely be evident that wetland archaeology has contributed a variety of evidence to help our understanding of the past and that the extraction of the evidence is both time-consuming and costly. From our own experience in Britain and elsewhere we know that the technique of field survey in wetlands is not much different from that in other environments, but wet site excavation has different implications and costs from those of dry sites. It is a debatable set of figures, but if a wet site takes x amount to excavate, the associated environmental work on site will cost a bit less, the post-excavation work for the archaeology will cost 5 times x, the environmental analyses may cost 10 times x, the conservation on and off site may cost 10 times x, the curation will cost as much as conservation, and the publication preparation will cost anything from 10 times x upwards. This makes a full excavation and study of a large wet site very costly. The alternative is to leave the site alone, and then face up to a cost that is impossible to quantify in theoretical terms, but generally a high one, of preserving the site in its wetland from drying-out or from other damage. At the end of the day, questions have to be asked about the ultimate worth of such expense, whether of excavation or preservation, measured against such criteria as the current state of knowledge, the likely yield of information, the importance of the wetland for other interests, national and local attitudes, financial implications and other concerns that are applied to the individual case. It is debatable whether or not we will be faced with even this set of questions, given that a majority of wet sites are found not by archaeologists but by others whose concerns are in no way reflective of our interests. The choice of major sites for the Rhind Lectures was random in terms of their discovery, and at this late stage in the writing we decided to list them along with their discoverers insofar as we could determine the latter. The list needs no comment.

Site	*Discoverer*
Key Marco	muck digger
Star Carr	amateur archaeologist
Friesack	archaeologist and old sighting
Noyen	archaeologist exploring Neolithic site
Windover	builder
Torihama	dredger
Sweet Track	peat digger
Hauterive	archaeologist and old sighting
Hornstaad	archaeologist and old sighting
Alvastra	builder
Biskupin	school teacher
Llyn Cerrig Bach	Royal Air Force
Nydam	peat cutter
Lindow, Tollund *et al*	peat cutters
Ballachulish	wall builder
Charavines-Colletière	lifeguard and early reports by fishermen
Glastonbury	medical student
Monte Verde	geologist
Ozette	native people (tradition)
Kückhoven	machine driver during archaeological survey
Huseby Klev	archaeologist exploring Iron Age site

For Scotland and its wide wetlands, the evidence has yet to be fully revealed, the story has yet to be told. Enough has already emerged from the work of a century

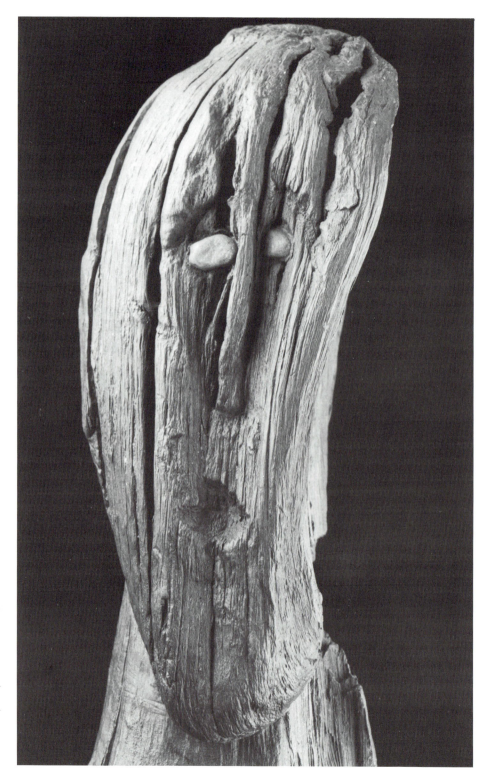

84
A recent
photograph of the
head of the
Ballachulish figure,
an evocative face
from the past that
epitomises the
potential wealth of
evidence preserved
in the wetlands of
Scotland.
Photograph
National Museums
of Scotland.

or more in the bogs and silts to show the potential wealth of information that remains to be recovered (Barber & Crone 1993; Crone 1993; Dixon 1991). The evidence of wooden structures, boats, containers and other organic pieces, of metal and pottery artefacts, of humans and other animals, and of the details of past environments and economics, all are known to have existed, and some are still in place for a determined survey, assessment, examination or active preservation. We need hardly remind Scottish readers of the international importance of the Ballachulish figure (illus 84), the Blairdrummond disc wheel, the Rotten Bottom bow and a few other single finds, and above all else of the crannogs, submerged both by water and peat. There are other finds too, certainly of national importance, such as the logboats, the Kincardine Moss corduroy road, bog butter and its containers, and the textiles from human burials or accidents in the bogland. And many wooden bowls, planks and other things have come up from the peat over the past century. The palaeoenvironmental record, surviving in the wet peats, is surely of national if not international importance.

Time is now not on our side, however, and opportunities will slip away as the actions of other agencies take effect. The stage now seems set for a project or projects that we all know must be pro-active and not merely passive. For too long, in many places in the world's wetlands, archaeologists and heritage managers have waited for the finds to come, relying upon the goodwill of those who exploit the wetlands for their own purposes. Meanwhile, the deterioration of the conditions that originally allowed the evidence to survive goes on apace, at rates from the truly dramatic in terms of loss, to a more leisurely decay, and most of it below ground where monitoring is impossible and detection virtually so – the Disappearance of the Invisible. So an active effort must be made to advance our knowledge of ancient use and exploitation of wetlands, and to take steps to protect those areas of the highest potential and demonstrable importance. How can this be done? We venture to suggest a few items in a rather long list of active involvements:

1 A national acceptance of the idea that Scottish wetlands contain much useful information and that serious damage is being done to the heritage.

2 A recognition that certain regions, and local areas within regions, hold the greatest potential for important evidence.

3 A realisation that the work of wildlife agencies may well be broadly in line with archaeological objectives but sometimes there will be conflicts of interests.

4 An acknowledgement that trained wetland archaeologists cannot be in the right place at the right time, when discoveries are made in the course of developments or other aggressive actions.

5   A scheme to inform and train regional and local archaeologists and others in the benefits, techniques and problems of wetlands – in recognition, in temporary conservation, in emergency recovery, and in education.

6   A plan to publicize the discoveries and potential of Scottish wetlands, to interest and inform the public, and to encourage observation and report.

7   A survey of those wetlands most at risk and of highest potential, to obtain the best possible data under the best possible conditions, knowing that the evidence will deteriorate year by year.

8   A project to assess the condition of sites identified by survey, with a view to further examination or to the establishment of regimes to arrest the agencies of decay.

9   A suitably-experienced team, able to be assembled at short notice, to undertake the recovery of material that is fragile and deteriorating by the hour.

10 A select force of specialists to engage in the collection, analysis and interpretation of economic and environmental evidence throughout all wetland surveys and excavations and to undertake further research into past environments particularly characteristic of Scottish landscapes.

11 A guide to all museums able to receive, store, conserve and curate wet-site material, or at least to act as an emergency holding office prior to transfer to more suitable premises.

12 An active encouragement and support by national and other agencies for the implementation of research projects into particular environments or monuments, to build on the solid base we now have in place. Crannogs, raised bogs, and estuarine/coastal areas are but three major areas for research, with only the first partially under way.

13 A forum, directed through the Society of Antiquaries of Scotland, in which periodic meetings may expose, debate, refine and direct the facilities that are made available for research into the wetlands.

What will all this cost? Very little, compared with the yield of information that will come. Even a modest input will be repaid tenfold. Unlike many areas of the world where wetland archaeology suffers almost total starvation of funds and rejection of its qualities, Scottish wetlands have had some serious studies, (and continue to prompt them, as the Society's Newsletter of September 1995 describes). They have revealed evidence widely acknowledged to be important, but more, much more, remains to be found and protected. We hope these Rhind Lectures will have created additional interest and will strengthen, and perhaps guide, the hands of those committed wetlanders and those who will soon fall under the spell of the endless variations of dark earth and broad sky, the bright sun and the lashing rain, the medley of calls from the wild, and the first glimpse of long-buried things.

REFERENCES

Andersen, SH 1985 'Tybrind Vig. A preliminary report on a submerged Ertebølle settlement on the west coast of Fyn', *J Danish Archaeol*, 4 (1985), 52-69.

Atkinson, RJC & Piggott, S 1955 'The Torrs Chamfrein', *Archaeologia*, 96 (1955), 197-235.

Barber, JW & Crone, BA 1993 'Crannogs: a diminishing resource? A survey of the crannogs of southwest Scotland and excavations at Buiston crannog', *Antiquity*, 67 (1993), 520-33.

Bartholin, T 1978 'Alvastra pile dwelling: tree studies. The dating and the landscape', *Fornvännen*, 73 (1978), 213-19.

Bartholin, T 1987 'Oak and willow: active and passive periods at Alvastra pile dwelling', *in* Burenhult *et al* 1987, 123-32.

Bell, M 1993 'Intertidal archaeology at Goldcliff in the Severn estuary', *in* Coles *et al* 1993, 9-13.

Bennike, P & Ebbesen, K 1986 'The bog find from Sigersdal', *J Danish Archaeol*, 5 (1986), 85-115.

Bennike, P, Ebbesen, K & Jorgensen, LB 1986 'Early Neolithic skeletons from Bolkilde bog, Denmark', *Antiquity*, 60 (1986), 199-209.

Billamboz, A 1990 'Das Holz der Pfahlbausiedlungen Südwestdeutschlands', *in Siedlungsarchäologische Untersuchungen im Alpenvorland*, 187-207. Mainz am Rhein: Verlag Philipp von Zabern. (= *Sonderdruck aus Bericht der Römisch-Germanischen Kommission*, 71.)

Billamboz, A, Dieckmann, B, Maier, U & Vogt, R 1992 'Exploitation du sol et de la forêt à Hornstaad-Hörnle I (RFA, Bodensee)', *in Archéologie et environnement des milieux aquatiques: lacs, fleuves et tourbières du domaine alpin et de sa périphérie*, 119-48. Paris: Editions du Comité des Travaux historiques et scientifiques.

Bocquet, A 1994 *Charavines il y a 5000 ans*. Dijon: Editions Faton.

Bradley, R 1990 *The passage of arms*. Cambridge: Univ Press.

Brandt, R, Groenman-van Waateringe, W & van der Leeuw, S (eds) 1987 *Assendelver Polder Papers*, 1. Amsterdam: Cinggula.

Browall, H 1986 *Alvastra pålbyggnad. Social och ekonomisk bas*. Stockholm: Univ Press.

Bulleid, A & Gray, HStG 1911 *The Glastonbury Lake Village*. 1. Glastonbury: Antiquarian Society.

Bulleid, A & Gray, HStG 1917 *The Glastonbury Lake Village*. 2. Glastonbury: Antiquarian Society.

Burenhult, G, Carlsson, A, Hyenstrand, A & Sjøvold, T (eds) 1987 *Theoretical approaches to artefacts, settlement and society*. Oxford: Brit Archaeol Rep. (= *Brit Archaeol Rep Int Ser*, S366.)

Burri, N, Joye, C, Rychner-Faraggi, A-M & Schifferdecker, F 1987 'Découverte d'un village littoral de la civilisation de Cortaillod à Hauterive-Champréveyres', *Jahrbuch der Schweizerischen Gesellschaft für Ur- und Frühgeschichte*, 70 (1987), 35-50.

Christison, R 1881 'On an ancient wooden image, found in November last at Ballachulish Peat Moss', *Proc Soc Antiq Scot*, 15 (1881), 158-78.

Clark, JGD 1954 *Excavations at Star Carr*. Cambridge: Univ Press.

Clark, JGD 1972 *Star Carr: a case study in bioarchaeology*. Reading, Massachusetts: Addison-Wesley Modular Publications.

Clarke, C 1995 *Scottish archaeological database for the raised bogs*. Edinburgh: Univ Centre for Field Archaeology. (= *Edinburgh Univ Centre Field Archaeol Rep*, 199.)

Colardelle, M & Verdel, E 1993a *Les habitats du lac de Paladru (Isère) dans leur environnement*. Paris: Editions de la Maison des Sciences de l'Homme.

Colardelle, M & Verdel, E 1993b *Chevaliers-Paysans de l'an Mil*. Paris: Editions Errance.

Coles, B 1990 'Anthropomorphic wooden figures from Britain and Ireland', *Proc Prehist Soc*, 56 (1990), 315-33.

Coles, B (ed) 1992a *The Wetland revolution in prehistory*. Exeter: Wetland Archaeol Res Project. (= *Wetland Archaeol Res Project Occas Pap*, 6.)

Coles, B 1992b 'Further thoughts on the impact of beaver on temperate landscapes', *in* S Needham & MG Macklin (eds) *Alluvial archaeology in Britain*, 93-9. Oxford: Oxbow Books (= *Oxbow Monogr*, 27.)

Coles, B 1993 'Roos Carr and Company', *in* J Coles *et al* 1993, 17-22.

Coles, B 1995 *Wetland management. A survey for English Heritage*. Exeter: Wetland Archaeol Res Project. (= *Wetland Archaeol Res Project Occas Pap*, 9.)

Coles, B & Coles, J 1986 *Sweet Track to Glastonbury*. London: Thames & Hudson.

Coles, B & Coles J 1989 *People of the Wetlands. Bogs, bodies and lake dwellings*. London: Thames & Hudson.

Coles, J 1971 'The early settlement of Scotland: excavations at Morton, Fife', *Proc Prehist Soc*, 37 (2) (1971), 284-366.

Coles, J 1984 'Irish bogs: the time is now', *North Munster Antiq J*, 26 (1984), 3-7.

Coles, J 1986 'The preservation of archaeological sites by environmental intervention', *in* H Hodges (ed) *In Situ Archaeological Conservation*, 32-55. Institutio Nacional de Antropologia e Historia de Mexico and The Getty Conservation Institute, Century City California.

Coles, J 1987 *Meare Village East. The excavations of A. Bulleid and H. St. George Gray 1932-1956*. (=*Somerset Levels Pap*, 13.)

Coles, J 1989 'Prehistoric settlement in the Somerset Levels', *Somerset Levels Pap*, 15, 14-33.

Coles, J 1991 *From the waters of oblivion*. Reuvens – Lezing 2, Assen.

Coles, J, Fenwick, V & Hutchinson, G (eds) 1993 *A Spirit of Enquiry. Essays for Ted Wright*. Exeter and London: Wetland Archaeol Res Project, Nautical Archaeol Soc & Nat Maritime Mus (= *Wetland Archaeol Res Project Occas Pap*, 7).

Coles, J, Goodall, A & Minnitt, S 1992 *Arthur Bulleid and the Glastonbury Lake*

Village 1892–1992. Somerset Levels Project & Somerset County Counc Mus Service.

Coles, J, Hibbert, FA & Orme, BJ 1973 'Prehistoric roads and tracks in Somerset: 3. The Sweet Track', *Proc Prehist Soc*, 39, 256-93.

Coles, J & Jones, RA 1975 'Timber and radiocarbon dates', *Antiquity*, 49 (1975), 123-5.

Coles, J & Lawson, A 1987 *European wetlands in prehistory*. Oxford: Clarendon Press.

Coles, J & Minnitt, S 1995 *'Industrious and Fairly Civilized'. The Glastonbury Lake Village.* Somerset Levels Project Somerset County Counc Mus Service.

Coles, J & Orme, BJ 1983 *'Homo sapiens* or *Castor fiber?'*, *Antiquity*, 57 (1983), 95-102.

Croes, D (ed) 1976 *The excavation of water-saturated archaeological sites (wet sites) on the northwest coast of North America.* Ottawa: Nat Mus.

Croes, D 1992 'An evolving revolution in wet site research on the northwest coast of North America', *in* B Coles 1992a, 99-111.

Crone, A 1993 'Crannogs and chronologies', *Proc Soc Antiq Scot*, 123 (1993), 245-54.

Crumlin-Pedersen, O & Rieck, F 1993 'The Nydam ships. Old and new investigations at a classic site', *in* J Coles *et al* 1993, 39-45.

Cushing, FH 1896 'Exploration of Ancient Key Dwellers' Remains on the Gulf Coast of Florida', *Proc American Philosoph Soc*, 35 (1896), 329-448.

Daugherty, R 1988 'Problems and responsibilities in the excavation of wet sites', *in* Purdy 1988, 15-29.

Day, SP & Mellars, PA 1994 'Absolute dating of Mesolithic human activity at Star Carr, Yorkshire: new palaeoecological studies and identification of the 9600 BP radiocarbon plateau', *Proc Prehist Soc*, 60 (1994), 417-22.

Dieck, A 1965 *Die europäischen Moorleichenfunde.* Neumünster.

Dieckmann, B 1990 *Zum Stand der archäologischen Untersuchungen in Hornstaad. Siedlungsarchäologische Untersuchungen in Alpenvorland.* Mainz am Rhein: Verlag Philipp von Zabern. (= *Sonderdruck aus Bericht der Römisch-Germanischen Kommission,* 71)

Dillehay, TD 1984 'A Late Ice-Age settlement in southern Chile', *Scientific American*, 251 (1984), 106-18.

Dillehay, TD 1988 'Early rainforest archaeology in Southwestern South America: research context, design, and data at Monte Verde', *in* Purdy 1988, 177-206.

Dillehay, TD 1989 *Monte Verde. A Late Pleistocene settlement in Chile. 1. Palaeoenvironment and site context.* Washington: Smithsonian Inst.

Dillehay, T 1996 *Monte Verde. A Late Pleistocene settlement in Chile. 2. The archaeological context.* Washington: Smithsonian Inst.

Dixon, N 1991 'The history of crannog survey and excavation in Scotland', *Internat J Nautical Archaeol*, 20 (1991), 1-8.

Doran, G 1992 'Problems and potential of wet sites in North America: the example of Windover', *in* B Coles 1992a, 125-34.

Doran, G & Dickel, D 1988 'Multi-disciplinary investigations at the Windover site', *in* Purdy 1988, 263-89.

During, E 1987 'Animal bone material from the Alvastra pile dwelling', *in* Burenhult *et al* 1987, 133-51.

Ebbesen, K 1986 *Døden i mosen*. Copenhagen: Carlsen.

Egloff, M 1987 '130 years of archaeological research in Lake Neuchâtel, Switzerland', *in* J Coles & Lawson 1987, 23-32.

Egloff, M 1989 *Des premiers chasseurs au début du christianisme*. Editions Gilles Attinger à Hauterive, Suisse.

Fairweather, AD & Ralston, IBM 1993 'The Neolithic timber hall at Balbridie, Grampian Region Scotland: the building, the date, the plant macrofossils', *Antiquity*, 67 (1993), 313-23.

Fischer, C 1980 'Bog bodies of Denmark', *in* A & E Cockburn (eds) *Mummies, disease and ancient cultures*, 177-93. Cambridge.

Fox, C 1947 *A find of the Early Iron Age from Llyn Cerrig Bach, Anglesey*. Cardiff: Nat Mus Wales.

Frödin, O 1910 'En svensk pålbyggnad från stenåldren', *Fornvännen*, 5 (1910), 29-77.

Gilliland, M 1989 *Key Marco's buried treasure. Archaeology and adventure in the nineteenth century*. Gainesville: Univ Florida.

Gleeson, P & Grosso, G 1976 'Ozette site', *in* Croes 1976, 13-44.

Glob, PV 1965 *Mosefolket: Jernalderens Mennesker bevaret i 2000 Ar*.

Glob, PV 1969 *The Bog People. Iron Age man preserved*. London: Faber.

Godwin, H 1978 *Fenland: its ancient past and uncertain future*. Cambridge: Univ Press.

Godwin, H 1981 *The archives of the peat bogs*. Cambridge: Univ Press.

Göransson, H 1995 *Alvastra pile dwelling. Palaeoethnobotanical studies*. Lund: Univ Press.

Gramsch, B 1992 'Friesack Mesolithic wetlands', *in* B Coles 1992a, 65-72.

Grøn, O 1995 'Use of sediment echo-sounding for location of archaeological sites under water', *Maritime Archaeol Newsletter Roskilde*, 4 (1995), 13-15.

Hall, D & Coles, J 1994 *Fenland Survey. An essay in landscape and persistence*. London: English Heritage.

Hayen, H 1987 *Die Moorleichen im Museum Am Damm*. Oldenburg.

Herneck, R & Nordqvist, B 1995 *Världens äldsta tuggummi?* Kungsbacka: Riksantikvariembetet.

Hillman, J, Groves, CM, Brown, DM, Baillie, MGL, Coles, JM & Coles, BJ 1990 'Dendrochronology of the English Neolithic', *Antiquity*, 64 (1990), 210-20.

Holden, TG 1995 'The last meals of the Lindow bog men', *in* Turner & Scaife 1995, 76-82.

Hongo, H 1989 'Freshwater fishing in Early Jomon Period: an analysis of fish remains from the Torihama shell-mound', *J Archaeol Sci*, 16 (1989), 333-54.

Housley, R 1988 'The environmental context of Glastonbury Lake Village', *Somerset Levels Pap*, 14 (1988), 63-82.

Housley, R 1995 'The environment', *in* J Coles & Minnitt 1995, 121-36.

Jaskanis, J (ed) 1991 *Prahistoryczny gród w Biskupinie*. Warsaw: Panstwowe Mus.

Jørgensen, MS & Sigurdsson, T 1991 'Looking into the wetland – using a new ground-penetrating radar system', *NewsWARP* (= *Newsletter Wetland Archaeol Res Project*), 10 (1991), 2-5.

Kasahara, Y 1981 'Analysis of seeds from Torihama shell-mound', *Torihama Shell-Mound Res Grp*, 2 (1981), 65-87.

Kasahara, Y 1983 'Analysis of plant seeds from Torihama shell-mound', *Torihama Shell-Mound Res Grp*, 3 (1983), 47-64.

Keller, F 1878 *The Lake-dwellings of Switzerland and other parts of Europe.* London: Longman.

Kjaerum, P & Olsen, RA 1990 *Oldtidens Ansigt. Faces of the Past.* Nordiske Oldskriftselskab & Jysk Arkaeologisk Selskab.

Kostrzewski, J (ed) 1950 *III Sprawozdanie z prac wykopaliskowych w grodzie kultury Luzyciej w Biskupinie w powiecie zninskim za lata 1938–1939 i 1946–1948.* Poznan.

Lane, T & Reeve, J (eds) 1996 *Fenland investigations 1991–1995.* Sleaford: Heritage Lincolnshire.

Legge, AJ & Rowley-Conwy, PA 1988 *Star Carr Revisited.* London: Birkbeck College.

Louwe Kooijmans, LP 1985 *Sporen in het land. De Nederlandse delta in de prehistorie.* Amsterdam: Meulenhoff.

Lynn, C 1977 'Trial excavations at The King's Stables, Tray townland, Co Armagh', *Ulster J Archaeol*, 40 (1977), 42-62.

MAFF 1991 *Conservation Guidelines for Drainage Authorities.*

MAFF 1994 *Water Level Management Plans. A procedural guide for operating authorities. PB 1793*, MAFF.

Malmer, MP 1986 'Aspects of Neolithic ritual sites', *in* G Steinsland (ed) *Words and objects*, 91-110. Oslo: Univ Press.

Malmer, MP 1991 'Social space in Alvastra and other pile dwellings', *in* O Grøn, E Engelstad & I Lindblom (eds) *Social space, human spatial behaviour in dwellings and settlements*, 118-22. Odense.

Malmer, MP & Bartholin, T 1983 'Paelbygning', *Skalk*, 1983 (4), 18-27.

Mapleton, RJ 1867 'Notice of an artificial island in Loch Kielziebar', *Proc Soc Antiq Scot*, 7 (1867), 322-4.

Matsui, A 1992 'Wetland sites in Japan', *in* B Coles 1992a, 5-14.

Middleton, R, Wells, C & Huckerby, E 1995 *The wetlands of North Lancashire.* Lancaster: North West Wetlands Survey.

Moloney, A (ed) 1993a *Survey of the raised bogs of County Longford.* (=*Irish Archaeol Wetland Unit Trans*, 1.)

Moloney, A 1993b *Excavations at Clonfinlough Co Offaly.* (=*Irish Archaeol Wetland Unit Trans*, 2.)

Mordant, C & Mordant, D 1992 'Noyen-sur-Seine: a mesolithic waterside settlement', *in* B Coles 1992a, 55-64.

Morgan, R 1988 *Tree-ring studies of wood used in Neolithic and Bronze Age trackways from the Somerset Levels.* Oxford: Brit Archaeol Rep. (= *Brit Archaeol Rep*, 184)

Morrison, A 1985 *Landscape with lake dwellings. The crannogs of Scotland.* Edinburgh: Univ Press.

Moss, M & Erlandson, J 1995 'Reflections on North American Pacific coast prehistory', *J World Prehist*, 9 (1995), 1-45.

Mowat, R 1996 *The Logboats of Scotland, with notes on related artifact-types.* Oxford: Oxbow Books.

Munksgaard, E 1974 *Oldtidsdragter.* Copenhagen: Nat Mus.

Munksgaard, E 1984 'Bog bodies – a brief survey of interpretation', *J Danish Archaeol,* 3 (1984), 120-33.

Munro, R 1882 *Ancient Scottish lake dwellings or crannogs.* Edinburgh: Douglas.

Munro, R 1890 *The Lake-Dwellings of Europe.* London: Cassell.

NRA National Rivers Authority 1993 *NRA Conservation Strategy.* Bristol: Nat Rivers Authority.

Niewiarowski, W, Noryskiewicz, B, Piotrowski, W & Zajaczkowski, W 1992 'Biskupin fortified settlement and its environment in the light of new environmental and archaeological studies', *in* B Coles 1992a, 81-92.

Nordqvist, B 1994 'Huseby Klev – marine archaeology on land', *NewsWARP (= Newsletter Wetland Archaeol Res Project),* 16 (1994), 24-7.

Nordqvist, B 1995 'The Mesolithic settlements of the Swedish west coast – with special emphasis on chronology and topography of coastal settlements', *in* A Fischer (ed) *Man and sea in the Mesolithic,* 185-96. Oxford: Oxbow Books.

O'Donnell, T 1993 'Conservation of Iron Age roadway and associated peatlands at Corlea, Co Longford', *Engineers J,* 46(3) (1993), 44-7.

O Floinn, R 1995 'Recent research into Irish bog bodies', *in* Turner & Scaife 1995, 137-45.

Orme, BJ, Coles, JM, Caseldine, AE & Bailey, GN 1981 'Meare Village West 1979', *Somerset Levels Pap,* 7 (1981), 12-69.

Painter, T 1991 'Lindow man, Tollund man and other peat-bog bodies: the preservative and antimicrobial action of *Sphagnan,* a reactive glycuronoglycan with tanning and sequestering properties', *Carbohydrate Polymers,* 15, 123-42.

Parfitt, K & Fenwick, V 1993 'The rescue of Dover's Bronze Age boat', *in* Coles, Fenwick & Hutchinson 1993, 77-80.

Parry, S & McGrail, S 1991 'A prehistoric plank boat fragment and a hard from Caldicot Castle Lake, Gwent, Wales', *Internat J Nautical Archaeol,* 20 (1991), 321-4.

Piggott, S 1971 'Excavation of the Dalladies long barrow, Fettercairn, Kincardineshire', *Proc Soc Antiq Scot,* 104 (1971), 23-47.

Piggott, S & Henderson, K 1958 *Scotland before history.* Edinburgh: Nelson.

Piotrowski, W 1995 'Biskupin – the fortified settlement from the first millennium BC', *Quaternary Stud Poland,* 13 (1995), 89-99.

Piotrowski, W & Zajaczkowski, W 1993 'Protecting Biskupin by an artificial barrier', *NewsWARP (= Newsletter Wetland Archaeol Res Project),* 14 (1993), 7-11.

Pollard, T 1993 *Ballachulish Moss Archaeological Assessment.* Glasgow: Univ Archaeol Res Division.

Pryor, F 1991 *Flag Fen. Prehistoric Fenland centre.* London: Batsford.

Pryor, F 1992 'Current research at Flag Fen, Peterborough', *Antiquity,* 251 (1992), 439-57.

Purdy, B (ed) 1988 *Wet-site archaeology.* Caldwell, New Jersey: Telford.

Purdy, B 1991 *The art and archaeology of Florida's wetlands.* Boca Raton: CRC Press.

Pyatt, FB, Beaumont, EH, Buckland, PC, Lacy, D, Magilton, JR & Storey, DM 1995 'Mobilisation of elements from the bog bodies Lindow II and III, and some observations on body painting', *in* Turner & Scaife 1995, 62-73.

Raftery, B 1990 *Trackways through time.* Dublin: Headline.

Raftery, B 1993 'Preface', *in* Moloney 1993a, vii.

Rajewski, Z 1970 *Biskupin. A fortified settlement dating from 500 BC.* Poznan: Wydawnictwo.

Rieck, F 1993 'The Man from Nydam Mose', *Maritime Archaeol Newsletter Roskilde*, 1 (1993), 3-4.

Rieck, F 1994 'The Iron Age boats from Hjortspring and Nydam – new investigations', *in* C Westerdahl (ed) *Crossroads in ancient shipbuilding*, 45-54. Oxford: Oxbow Books. (= *Oxbow Monogr*, 40.)

Rimes, C 1992 *Freshwater acidification of SSSIs in Great Britain. 1: Overview.* Peterborough: English Nature.

Ruoff, U 1992 'The Pfahlbauland exhibition, Zürich 1990', *in* B Coles 1992a, 135-46.

Samuels, SR 1994 *Ozette archaeological project research report 2. Fauna.* Seattle: Washington State Univ.

Schlichtherle, H & Wahlster, B 1986 *Archäologie in Seen und Mooren.* Stuttgart: Konrad Theiss.

Sears, WH 1982 *Fort Center: an archaeological site in the Lake Okeechobee basin.* Gainesville: Univ Press.

Sheridan, A 1992 'A longbow from Rotten Bottom, Dumfriesshire, Scotland', *NewsWARP* (=*Newsletter Wetland Archaeol Res Project*), 12 (1992), 13-15.

Słupecki, LP 1994 *Slavonic pagan sanctuaries.* Warsaw: Polish Acad Sci.

Speck, J 1981 'Pfahlbauten: Dichtung oder Wahrheit? Ein Querschnitt durch 125 Jahre Forschungsgeschichte', *Helvetia Archaeologica*, 45-8 (1981), 98-138.

Stead, IM, Bourke, JB & Brothwell, D 1986 *Lindow Man. The body in the bog.* London: Brit Mus.

Torihama Shell-Mound Research Group (ed) 1979-1987 *Torihama Shell-Mound*, 1-7. Wakasa.

Turner, RC 1995a 'Discoveries and excavations at Lindow Moss 1983-8', *in* Turner & Scaife 1995, 10-18.

Turner, RC 1995b 'Recent research into British bog bodies', *in* Turner & Scaife 1995, 108-22.

Turner, RC 1995c 'The Lindow Man phenomenon: ancient and modern', *in* Turner & Scaife 1995, 188-204.

Turner, RC & Scaife, RG (eds) 1995 *Bog Bodies: new discoveries and new perspectives.* London: Brit Mus.

Van de Noort, R & Ellis, S 1995 *Wetland heritage of Holderness.* Hull: Humber Wetlands Project.

van der Sanden, WAB 1990 *Mens en moeras.* Assen: Drents Mus.

van der Sanden, WAB 1995 'Bog bodies on the continent: the developments since 1965, with special reference to the Netherlands', *in* Turner & Scaife 1995, 146-67.

Warner, R 1986 'Preliminary schedule of sites and stray finds in the Navan Complex', *Emania*, 1 (1986), 5-9.

Wazny, T 1993 'Dendrochronological dating of the Lusatian Culture settlement at Biskupin, Poland – first results', *NewsWARP* (= *Newsletter Wetland Archaeol Res Project*), 14 (1993), 3-5.

Weiner, J 1992a 'Eine bandkeramische Siedlung mit Brunnen bei Erkelenz-Kückhoven', *Aus der Geschichte des Erkelenzer Landes. Schriften des Heimatvereins der Erkelenzer Lande*, 12 (1992), 17-33.

Weiner, J 1992b 'Der früheste Nachweis der Blockbauweise. Zum Stand der Ausgrabung des bandkeramischen Holzbrunnens', *Archäologie in Rheinland 1991*, 30-3. Köln: Rheinland Verlag.

Weiner, J 1992c 'The Bandkeramik wooden well of Erkelenz-Kückhoven', *NewsWARP* (= *Newsletter Wetland Archaeol Res Project*), 12 (1992), 3-11.

Weiner, J 1994 'Well on my back – an update on the Bandkeramik wooden well of Erkelenz-Kückhoven', *NewsWARP* (= *Newsletter Wetland Archaeol Res Project*), 16 (1994), 5-17.

Willey, GR 1949 *Excavations in southeast Florida*. New Haven: Yale Univ. (= *Yale Univ Pub Anthropol*, 42.)

Wood-Martin, WG 1886 *The Lake dwellings of Ireland*. Dublin: Hodges, Figgis.

Wright, EV 1990 *The Ferriby boats. Seacraft of the Bronze Age*. London: Routledge.

INDEX